SECRET OF THE SWAMP THING

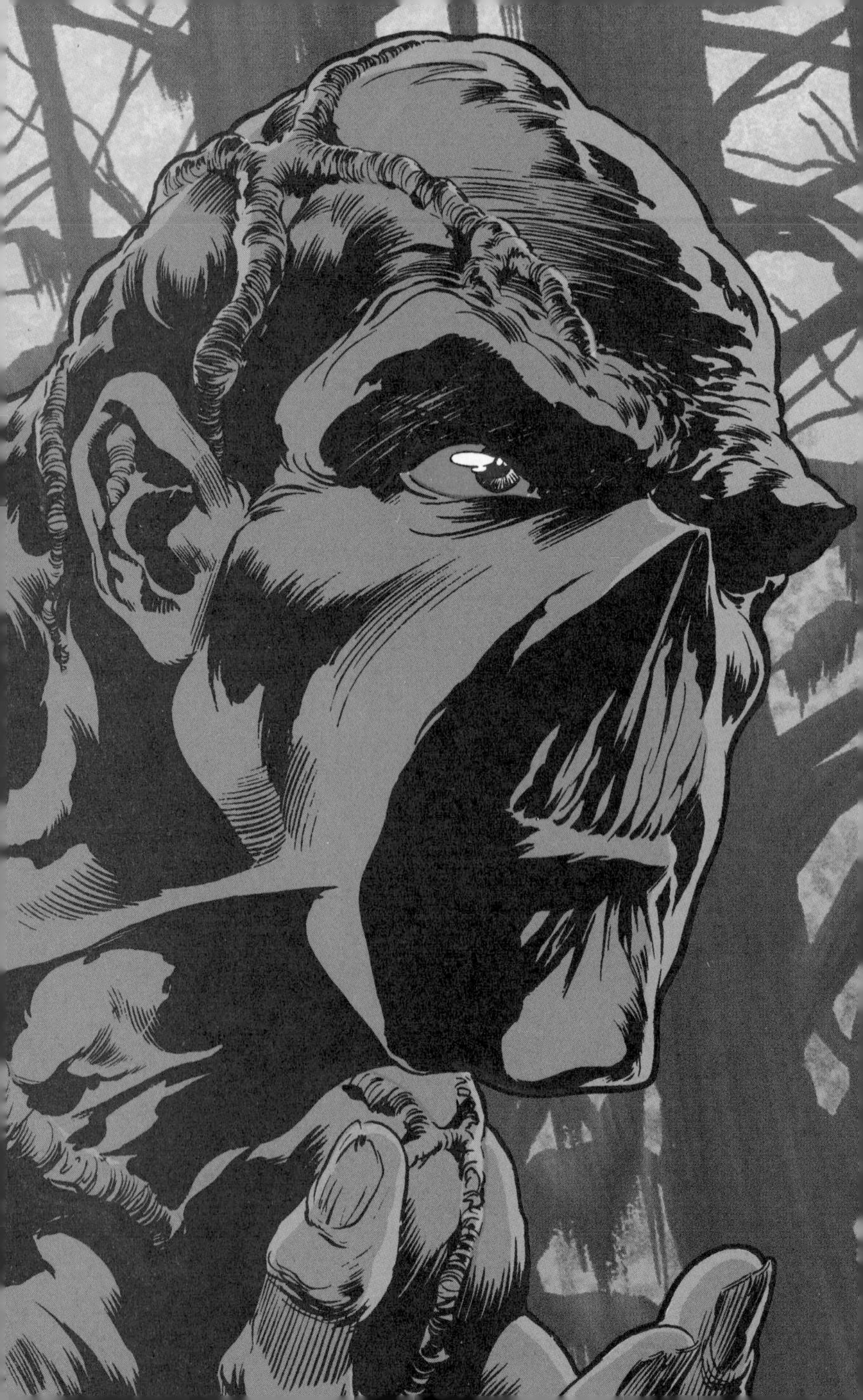

SECRET OF THE SWAMP THING

WRITTEN BY
LEN WEIN

ILLUSTRATED BY
BERNI WRIGHTSON

COLORED BY
TATJANA WOOD

LETTERED BY
BEN ODA
GASPAR SALADINO

SWAMP THING CREATED BY
LEN WEIN AND **BERNI WRIGHTSON**

SECRET OF THE SWAMP THING

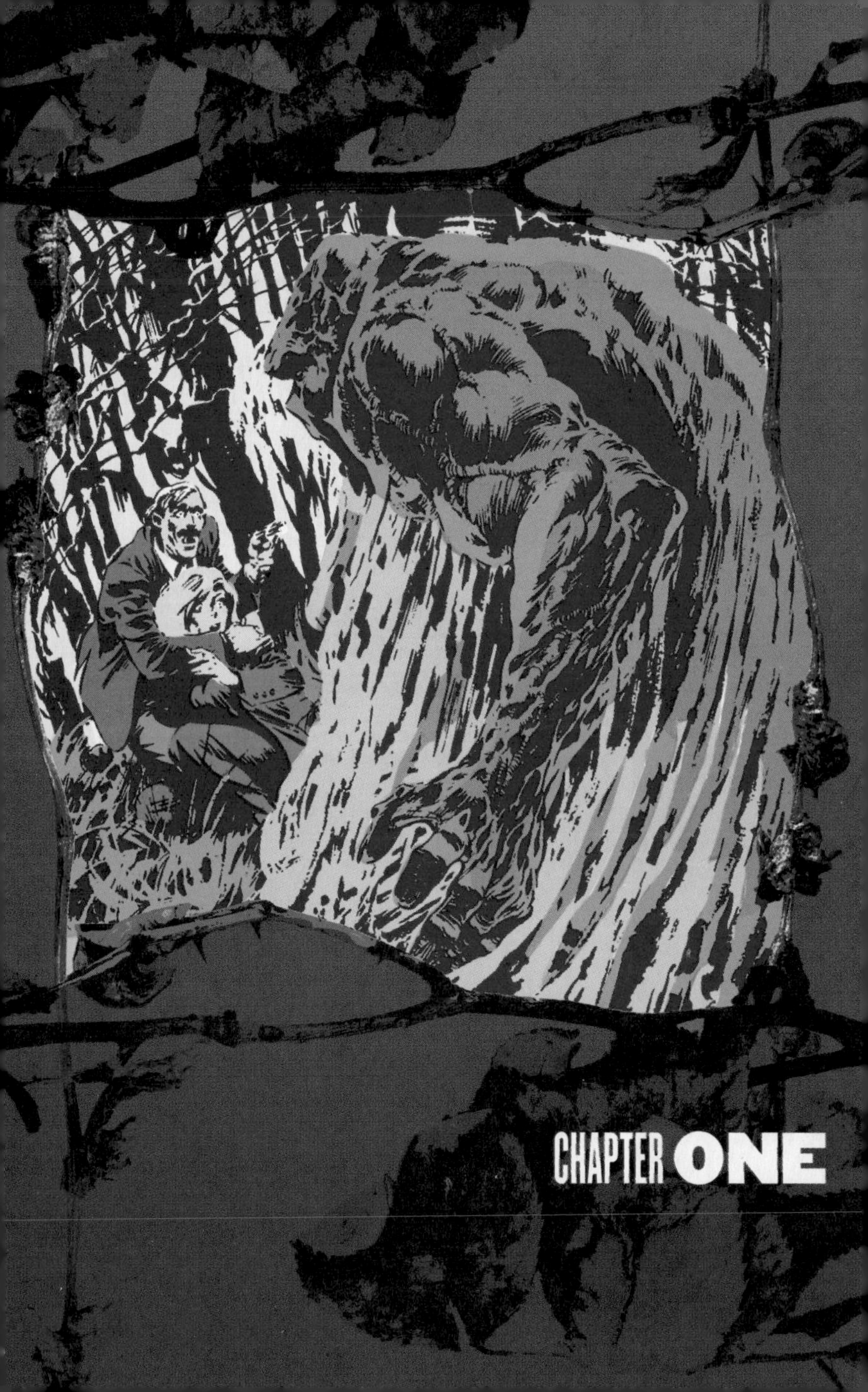

CHAPTER ONE

THE DARKNESS **CRIES**--A LONG, MOURNFUL **WAIL** THAT WRITHES THROUGH THE GNARLED CYPRESS BRANCHES LIKE A BREATH OF HADES' WIND, SKIPPING OVER THE PLACID SURFACE OF THE STAGNANT **MIRE** BELOW...

THIS IS **BAYOU COUNTRY:** A SWAMPY, DESOLATE MARSHLAND FORSAKEN BY CIVILIZED **MAN**-- AND NOW INHABITED BY FAR LESS **DEMANDING** CREATURES...

SCREAMING **HERONS** STRETCH THEIR SLEEK WINGS TOWARD THE ANGRY HEAVENS...

MOTTLED **BULL- FROGS** SING THEIR CROAKING NIGHT-SONG IN EAGER ANTICIPATION..

GREAT **REPTILES** LOLL UNCARINGLY BE- NEATH THE CLOUD- CLOAKED MOON ...

AND **THIS** NIGHT, THIS RAINY, WIND-SWEPT NIGHT, IMPATIENT **HUMANITY** INTRUDES ITSELF INTO THIS PRIMI- TIVE REGION ONCE MORE...

HUMANITY--AND SOMETHING FAR *LESS* THAN HUMAN!

THE MISSHAPEN *MONSTROSITY* PRESSES DEEPER INTO THE SHADOWS SURROUNDING THE SINGLE WOODEN STRUCTURE THAT RISES FROM THE *BOG...*

...AND HIS PUZZLED *MIND* FAIRLY CRACKLES WITH *THOUGHT...*

THEY WILL *RETURN...* THOSE WHO *KILLED* ME! THEY *WILL* RETURN...

...AND I WILL BE *WAITING!*

SILENTLY, THE **CREATURE** LURCHES FORWARD, INTO A DRIVING WIND-- AND A RAIN FILLED WITH **MEMORIES**...

THAT **HOUSE**...THAT SMIRKING SHELL OF A **HOUSE**...

...STANDS THERE **TAUNTING** ME...**LAUGHING**...

...AS IF IT WERE **RESPONSIBLE** FOR ALL THAT HAS **HAPPENED** HERE!

COLOR THE FIRST DAY A BRIGHT **BLUE**-- CRISP, SHINING--FULL OF **PROMISE** AND OPEN-EYED **DREAMS**...

...ONLY A **REFURBISHED BARN**...

...BUT WE DIDN'T HAVE MUCH **NOTICE** OF YOUR COMING!

WELL, DOCTORS HOLLAND-- **THERE** IT IS...

WE UNDERSTAND, LT. CABLE-- **WASHINGTON** WANTS TO KEEP OUR PRESENCE HERE **TOP-SECRET!**

SEEMS WE'RE **PRIORITY-ONE** MERCHANDISE!

ALEC, **PLEASE**-- YOU MAKE US SOUND LIKE SOMETHING AT A **SHOPPER'S SALE!**

MAYBE YOU **ARE**, MRS. HOLLAND...

...THE WORK YOU TWO ARE DOING IN **BIO-RESTORATIVE RESEARCH** IS **IN-VALUABLE** TO THE GOVERNMENT!

THAT'S WHY WE'RE **STASHING** YOU HERE -- IN THIS SUBURB OF **NOWHERE**...

...TO KEEP YOU OUT OF THE HANDS OF **OTHER** PRO-SPECTIVE **"SHOPPERS"!**

OH, BY THE WAY-- IF YOU HEAR *TRAFFIC*, DON'T LET IT *SPOOK* YOU...

...THERE'LL BE A *PATROL CAR* IN THE AREA CONSTANTLY!

WOULDN'T WANT TO *LOSE* THE "MERCHANDISE"!

ALEC, LET'S GO *INSIDE*--!

GLEAMING NEW DOOR HINGES WHINE OPEN AS THE HUSBAND-WIFE RESEARCH TEAM ENTERS THE RESURRECTED STABLE--THEIR VOICES ECHOING HOLLOW AMONG THE RAFTERS...

THOUGHT OF *EVERYTHING*, DIDN'T THEY? WE'VE GOT ENOUGH EQUIP-MENT HERE FOR A *DOZEN* DR. FRANKENSTEINS!

SEEMS ALMOST A SHAME WE'RE NOT BUILD-ING A *MONSTER!*

SILLY! I ONLY HOPE THEY REMEMBERED TO STOCK A *REFRIGERATOR!*

...BECAUSE RIGHT NOW, *THIS* LITTLE SCIENTIST IS *STARVING!*

9

EVENING, A FEW DAYS LATER--AND THE PROJECT IS WELL UNDER WAY...

WELL, SWEETHEART-- WHAT DO YOU *THINK?*

ARE WE READY TO *TRY* IT?

THEORETICALLY, *YES*--BUT I WOULDN'T WANT YOU TO *QUOTE* ME!

I'D *HATE* TO BE PROVEN *WRONG!*

BUT IF WE'RE *RIGHT*, LARGER QUANTITIES OF OUR *CHEMICAL* WILL BE USED TO CREATE *GARDENS* OUT OF SWELTERING *DESERTS*...

...AND *THAT* IS DEFINITELY WORTH THE EFFORT!

WELL-- CAN I QUOTE YOU *NOW?*

THE *COMPOUND* WORKED *BETTER* THAN...

UH, OH--OL' MATT CABLE AT·THE DOOR! WE'D BETTER LET HIM *IN*, LINDA!

KNOK! KNOK!

DR. HOLLAND? MY NAME IS *FERRETT!*

MY ASSOCIATES AND I WOULD LIKE A *WORD* WITH YOU IF WE COULD...

...IN *PRIVATE!*

10

HOLD ON, FRIEND-- THERE'S SUPPOSED TO BE A *CAR* PATROLLING THIS AREA!

JUST *HOW* DID YOU AND YOUR *CRONIES* GET *PAST*--?

PLEASE, DR. HOLLAND-- WE HAVE MORE *IMPORTANT* THINGS TO DISCUSS!

WE THREE REPRESENT A *PRIVATE* ORGANIZATION INTERESTED IN *PURCHASING* YOUR *BIO-RESTORATIVE FORMULA*...

...*SO* INTERESTED, IN FACT, THAT WE'VE BEEN AUTHORIZED TO OFFER YOU A *BLANK CHECK* FOR THE EXCLUSIVE RIGHTS...

...AND IF I WERE *YOU*, DR. HOLLAND... I'D *ACCEPT* OUR OFFER!

BUT YOU'RE *NOT* ME, FRIEND--AND OUR FORMULA *ISN'T* FOR SALE!

PERHAPS YOU CAN BE CONVINCED *OTHERWISE*, DOCTOR...

BRUNO, *CONVINCE* THE GENTLEMAN!

YOU'D BETTER *SAVE* THE CONVINCIN', FERRETT...

...'CAUSE WE GOT *COMPANY*!

THERE'S ANOTHER *CAR* COMIN' UP THE ROAD!

HATE TO CUT OUR LITTLE CHAT *SHORT*, DOCTOR--BUT WE REALLY HAVE TO *RUN*!

WHY DON'T YOU THINK ABOUT *ACCEPTING* OUR GENEROUS OFFER?

YOU WILL SAVE US *ALL* A LOT OF *TROUBLE* IF YOU *DO*!

WE'LL BE *SEEING* YOU, DR. HOLLAND... *SOON*!

THE SOUND OF ONE CAR MOTOR DIES AWAY TO BE REPLACED BY THE ROAR OF ANOTHER... THEN...

CABLE! IT'S ABOUT TIME YOU GOT HERE!

SORRY I'M *LATE*-- BUT THE PATROLMAN THOUGHT HE SAW AN UNREGISTERED *CAR* IN THE AREA...

...WE WERE CHECKING IT OUT!

WELL, YOU SHOULD HAVE CHECKED *HERE* FIRST!

THREE VERY *UN-FRIENDLY* PEOPLE WERE JUST HERE-- ATTEMPTING TO BUY OUR FORMULA!

WHAT--? AND YOU LET THEM GET *AWAY*?

YOU SHOULD HAVE NOTIFIED THE *PATROL GUARD* IMMEDIATELY

AFRAID WE WERE A TRIFLE *BUSY* AT THE TIME, LT.!

YEAH? WELL, LET ME *TELL* YOU SOMETHING...

...THAT CONVERSATION WE HAD ABOUT YOU TWO BEING *MERCHANDISE* WAS NO *JOKE*!

YOU'RE *COMMODITIES*, DOCTOR--YOU AND YOUR WIFE--TO BE BOUGHT, SOLD OR TRADED BY WHOEVER CAN MANAGE TO *OWN* YOU!

WHEN YOU'RE *FINISHED* HERE, DOCTOR--THE COUNTRY THAT CONTROLS YOUR *FORMULA* WILL BE ABLE TO CONTROL THE *WORLD*!

THINK ABOUT THAT! THINK HOW MANY PEOPLE WOULD DO *ANYTHING* TO HOLD YOUR *SECRET* IN THEIR HANDS--!

AND THINK HOW MANY PEOPLE WOULD RATHER SEE YOU *DEAD* THAN TO LET THEIR *ENEMIES* HAVE YOUR FORMULA!

REMEMBER THAT, DOCTOR--THEY'D RATHER SEE YOU *DEAD*!

NEXT TIME YOU *OPEN* THAT DOOR, YOU'D BETTER KNOW WHO'S *BEHIND* IT!

DON'T YOU THINK **LT. CABLE** WAS BEING OVERLY **MELODRAMATIC,** ALEC?

I'M NOT SO **SURE,** LINDA!

THOSE THREE **GANGSTER MOVIE REJECTS** DIDN'T THREATEN US FOR **PRACTICE!** THERE'S...

HEY! DO **YOU** HEAR WHAT **I** HEAR?

SOMEONE'S **MOVING AROUND** OUTSIDE!

BUT IT **CAN'T** BE MATT CABLE--! HE DROVE AWAY TEN MINUTES AGO!

FILE C
§12-942 GP

SCRATCH
SCRATCH

ALEC? WHAT ARE YOU **DOING?**

JUST TAKING PRECAUTIONS, LINDA! YOU REMEMBER WHAT CABLE SAID!

THERE'S SOMETHING OUTSIDE THAT DOOR--

--AND I'M GOING TO **FIND OUT** WHAT IT **IS!**

BUT AS THE WARY SCIENTIST FLINGS OPEN THE DOOR...

HA, HA! THERE'S YOUR **KILLER,** ALEC...

...AN OLD **HOUND DOG!**

WELL, IT MIGHT JUST AS WELL **BE A MURDERER!**

THE BLASTED THING ALMOST **SCARED** ME TO DEATH!

ALEC, HOW CAN YOU *SAY* THAT?

THE POOR DARLING LOOKS *LOST* AND HUNGRY!

CAN WE *KEEP* HIM?

ARE YOU *KIDDING?* WE'RE *OFF-LIMITS...*

...TO *EVERY-BODY!*

I MEAN--*LOOK* AT THE MUTT! IT'S *DIRTY...* AND *FLEA-BITTEN...* AND...

...AND... *DON'T* LOOK AT ME WITH THOSE *SOULFUL* EYES! THE ANSWER IS *NO!*

I *MEAN* IT, LINDA, WE'RE *NOT* KEEPING THAT...

...OH, WHAT'S THE *USE?*

YOU KNOW--FOR A WOMAN *SCIENTIST,* YOU SURE FIGHT *DIRTY!*

YOU CAN *HAVE* THE SHAGGY MUTT...

...AND *I* OUGHT TO HAVE MY *HEAD* EXAMINED!

...OUGHT TO HAVE MY *HEAD* EXAMINED!

NO, DR. HOLLAND... YOU OUGHT TO HAVE THE *DOG'S* HEAD EXAMINED...

...THEN PERHAPS YOU WOULD FIND THE TINY *RADIO TRANSMITTER* WE PLANTED THERE!

PERHAPS-- BUT I *DOUBT* IT!

LOUISIANA BLUE TO MISTER E.! REPORTING AS INSTRUCTED!

THE HOLLANDS HAVE TAKEN IN THE DOG AS EXPECTED-- ENABLING US TO MONITOR THEIR LAB AT ALL TIMES!

EVERYTHING PROCEEDING ON SCHEDULE!

SPLENDID, AGENT BLUE-- YOU HAVE DONE WELL!

AS SOON AS THE GOOD DOCTORS COMPLETE THEIR EXPERIMENTATION, YOU KNOW WHAT MUST BE DONE!

SEND FERRETT AROUND TO SEE THEM AGAIN--WITH A REPEAT OF OUR OFFER!

IF WE CAN GET THE FORMULA WITHOUT ANY DIFFICULTY, ALL WELL AND GOOD--BUT IF NOT...

THE CONCLAVE HAS MANY ENTERPRISES THAT WOULD BE JEOPARDIZED BY OUTSIDE USE OF THAT COMPOUND...

THUS, IF WE CAN'T HAVE IT, NOBODY WILL!

THE HOLLANDS AND THEIR FORMULA MUST BE DESTROYED!

BUT WHEN *FERRETT* AND HIS COHORTS ATTEMPT TO RENEW THEIR OFFER...

BUT, DR. HOLLAND-- WE CAME TO YOU IN *GOOD FAITH!*

SAVE IT FOR THE *BOYS IN BLUE,* FERRETT!

MY WIFE AND I'LL *SLEEP* A LOT BETTER-- KNOWING YOU THREE ARE *BEHIND BARS!*

SORRY WE CAN'T *ACCOMMODATE* YOU, DOC!

BRUNO-- TAKE *HIM!*

W-OK!

UUNNGG!

HE WILL NOT *BOTHER* US, FERRETT.

SWELL! THEN WE CAN *PLANT* OUR LITTLE *"SURPRISE PACKAGE"...*

...AN' GET THE HECK *AWAY* FROM THIS DUMP!

AGREED! I WANT TO BE *MILES* FROM HERE WHEN OUR GRACIOUS GIFT *BLOWS!*

FOR A TIME, *DARKNESS* REIGNS--AND WHEN *DR. ALEC HOLLAND* CRAWLS OUT OF THE *SHADOWLAND* AT LAST...

UUNHH... FEELS LIKE THEY DROPPED A *MOUNTAIN* ON MY HEAD! THEY'VE...

HEY, SEEMS MY PLAYMATES HAVE DECIDED TO *SKIP OUT!*

OH... MY DEAR *GOD!*

THAT THING IS-- *TICKING!*

I WONDER *WHY* THEY...

TICK TICK TICK TICK

GOTTA TRY TO *DEFUSE* IT BEFORE...

CRACK!

CLICK

BWAROOOOMM!

IMAGINE *PAIN*--SO INTENSE IT DEFIES DESCRIPTION-- AS COUNTLESS UNCLASSIFIED *CHEMICALS* SEEP DEEP INTO THROBBING, FUME-ENVELOPED *FLESH*...

OH, MY GOD...

OH, MY DEAR, DEAR GOD--!

IMAGINE WHAT SUCH TERRIBLE *SUFFERING* CAN DO TO THE FRAGILE *MIND*...

...AS IT DRIVES THE STRICKEN *BODY* FORWARD, CLAWING DESPERATELY AT THE COOL NIGHT AIR IN HOPES OF SOME SMALL *COMFORT*...

IMAGINE *RELIEF*--AS THE SMOLDERING MAN-SHAPE REACHES THE SOOTHING WATERS OF THE EVER-PRESENT *BOG*...

HSSSS

...THEN DISAPPEARS SOUND-LESSLY BENEATH ITS BUBBLING SURFACE...

17

A BITTER WIND WHISTLES PAST THE HANDFUL OF SADDENED FORMS WHO STAND TOGETHER BEFORE A FRESHLY-FILLED GRAVE...

P-POOR ALEC--! IF ONLY I HAD BEEN THERE--! MAYBE...

IT WOULDN'T HAVE *HELPED*, MRS. HOLLAND...LINDA...

...THE *BOMB* DESTROYED *EVERY* TRACE OF YOUR *HUSBAND!* IF YOU *HAD* BEEN THERE--

--IT WOULD'VE FINISHED *YOU*, TOO!

C'MON... LET'S HEAD BACK TO THE *LAB!*

LOOK AT THIS PLACE-- SPOTLESSLY *CLEAN!*

YOU CAN HARDLY TELL A *MAN* DIED HERE A FEW DAYS AGO...

...A *GOOD* MAN...*MY* MAN...

...MY POOR, DEDICATED *ALEC*--!

THEY PUT IT BACK TOGETHER AS *QUICKLY* AS THEY COULD, LINDA...

...DIDN'T WANT TO LOSE ANY TIME ON THE *PROJECT!*

OF COURSE-- THE *PROJECT!* THAT GOES ON, REGARDLESS... DOESN'T IT, CABLE?

NOBODY *CARES* ABOUT THE *PEOPLE* THAT LIVE OR DIE HERE...

...ONLY THE *MISERABLE PROJECT!*

AFRAID *SO*, LINDA--BUT WITH *ALEC* GONE, YOU'RE THE *ONLY* ONE LEFT WHO CAN *HANDLE* IT!

NOW WE'D BETTER GET OUT OF THE *RAIN!*

FUNNY--WHEN I WAS A *KID*, IT USED TO RAIN LIKE *THIS*--DARK, CHILLING...

AS IF THE SKY WERE *ALIVE*--AND LIVING, FELT *PAIN!*

IT FEELS THAT WAY *AGAIN* TO-NIGHT...AND LADY, I DON' *LIKE* IT!

18

RAIN: SOME SAY IT CLEANSES THE ALL-TOO-IMPURE *EARTH*-- OTHERS PROCLAIM IT THE SORROW OF THE *GODS*, REGRETTING THE *TRAGEDY* THEIR GOLDEN HANDS HAVE WROUGHT...

...THE *TRAGEDY* THAT HAS LONG BEEN KNOWN AS *MAN!*

BUT THOSE WHO DWELL IN THIS TIME-LESS LAND CARE NOT FOR IDLE *OPINION.* THEY ARE CONTENTED TO BASK IN THE TEEMING *TORRENT*...

...UNTIL SOMETHING SUDDEN *DISTURBS* THEIR REPOSE...

...SOMETHING THAT *CLAWS* ITS WAY OUT OF THE GRASPING *MIRE*...

...AND INTO THE *LIGHT* ONCE MORE!

SOMETHING THAT PULLS ITSELF *UPRIGHT* ON UNSTEADY LEGS, SEARCHING ITS CLOUDY MIND FOR A FRAGMENT OF *MEMORY*...

...THEN *PAUSES*, STUDYING ITS GNARLED, MISSHAPEN *HANDS*... EXAMINING THE CLUSTERS OF *ROOT*, THE CRUMBLING CHUNKS OF *MOSS*...

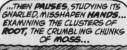

...AND IN THAT FRIGHTENING, MIND-SHATTERING SECOND-- **KNOWS** WHAT IT HAS BECOME!

A MUCK-ENCRUSTED, SHAMBLING **MOCKERY** OF LIFE...A TWISTED **CARICATURE** OF HUMANITY THAT CAN ONLY BE CALLED...

SWAMP THING!

BUT TRAVESTY THOUGH IT MAY BE, THE CREATURE BREATHES--AND *THINKS*...

MUST BE *LOGICAL*... MUST *GATHER MY THOUGHTS*...

EXPLOSION SHOULD HAVE *KILLED* ME... IT *DIDN'T*!

WHY? WHY?

THE *FORMULA*... *BIO-RESTORATIVE*... ON THE TABLE WHEN IT BLEW...

...I SAID IT COULD MAKE *FORESTS* OUT OF *DESERTS*...AND IT DID... *IT DID*...

...CHEMICAL MINGLED WITH MY FLESH... RE-ACTED WITH SWAMP *OOZE*...

...TURNED ME INTO... INTO... *WHAT?*

THE *LAB*... STILL STANDS... AND *LIGHTS* ARE ON...

LINDA WILL BE THERE...SHE'LL *KNOW* WHAT TO DO...

...SHE'LL *HELP* ME...

DETERMINEDLY, THE MONSTROSITY LUMBERS CLOSER TO THE BARN--CLOSE ENOUGH TO SEE...

THAT *REFLECTION* IN THE GLASS... CAN'T BE...CAN'T BE...

AARGH!

STRANGE-- COULD'VE SWORN *I HEARD* SOMETHING OUT THERE!

PROB'LY JUST THE *WIND* IN THE *CYPRESS TREES*-- BUT I'D BETTER *WATCH* IT!

I'M LETTING THOSE CHILD-HOOD NIGHTMARES *GET* TO ME!

NEXT THING YOU KNOW-- I'LL BE SEEING *BOOGIE-MEN* AND BUG-EYED *MONSTERS!*

COULDN'T LET LINDA *SEE* ME... NOT THE WAY I AM!

...BETTER TO STAY IN THE *SHADOWS*... AND KEEP *WATCH* ON THE HOUSE!

THEY WILL BE BACK... THE ONES WHO THOUGHT THEY *KILLED* ME...

...*FERRETT* AND THE OTHERS WILL BE BACK...

...AND I WILL BE *WAITING!*

WAIT-- *WAIT!!* YOU SILLY DOG--COME *BACK* HERE! OHHHH--!

SAVE YOUR BREATH, LINDA--IT CAN'T *HEAR* YOU! GOT A *FLEA* IN ITS EAR, I GUESS!

I'LL GO FETCH IT--BUT I WANT YOU TO *BOLT* THE DOOR BEHIND ME WHILE I'M GONE!

RUN, DOG-- FOLLOW YOUR MASTER'S VOICE--!

*U*NAWARE OF THE SILENT COMMANDS DRAWING THE HOUND ONWARD, *MATT CABLE* MOVES THROUGH THE DOWNPOUR IN DETERMINED PURSUIT...

YOU *STUPID* MUTT-- *WHERE ARE YOU?*

COME BACK HERE BEFORE YOU *KILL* YOURSELF!

THERE ARE *BOGS* IN THIS AREA! THEY...

22

LISTEN TO ME-- TRYING TO *RATIONALIZE* WITH A *DOG!* I'M GOING...

SNAT!

HUH?

UNLESS THAT POOCH HAS STARTED WEARING *SIZE 12 WORK-SHOES,* THERE'S SOMEBODY *PROWLING* AROUND THE LAB...

...AND IF I FIGURE TO *EARN* MY SALARY, I'D BETTER FIND OUT *WHO* IT IS!

BUT AS THE *SECURITY OFFICER* RETURNS TO THE LAB...

CRAK!

SORRY, MISTER-- BUT *BRUNO* HAS HIS *ORDERS!*

THAT *NOISE--* OUTSIDE--!

CABLE, IS THAT *YOU?* DID YOU *FIND* THE DOG?

WHO--?

KRUMP!

AFRAID YOUR FRIEND ISN'T GONNA BE FINDING *ANYTHING* FOR A WHILE, LITTLE LADY! BUT THAT'S OKAY...

...BECAUSE RIGHT NOW, YOU AND I HAVE *THINGS* TO DISCUSS...

...*ALONE!* HEH, HEH, HEH...

23

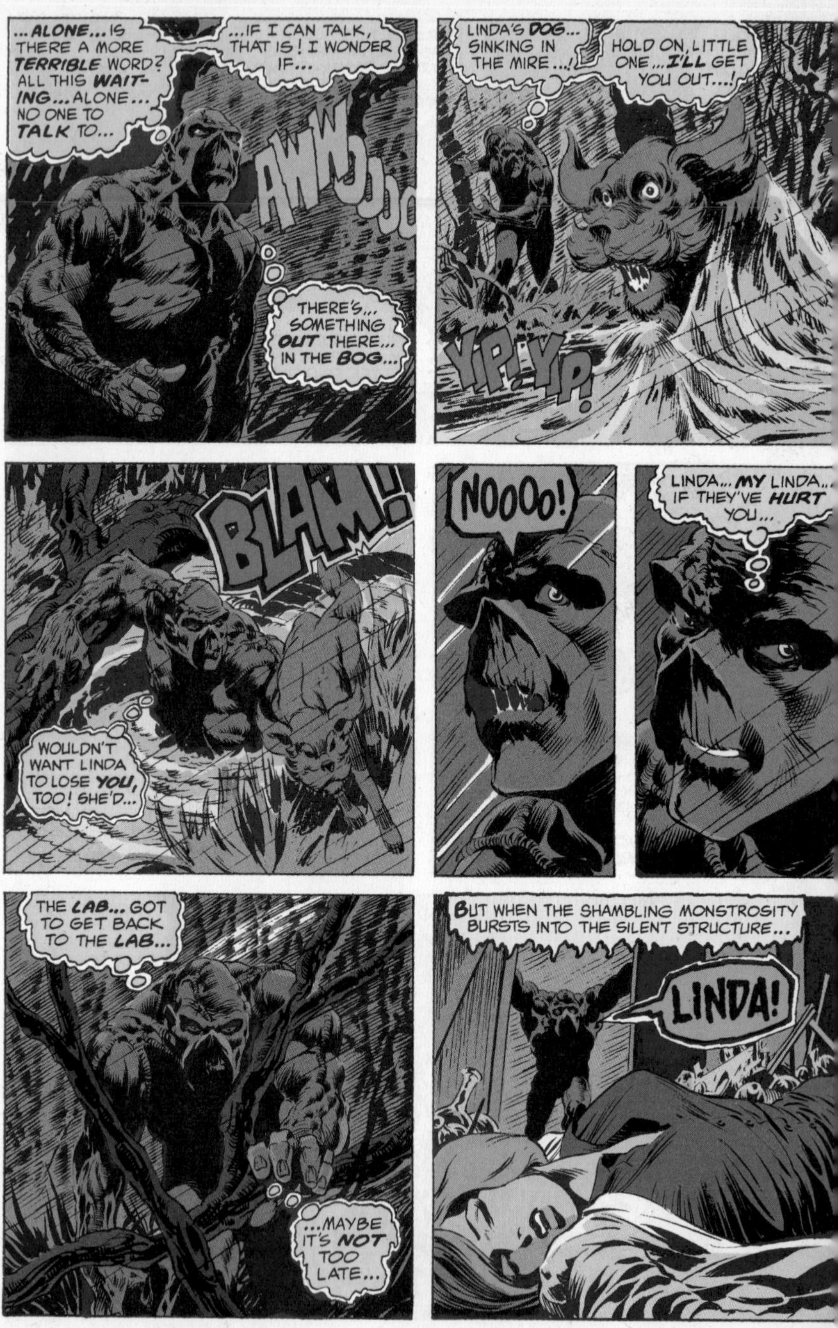
...ALONE... IS THERE A MORE TERRIBLE WORD? ALL THIS WAITING... ALONE... NO ONE TO TALK TO...
...IF I CAN TALK, THAT IS! I WONDER IF...
AWWOOOO
THERE'S... SOMETHING OUT THERE... IN THE BOG...
LINDA'S DOG... SINKING IN THE MIRE...!
HOLD ON, LITTLE ONE... I'LL GET YOU OUT...!
YIP! YIP!
BLAM!
WOULDN'T WANT LINDA TO LOSE YOU, TOO! SHE'D...
NOOOO!
LINDA... MY LINDA... IF THEY'VE HURT YOU...
THE LAB... GOT TO GET BACK TO THE LAB...
...MAYBE IT'S NOT TOO LATE...
BUT WHEN THE SHAMBLING MONSTROSITY BURSTS INTO THE SILENT STRUCTURE...
LINDA!

LINDA... LINDA... IT'S MY FAULT... MY FAULT...

...IF ONLY I HADN'T GONE FOR THE *DOG*... IF I HADN'T *TURNED AWAY!*

THEN THE ROAR OF AN AUTO- MOBILE CHURNING DOWN THE ROAD CUTS THROUGH THE SILENCE...

...AND THE MASSIVE MAN-MONSTER *ANSWERS* ITS GROWLING CALL...

KAWRAWW!

STOP!

F-F-*FERRETT*--! WHAT *IS* THAT THING?

DON'T ASK ME, BRUNO--JUST RUN IT *DOWN!*

STOP!

I SAID...

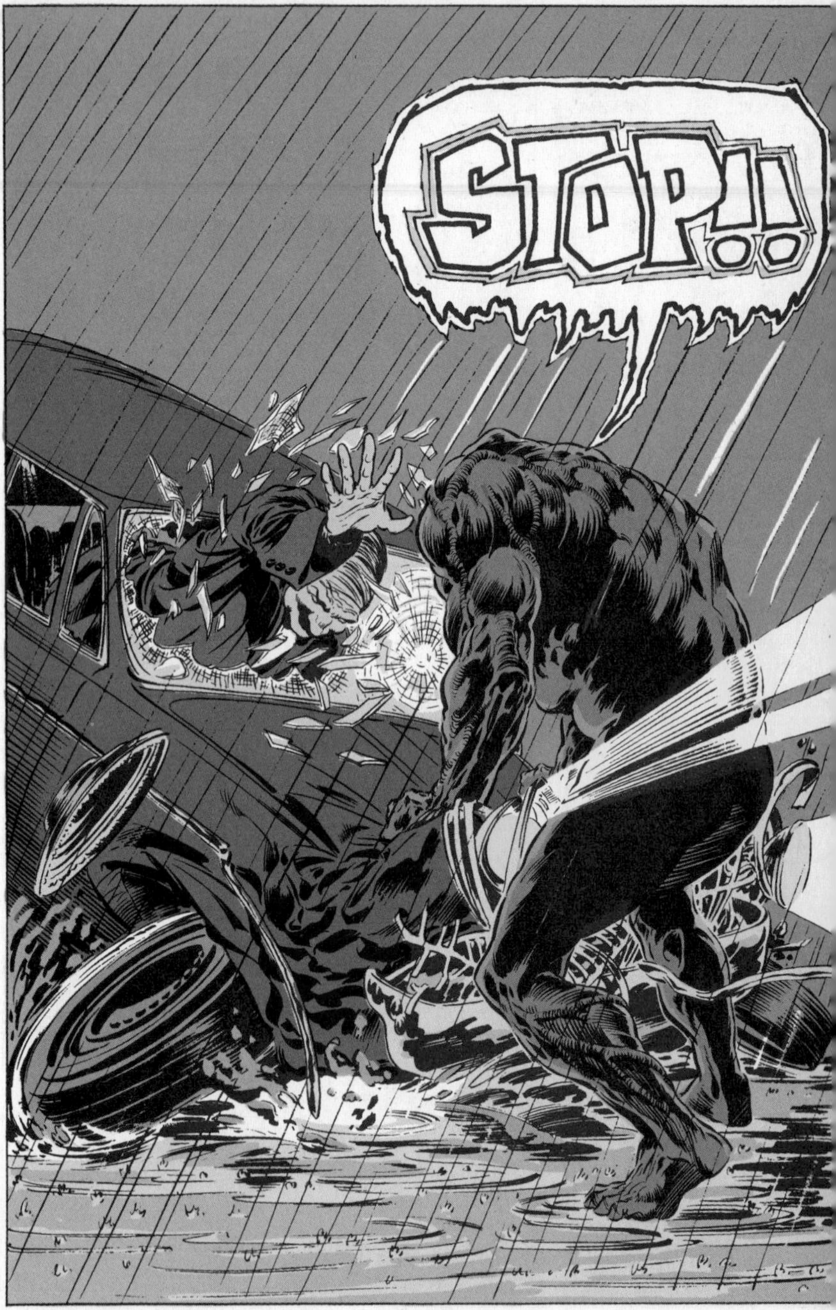
STOP!!

THEM AGAIN... FERRETT AND HIS FRIEND...

THE ONES WHO *KILLED* ME...AND MY *LINDA*...

THAT *MONSTER'S* NOT HUMAN...*NOT HUMAN!!*

NOT *HUMAN?* NO...I'M *NOT*...

...AND *YOU* ARE THE ONES WHO *MADE* ME THAT WAY...

NO... NO--!!

FRAGILE BONE AND CARTILAGE *SHATTER* BENEATH THE WEIGHT OF A MOSS-ENCRUSTED *FIST* AND...

IT'S *FINISHED* BRUNO...BUT IT *WON'T* GET *ME!*

ALL RIGHT, YOU FILTHY *MONSTER*--TURN AROUND AND *FACE* ME!

I WANT TO *SEE* THE LOOK IN YOUR EYES WHEN YOU-- *DIE!!*

BLAM!

C'MON, MONSTER-- *DIE!!*

WHY WON'T YOU *DIE?*

BLAM! BLAM!!

DIE! DIE! DIE!

BLAM! BLAM!

CLICK!

OH... MY... GOD...

AND WHEN FERRETT'S SCREAMING HAS FINALLY STOPPED...

YOU CAN'T KILL A DEAD MAN, FERRETT...

MAYBE YOU'LL REST EASIER NOW, LINDA! MAYBE WE BOTH WILL--!

SNIK!

HUH?

BLAM

...AND THE MAN I WAS IS MOST DEFINITELY DEAD!

IT'S CABLE... THAT BLASTED FOOL! I'LL...

OKAY, YOU--YOU THING! HANDS HIGH!

YOU'RE UNDER ARREST-- FOR MURDER...

...AND YOU'RE COMING WITH ME!

NO, CABLE... I'M AFRAID NOT!

MUCH AS I WANT TO...I CAN'T GO WITH YOU...

...AND, LORD HELP ME... I CAN'T TAKE YOU WITH ME!

COME BACK HERE, YOU MONSTER...

...COME BACK--!

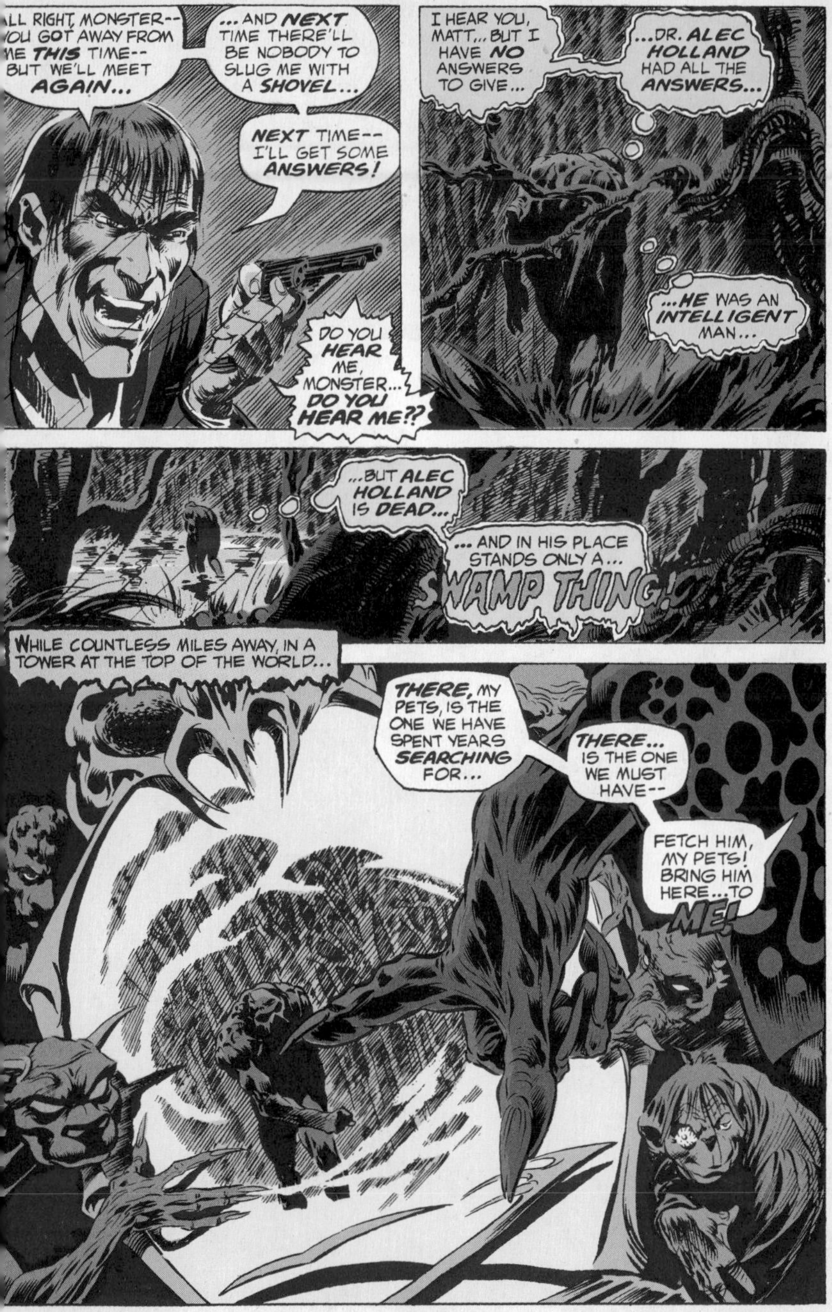

ALL RIGHT, MONSTER--YOU GOT AWAY FROM ME THIS TIME--BUT WE'LL MEET AGAIN...
...AND NEXT TIME THERE'LL BE NOBODY TO SLUG ME WITH A SHOVEL...
NEXT TIME--I'LL GET SOME ANSWERS!
DO YOU HEAR ME, MONSTER...DO YOU HEAR ME??
I HEAR YOU, MATT... BUT I HAVE NO ANSWERS TO GIVE...
...DR. ALEC HOLLAND HAD ALL THE ANSWERS...
...HE WAS AN INTELLIGENT MAN...
...BUT ALEC HOLLAND IS DEAD...
...AND IN HIS PLACE STANDS ONLY A...
SWAMP THING!
WHILE COUNTLESS MILES AWAY, IN A TOWER AT THE TOP OF THE WORLD...
THERE, MY PETS, IS THE ONE WE HAVE SPENT YEARS SEARCHING FOR...
THERE... IS THE ONE WE MUST HAVE--
FETCH HIM, MY PETS! BRING HIM HERE...TO ME!

CHAPTER **TWO**

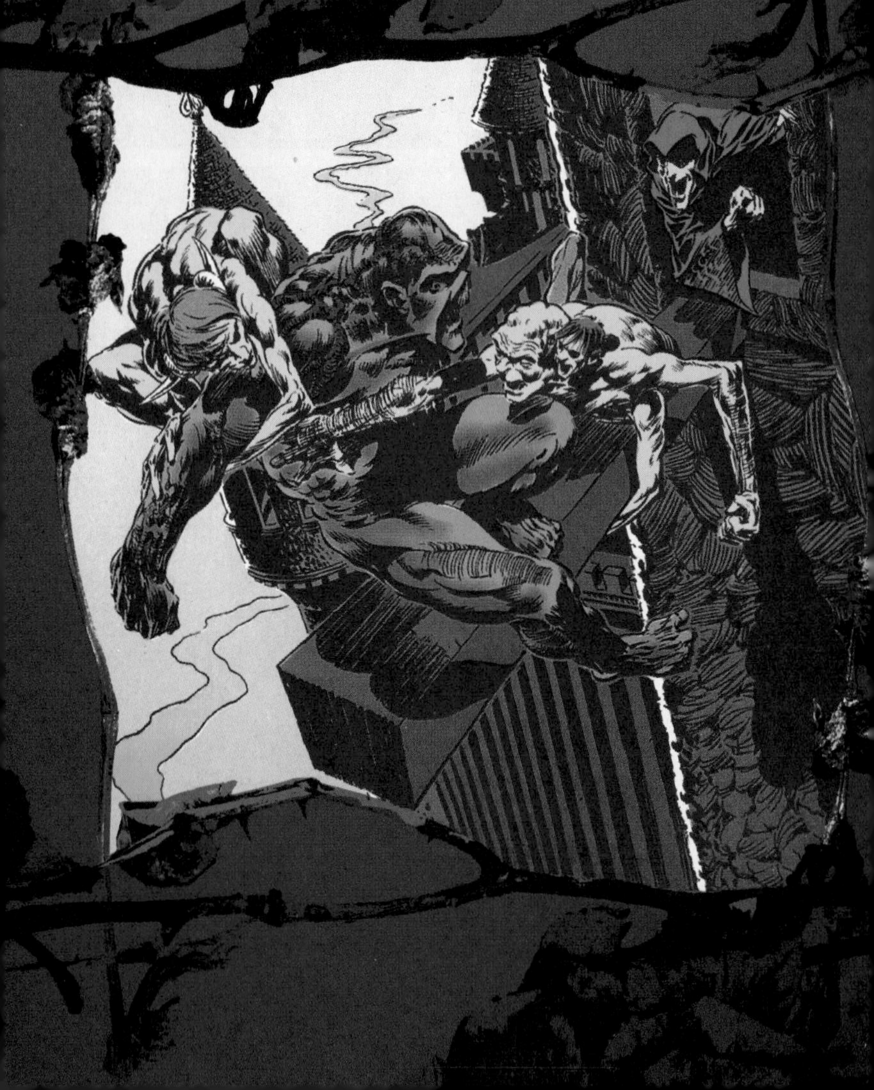

RAIN, 'TIS SAID, CAN WASH AWAY THE *PAST*--COVER OVER *MEMORIES* WITH A BITTERSWEET, GLISTENING HAZE...

FOR THE GROTESQUE *FIGURE* WHO CROUCHES IN THE SHADOWS, WATCHING GRIMLY AS TWO BROKEN BODIES ARE SILENTLY CARRIED AWAY, THE SUDDEN *STORM* HAS ENDED FAR TOO SOON...

...FOR THE *MEMORIES* LINGER...AND THEY BURN...

LORD, HOW THEY *BURN*!

BUT NO MERE SKY-BORN MOISTURE CAN QUENCH THE FLAMING IMAGES THAT FILL THE **SWAMP THING'S** MIND...

...IMAGES OF **ANGRY CONFRONTATION** SEVERAL DAYS EARLIER--WHEN MONSTER HAD BEEN **MAN**...

FOR THE **LAST TIME,** FERRETT--MY BIO-RESTORATIVE FORMULA IS **NOT FOR SALE!**

YOU MAY **REGRET** THAT **DECISION,** DOCTOR!

...IMAGES OF PAIN--AS A FEARSOME EX-**PLOSION** HURLED ALEC HOLLAND'S SMOLDERING BODY DEEP INTO THE SURROUNDING **SWAMP**...

...AND THE MAN CALLED FERRETT EXACTED HIS MEASURE OF **VENGEANCE**...

...IMAGES OF **RESURRECTION**--AS A GREAT, TWISTED FORM **ROSE** FROM THE GRASPING MIRE...

...AND TASTED **LIFE** ONCE MORE...

...BUT WITH RENEWED LIFE CAME THE **GRISLY** SHADOW OF **DEATH**--IN THE STILL, SILENT FIGURE OF DR. **LINDA HOLLAND,** ALEC'S ASSOCIATE...

...AND HIS **WIFE**...

...THEN, FINALLY, IMAGES OF A **DEBT** RE-**PAID** --AS THE HIDEOUS THING THAT WAS ONCE A MAN OF SCIENCE **BALANCED** FATE'S COLD SCALES...

IT'S *OVER*, LITTLE ONE...! *FERRETT* AND *BRUNO* WILL NEVER...*HURT* ANYONE AGAIN!

THEIR HELL IS ENDED... WHILE *MINE*...

...*MINE* IS JUST... *BEGINNING*..!

COME, LITTLE ONE...THERE IS NOTHING LEFT FOR US *HERE*...

...NOTHING LEFT FOR *ME*...*ANYWHERE*..!

ONLY *SILENCE*... COLD, UNENDING *SILENCE*..!

THEN, SUDDENLY, THE SILENCE HAS *HANDS*-- AND TALONS, CLUTCHING TENDRILS, SLICK-SCALED CLAWS...

...IT WRITHES IN COUNTLESS UN-HUMAN SHAPES THAT DROP FROM THE TOWERING TREETOPS LIKE A DEMONIC *RAIN*...

...COVERING THE MASSIVE MAN-MONSTER WITH A BLANKET OF SYNTHETIC FLESH...

SWIFTLY, MY *UN-MEN*-- *CAPTURE HIM* SWIFTLY!

THE *MASTER* WILL NOT TOLERATE YOUR *FAILURE*!

33

DON'T KNOW *WHAT* THESE THINGS ARE... OR WHAT THEY *WANT*...

...AND I DON'T *CARE* TO... *FIND OUT*...!

JUST WANT THEM TO... *LEAVE ME ALONE*..!

HE DISCARDS THEM ALL LIKE SO MUCH *CHAFF!* BUT THERE IS STILL ONE LEFT TO *CALL*--!

OPHIDIAN-- YOUR BROTHERS HAVE *NEED* OF YOU!

YESSSSS, CRANIUSSSSS-- OPHIDIAN COMESSSSS!

SWIFTLY, THE CREATURE CALLED *OPHIDIAN* UNDULATES ITS SERPENTINE BODY ACROSS THE MOSS-DAMP MIRE AND...

MY HEAD... *POUNDING*....! GOT TO TEAR HIM *LOOSE*...

...*TURN* THOSE EYES... *AWAY*...!

LOOK--LOOK AT ME! GAZE INTO OPHIDIAN'SSSSS EYESSSSS!

THAT'SSSSS SSSSSTRUGGLE-- TIRE YOURSSSSSELF-- --SSSSSO YOU WILL-- SSSSSLEEP--

34

THAT *STARE* BURNING INTO MY HEAD...

...MUST DO SOMETHING TO... *STOP* IT... BEFORE I... I...

...I DON'T... REMEMBER ANYMORE... DON'T UNDERSTAND...

...*WHAT*... WHAT AM I *DOING* HERE..?

WHY DO I FEEL SO... *STRANGE*..?

FOR A MOMENT, THE *SWAMP THING* SWAYS GENTLY IN THE BREEZE-- AND THEN WITH THE HINT OF A SIGH...

...HE *FALLS!*

YOU HAVE DONE *WELL*, OPHIDIAN-- HE WAS A MOST *FORMIDABLE* FOE, INDEED!

WELL--? YOU ALL KNOW YOUR *TASKS!* EVERY-ONE-- GET TO *WORK!*

K WUMPSH!

MOMENTS LATER--A SHORT DISTANCE AWAY...

HEAR WHAT, LT. CABLE? ALL I HEAR 'ROUND THIS BOG IS--BULLFROGS!

HEY--YOU DID YOU HEAR *THAT*?

NO--NOTHING *LIVING*--MORE LIKE AN *ENGINE*... A *BOAT*, MAYBE!

YEAH--I HEAR IT *NOW*--

--BUT THAT AIN'T NO *BOAT*!

SOUNDS MORE LIKE..

--AN *AIRPLANE*!

M-MY GOD, CABLE...THERE'S SOMETHING *CHAINED* TO THE UNDERCARRIAGE OF THAT JOB...

...SOMETHING *HUMAN*!

WHATEVER THAT *IS*, MIKE-- IT'S *NOT* HUMAN!

THAT'S THE MONSTER THAT *CLOBBERED* ME AND *KILLED* THOSE TWO...

YIP YIP!

WHA--? LINDA'S *MUTT*--!

AT LEAST, THAT... THAT *THING* DIDN'T GET *YOU*!

MAN, SHE'S OUT OF RANGE ALREADY--HEADING *DUE EAST* LIKE HER *TAIL* WERE ON FIRE!

WONDER WHERE THE HECK SHE'S *GOING*?

WELL, *STOP WONDERING*-- AND *FIND OUT*!

SOMEHOW, THAT CREATURE IS RESPONSIBLE FOR THE *DEATHS* OF SEVERAL PEOPLE--

--AND I'M NOT GOING TO *REST* TILL I *FIND* IT... AND *FINISH* IT OFF!

MORNING DWINDLES INTO *NOON*-- THE GREAT BLACK CRAFT CUTS THE SKY LIKE A TWIN-ENGINED *SCYTHE*...

DUE EAST: AN INK-DARK SHADOW SLIPS ACROSS THE RIPPLING *ATLANTIC*-- THE *IBERIAN PENINSULA*-- THE GLEAMING *MEDITERRANEAN*...

--AND THE DAY GROWS OLDER STILL...

UNTIL--THE SHADOW SETTLES SOFTLY UPON AN ICY BALKAN LAKE...

HAVE A CARE, FOOL! THE *MASTER* WANTS NO *HARM* TO BEFALL THE GIANT ONE!

HE HAS SOMETHING... *SPECIAL* PLANNED FOR *THIS* SPECIMEN!

THE *SWAMP THING* SLUMBERS ON, OBLIVIOUS, AS THE SMALL SHIP SWEEPS INTO DARKNESS--

--THE ANGRY MOUNTAIN'S *MAW*...

HE DOES NOT FEEL HIMSELF LIFTED FROM THE WATER BY UNHUMAN HANDS-- THEN TRUSSED LIKE SOME SAD MARTYR INTO A CREAKING WOODEN CART...

HE IS NOT BOTHERED BY THE PERSISTENT JOUNCE AND CLATTER-- AS HE IS DRAGGED DOWN TIMEWORN TUNNELS THAT TWIST THROUGH THE MOUNTAIN'S BREAST...

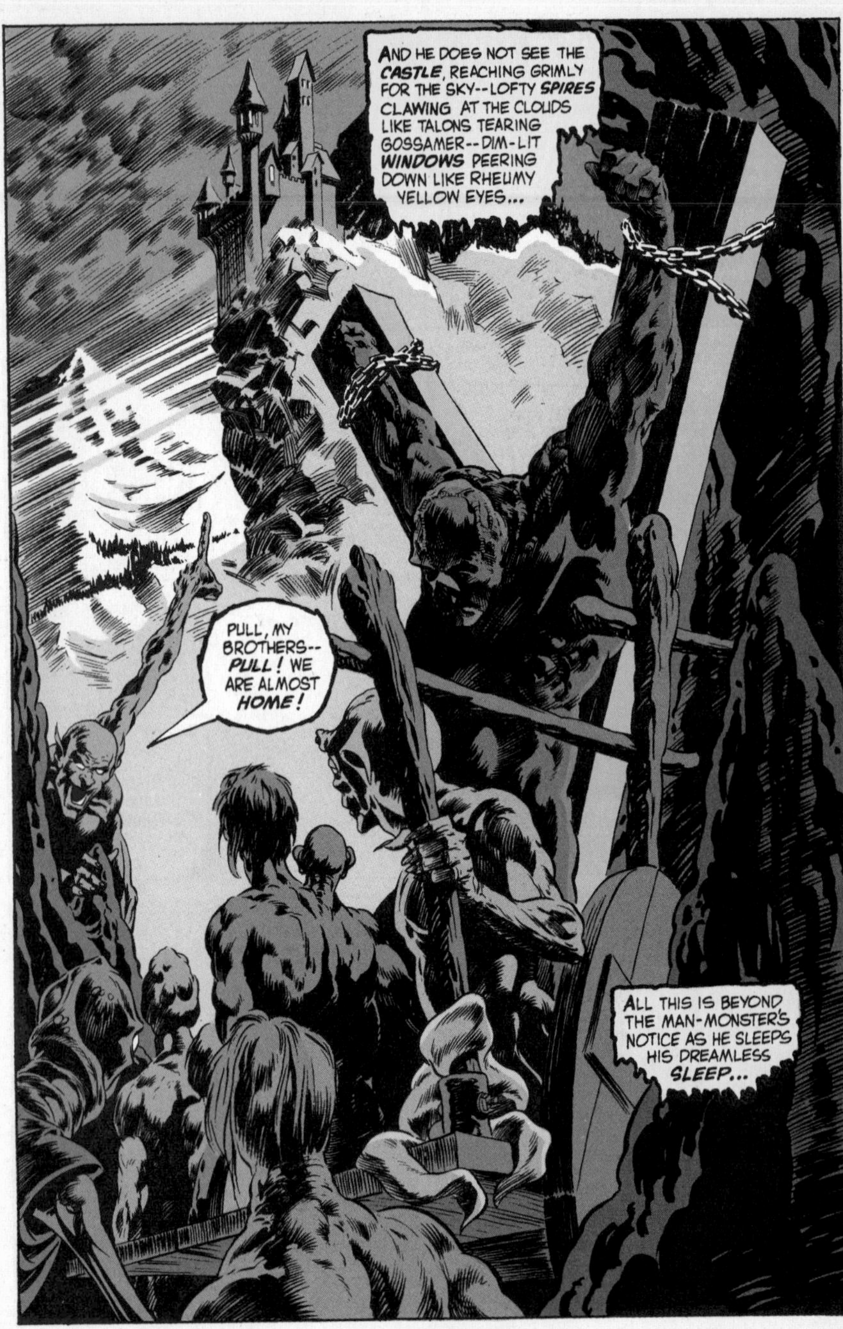
AND HE DOES NOT SEE THE CASTLE, REACHING GRIMLY FOR THE SKY--LOFTY SPIRES CLAWING AT THE CLOUDS LIKE TALONS TEARING GOSSAMER--DIM-LIT WINDOWS PEERING DOWN LIKE RHEUMY YELLOW EYES...
PULL, MY BROTHERS--PULL! WE ARE ALMOST HOME!
ALL THIS IS BEYOND THE MAN-MONSTER'S NOTICE AS HE SLEEPS HIS DREAMLESS SLEEP...

ONWARD AND UPWARD, THE BIZARRE PROCESSION PRESSES--ALONG A WINDING, ROCK-HEWN PATH--THROUGH A RUSTING PORTCULLIS--TO THE *CASTLE* ...

TO THE CASTLE--AND *HOME*...

MOTION...THE FLICKER OF A MOSS-LIDDED EYE...

...AND THE *SWAMP THING*--AWAKENS!

SNAK T

SNAKP T

CHAINED... THEY HAD ME CHAINED..!

THE *SCENERY* IS *DIFFERENT*...BUT THE *SITUATION* IS THE *SAME*...!

HOW *MANY* OF THEM... ARE THERE?

FOR EACH *ONE* THAT FALLS... *TWO OTHERS* TAKE ITS PLACE!

MUST BE A WAY OUT OF HERE... BUT WHERE... *WHERE*?

THAT *WINDOW*...! MAY BE...MY *ONLY* HOPE...!

CAN'T KEEP... *FIGHTING* THESE THINGS... *FOREVER*...!

HAVE TO *GET AWAY*... COLLECT MY *THOUGHTS*...

...*DISCOVER WHERE I AM*... BEFORE...

NO!!

REALLY *DID* IT... THIS *TIME*..!

NO PLACE LEFT... FOR ME TO *TURN*..!

BUT I'LL TAKE THESE...GOBLINS *WITH* ME...WHEN I *GO!*

THEY GIBBER AS THEY COME, THESE STRANGE SYNTHETIC BEINGS--AND THEY SPILL OVER THE MISSHAPEN MAN-MONSTER LIKE A WRITHING TIDE, GRASPING, CLUTCHING...

...UNTIL A VOICE LIKE FRACTURED CRYSTAL RINGS THROUGH THE COOL, CRISP AIR...

NOW, NOW, MY PETS--YOU SHOULDN'T BE SO ROUGH WITH YOUR NEW PLAYMATE!

WHO--?

I CAN READ THE QUESTION IN YOUR EYES, DEAR BOY...

MY NAME IS--*ARCANE!!*

REALLY, MY YOUNG FRIEND-- YOU NEEDN'T LOOK SO *DEFENSIVE* --

--I ASSURE YOU, MY"PETS"ARE QUITE HARMLESS!

NOW PLEASE-- TAKE MY HAND!

LET ME HELP YOU--INSIDE!

MOVEMENTS ECHO ALONG COBBLED CORRIDORS, STRANGE, UNFAMILIAR...

THE SOFT TREAD OF FEET GONE WITHERED WITH AGE...

THE MUCK-WET SHUFFLE OF LEGS NO LONGER HUMAN...

--BUT I COULD NOT CHANCE YOUR REFUSING MY INVITATION!

FORGIVE MY MANNER OF SUMMONING YOU, MY FRIEND--

YOU SEE, I HAVE A PROPOSITION TO MAKE YOU--A MOST UNUSUAL PROPOSITION, INDEED!

I AM OLD, MY BOY, FRIGHTFULLY OLD--

--BUT I HAVE LEARNED MANY THINGS IN MY TIME UPON THIS EARTH--OCCULT ENCHANTMENTS--SUPERNATURAL LORE!

I KNOW THE SECRET OF IMMORTALITY, FOR EXAMPLE--

--BUT IT IS A SECRET I DARE NOT PUT TO USE-- WHILE I STILL IN-HABIT THIS BENT AND WIZENED FORM!

USING MY GATHERED KNOWLEDGE, I SOUGHT TO BUILD MYSELF A NEW, MORE ENDURING FORM, SYNTHETICALLY!

MY UN-MEN ARE THE RESULT OF MY FIRST EXPERIMENTATIONS-- CRUDE, BUT TOTALLY DEDICATED TO ME!

I'M AFRAID I DID NOT FARE AS WELL WITH MY LATER CREATIONS!

THE BODIES, YOU WILL NOTICE, ARE MORE HUMAN IN FORM--BUT THE MINDS ARE NEARLY USELESS!

I KEEP THE POOR, ARTIFICIAL THINGS CONTAINED DOWN HERE--TO PREVENT THEM FROM DOING ANY ACCI-DENTAL HARM!

I'D ALMOST GIVEN UP HOPE OF OBTAINING THE NECESSARY BODY--WHEN I CHANCED TO SPY YOU IN THIS ANCIENT MYSTIC MIRROR!

I KNOW ALL ABOUT YOU--THE EXPERIMENTS--THE EXPLOSION--THE MURDER OF YOUR WIFE!

--AND THERE'S SOMETHING I CAN DO TO HELP YOU!

HOW WOULD YOU LIKE TO BE *HUMAN* ONCE AGAIN--*DOCTOR ALEC HOLLAND?*

BELIEVE ME, MY FRIEND--I AM MOST EARNEST!

I HAVE THE ABILITY TO RID YOU OF THIS MONSTROUS FORM--PERMANENTLY!

IT'S A SIMPLE PROCESS, ACTUALLY--BUT I MUST HAVE YOUR COMPLETE COOPERATION!

WELL, DOCTOR HOLLAND--? WHAT DO YOU SAY? HAVE WE A DEAL?

DOCTOR HOLLAND--? WHAT'S *WRONG* WITH YOU, MAN?

DON'T YOU *WANT* TO BE HUMAN?

DON'T YOU *CARE?*

I... CARE!!

SOON--IN A CAVERNOUS LABORATORY DEEP WITHIN THE CASTLE WALLS...

BEFORE WE CAN PROCEED, DR. HOLLAND, WE MUST KNOW MORE ABOUT YOUR-- *eh*-- CONDITION! VITAL STATISTICS AND SUCH, YOU UNDERSTAND!

MMMM--HEIGHT, 88 INCHES --WEIGHT, 547 POUNDS-- APPARENTLY ALL MUSCLE!

WE'D BEST CHECK YOUR RESPIRATION AND BLOOD PRESSURE NEXT!

WHY--Y-YOU HAVE *NO* BLOOD PRESSURE--

--AND YOUR RESPIRATION-- LIKE THAT OF A PLANT! YOU BREATHE IN CARBON DIOXIDE --AND EXHALE OXYGEN!

YOUR BODY, IT SEEMS, IS EQUALLY PLANT-LIKE! THERE ARE SEVERAL BULLETS LODGED INSIDE YOU--IN PLACES THAT WOULD BE FATAL TO ANYONE ELSE!

REMARKABLE, MY BOY--I MUST INVESTIGATE FURTHER!

ASTONISHING! THOSE ROOTS COVERING YOUR BODY--ARE *ALIVE!*

THEY MOVE OF THEIR OWN ACCORD!

YES, DOCTOR HOLLAND-- I WOULD SAY YOUR BODY IS EXACTLY WHAT I'VE BEEN LOOKING FOR!

BUT THE MAN CALLED *ARCANE* IS NOT THE ONLY ONE LOOKING FOR THAT PARTICULAR BODY...

THOUSANDS OF MILES DISTANT, SECURITY AGENT *MATT CABLE* IS PREPARING TO TAKE UP THE SEARCH...

ANOTHER MINUTE, LIEUTENANT--AND WE CAN *CLOSE* THIS PLACE UP!

SOONER THE *BETTER!* WITH THE *HOLLANDS* DEAD, THERE'S NO MORE REASON TO KEEP IT *OPEN!*

--AND THE QUICKER I CAN FINISH *HERE,* THE QUICKER I CAN START TRACKING DOWN THE *MONSTER* THAT *KILLED...*

HUH?

ARE YOU *CABLE?* I GOT THE *REPORT* YOU WANTED ON THAT CRAZY *PLANE!*

THEN *GIVE* IT TO ME, MISTER!

NOT *MUCH* TO GIVE! THE TRACKING STATION *LOST* HER SOME-WHERE OVER THE ATLANTIC--

--SO WE CONTACTED *INTERPOL*--AND THEY'VE GOT *THEIR* PEOPLE WORKING ON IT NOW!

ANYBODY THIS SIDE OF THE *SPHINX* SPOTS THAT SPOOK-JACKER-- AND *WE'LL* KNOW ABOUT IT!

SO WILL *WE,* MY FRIEND-- THANKS TO THE TINY *TRANS-MITTER* WE IMPLANTED IN *YOUR* MONGREL'S *HEAD*--

--FOR WE, TOO, HAVE A *SCORE* TO SETTLE WITH THIS SO-CALLED *"MONSTER"!*

TWO OF OUR *BEST MEN* WERE LOST TO THAT *SWAMP THING*--

--AND *THE CONCLAVE* DOES NOT TAKE SUCH LOSSES *LIGHTLY!*

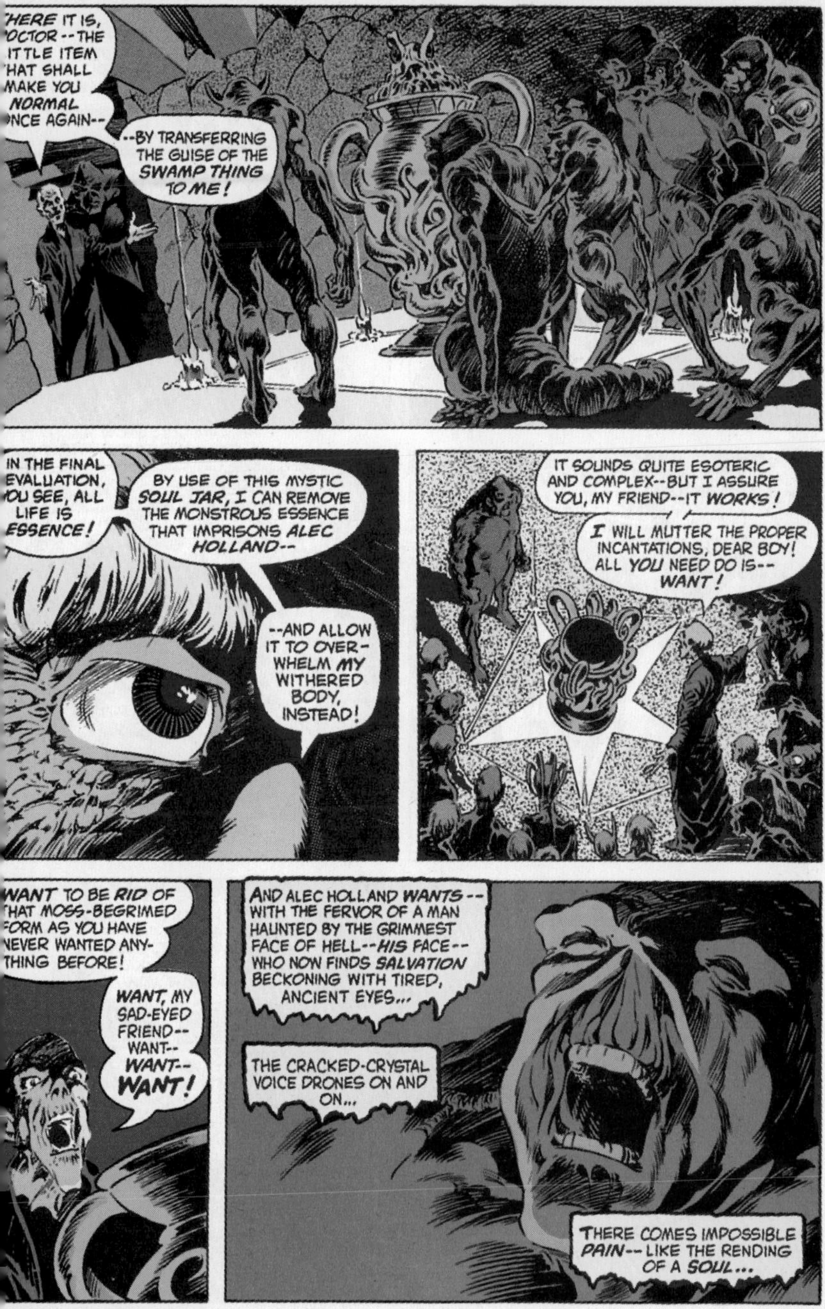
HERE IT IS, OCTOR -- THE ITTLE ITEM HAT SHALL MAKE YOU NORMAL NCE AGAIN--
--BY TRANSFERRING THE GUISE OF THE SWAMP THING TO ME!
IN THE FINAL EVALUATION, OU SEE, ALL LIFE IS ESSENCE!
BY USE OF THIS MYSTIC SOUL JAR, I CAN REMOVE THE MONSTROUS ESSENCE THAT IMPRISONS ALEC HOLLAND--
--AND ALLOW IT TO OVER-WHELM MY WITHERED BODY, INSTEAD!
IT SOUNDS QUITE ESOTERIC AND COMPLEX--BUT I ASSURE YOU, MY FRIEND--IT WORKS!
I WILL MUTTER THE PROPER INCANTATIONS, DEAR BOY! ALL YOU NEED DO IS-- WANT!
WANT TO BE RID OF THAT MOSS-BEGRIMED FORM AS YOU HAVE NEVER WANTED ANY-THING BEFORE!
WANT, MY SAD-EYED FRIEND-- WANT-- WANT-- WANT!
AND ALEC HOLLAND WANTS -- WITH THE FERVOR OF A MAN HAUNTED BY THE GRIMMEST FACE OF HELL--HIS FACE-- WHO NOW FINDS SALVATION BECKONING WITH TIRED, ANCIENT EYES...
THE CRACKED-CRYSTAL VOICE DRONES ON AND ON...
THERE COMES IMPOSSIBLE PAIN-- LIKE THE RENDING OF A SOUL...

...AND A QUEASY ALEC HOLLAND WATCHES THE *SWAMP THING* CLAMP THE SOUL JAR TIGHT...

WH-WHAT *HAPPENED*--?

IT'S *OVER,* MY BOY--TAKE A *LOOK* AT YOURSELF!

M-MY *ARMS*... MY *HANDS*... THEY'RE *NORMAL* AGAIN!

DEAR GOD...I'M *HUMAN!*

...AND I'LL SHOW YOU TO MORE *COMFORTABLE* QUARTERS!

AND SO YOU WILL *REMAIN*--PROVIDING THE ENCHANTMENT IS *NOT DISTURBED!*

COME-- TAKE THIS *ROBE*...

A *BENEFICENT* SIDE-EFFECT OF THE *ENCHANTMENT,* GOOD DOCTOR--BUT *ENOUGH* OF THAT FOR *NOW!*

YOUR *VOICE*--! IT WAS SO VERY *DIFFICULT* FOR ME TO MAKE THAT BODY *SPEAK*--!

HOW DO *YOU* MANAGE IT SO *EASILY?*

YOU MUST BE TERRIBLY *TIRED,* MY BOY--! REST A WHILE--AND THEN WE'LL TALK!

46

MOONLIGHT: FROM TIME IMMEMORIAL, IT HAS CHARTED THE COURSE OF LOVERS AND TIDES...

--HUMAN AGAIN! IT SEEMS TOO IMPOSSIBLE TO BE TRUE!

HUMAN AGAIN! TO BE ABLE TO SIT LIKE THIS--WITHOUT ANGER--WITHOUT FEAR...

...BUT HE WHO BASKS IN ITS QUICKSILVER GLOW THIS NIGHT HAS LITTLE INTEREST IN SUCH CELESTIAL CONCERNS...

I ONLY WISH LINDA COULD BE HERE TO SEE IT...

LORD--HOW I WISH LINDA COULD BE HERE!

I WONDER IF ARCANE KEEPS ANYTHING AROUND THIS PLACE TO DRINK?

RIGHT ABOUT NOW-- I NEED ONE!

AND AS THE DISPIRITED DOCTOR MAKES HIS WAY THROUGH CALIGARIAN CORRIDORS...

WHAT SORT OF MADHOUSE IS THIS PLACE?

IT APPEARS TO HAVE BEEN PUT TOGETHER IN THE THROES OF SOME ARCHITECT'S NIGHTMARE--!

AND AT LAST...

THESE MUST BE HIS *CHAMBERS!* I CAN HEAR *VOICES* FROM IN...

HUH?

...*GULLIBLE FOOL*-- PLAYED RIGHT INTO MY *HANDS!*

I'D HAVE GIVEN *ANYTHING* FOR THIS *BODY*-- ANYTHING--

--AND *HOLLAND* TRADED IT FOR A PALTRY TASTE OF FLEETING *HUMANITY!*

AN *ILL-CONSIDERED* BARGAIN ON *HIS* PART, INDEED...

...FOR THIS MALFORMED BODY MEANS FAR MORE THAN *IMMORTALITY,* MY *PETS*--

--IT MEANS *POWER!*

--POWER TO EXACT THE *VENGEANCE* THAT HAS GNAWED AT MY HEART FOR *YEARS*...

...*VENGEANCE* AGAINST THE UNTHINKING *CRETINS* WHO INHABIT THE *VILLAGE* BELOW...

...THE SELF-CENTERED *SNOBS* WHO SHUNNED ME IN MY YOUTH--WHO *SCORNED* ME AND MY *WORK!*

IN THIS *INDESTRUCTIBLE* BODY, I'M ABLE TO DO WHAT I'VE *LONGED* TO DO...

...I CAN GO DOWN THE MOUNTAIN-- AND *DESTROY* THEM ALL!

THE MAN IS *MAD*-- AND *I'VE* GIVEN HIM THE MEANS TO *CARRY OUT* HIS HOMICIDAL DREAM!

DEAR LORD-- WHAT HAVE *I DONE?*

I'VE *SOLD OUT*-- THAT'S WHAT I'VE DONE--

--TRADED THE LIVES OF *COUNTLESS* PEOPLE FOR THE SAKE OF *REGAINING* MY OWN--

--AND THERE'S *NOTHING* I CAN *DO* ABOUT IT-- *NOTHING!*

NO!

THERE *IS* A WAY TO STOP HIM--

EVEN IF IT COSTS ME MY *SOUL!*

"...AND SO YOU WILL *REMAIN*--PROVIDING THE ENCHANTMENT IS *NOT DISTURBED!*"

THE WORDS POUND IN ALEC HOLLAND'S MIND AS HE RACES UP CRUDE TOWER STAIRS--AND BURSTS INTO A DIMLY-LIT ROOM...

PARDON THE *INTRUSION*, FRIEND-- BUT YOU'RE STANDING IN MY *WAY!*

UNGH--THING IS *FASTER* THAN IT *LOOKS*--!

IT'S-- *BREAKING* MY--*BACK*!

THE *ROBE SASH*-- MY *ONLY* HOPE--!

HAVE TO PRAY THAT THE *NYLON CLOTH* IS *STRONGER*--

--THAN THIS *MONSTER'S* SYNTHETIC *THROAT*!

THE CREATURE IS *FINISHED*-- BUT THERE'S ONE THING *MORE* I MUST ATTEND TO!

HOLLAND-- *DON'T*!

FOR *GOD'S SAKE*, MAN-- YOU'LL RUIN *EVERYTHING*!

YES, ARCANE-- FOR *GOD'S* SAKE...

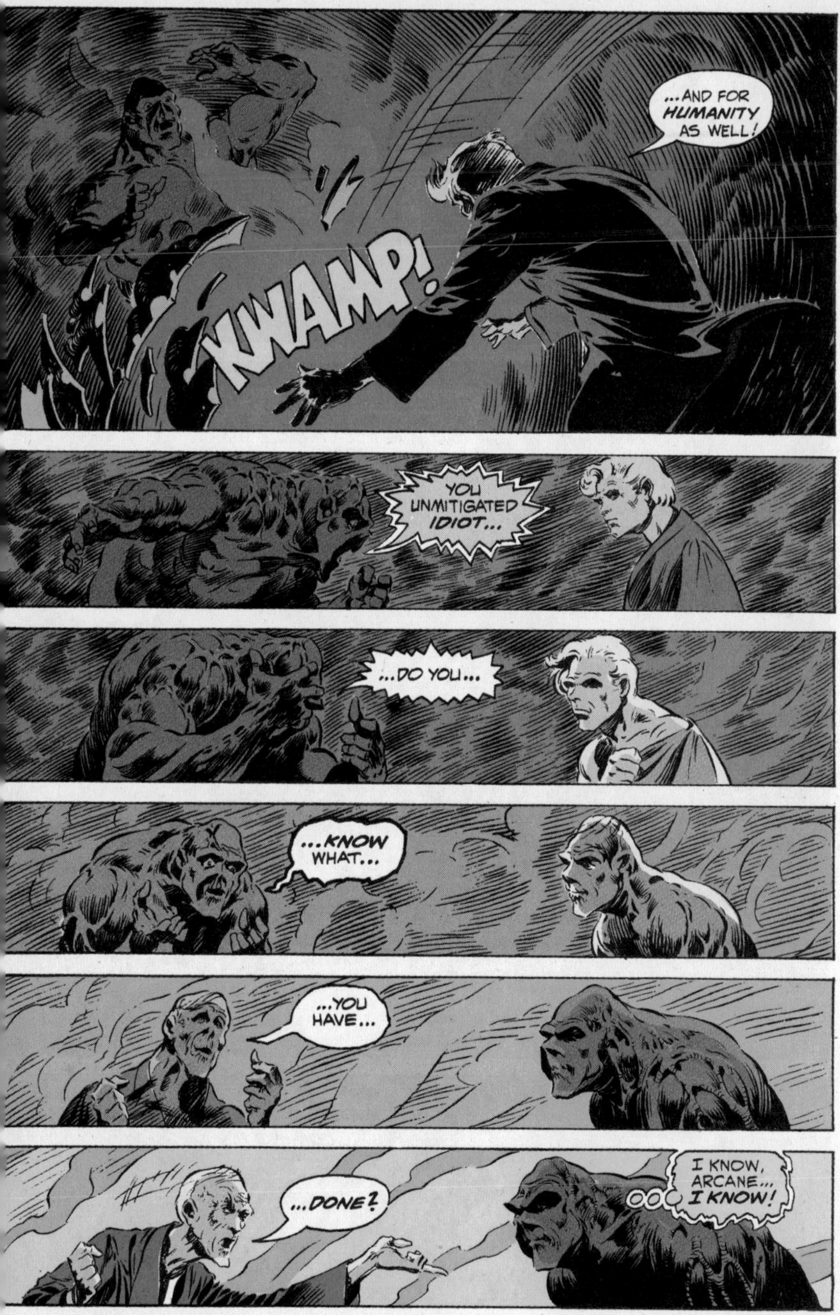
...AND FOR HUMANITY AS WELL!
KWAMP!
YOU UNMITIGATED IDIOT...
...DO YOU...
...KNOW WHAT...
...YOU HAVE...
...DONE?
I KNOW, ARCANE... I KNOW!

RUINED--EVERY-
THING RUINED--
BECAUSE OF YOUR
SELF-RIGHTEOUS
STUPIDITY!

AT HIM,
MY PETS--
TEAR HIM
APART!

ARCANE IS
ESCAPING...
THESE BEASTIES
ARE...HOLDING
ME BACK...

ARCANE!

THE SINGLE WORD ROLLS HARSHLY
FROM MOSS-ENCUMBERED LIPS--
BUT IT IS MUCH MORE THAN A
WORD...

...IT IS AN
EPITHET--
A CURSE--
A PROMISE OF
RETRIBUTION
NOT LONG IN
COMING...

...AND IT ECHOES
THROUGH THE ANCIENT
BATTLEMENTS LIKE
THE DEATH-KNELL OF
A DREAM...

STOP HIM,
MY PETS--
STOP
HIM!

NO CHANCE,
OLD MAN...I'M
COMING FOR
YOU...

...AND NOT ALL THE HOSTS OF *HELL* WILL STOP ME *NOW..!*

KRACK!

NO--KEEP AWAY FROM ME--STAY BACK--!

I GAVE YOU WHAT YOU WANTED--MADE YOU HUMAN AGAIN--!

IT'S *YOUR OWN* FAULT THAT YOU'VE *REVERTED* TO THE *MONSTER--* YOUR *OWN* FAULT--YOUR *OWN...*

FAULLLLLL

AND THE SOUND OF THE OLD MAN'S SCREAMING IS LOST IN THE CLOUDS BELOW...

THEIR MASTER GONE, THE UN-MEN PAUSE, UNCERTAIN OF WHAT TO DO...

THEY MUTTER AMONG THEMSELVES FOR A MOMENT--AND, AT LAST, A DECISION IS REACHED...

FOR ALL OF THEIR EXISTENCE, THEY HAVE FOLLOWED THEIR MASTER BLINDLY--WHEREVER HE MIGHT LEAD...

...AND THERE SEEMS NO GOOD REASON TO *CHANGE* THAT SITUATION *NOW...*

53

GONE-- ALL OF THEM!

THEY WERE *LOYAL*... TO THE *END*!

SHAKING HIS MOSSY HEAD SADLY, THE MAN-MONSTER TURNS FROM THE WINDOW--AND SILENTLY SHAMBLES AWAY...

...HIS THOUGHTS DWELLING ON AN AGED MADMAN AND HIS PATHETIC LITTLE FLOCK...

...SO HE *WON'T* HAVE TO THINK OF-- *HIMSELF*!

LOST IN CONTEMPLATION, THE *SWAMP THING* DOES NOT HEAR THE PONDEROUS FORM THAT RISES UP TO *FOLLOW*...

54

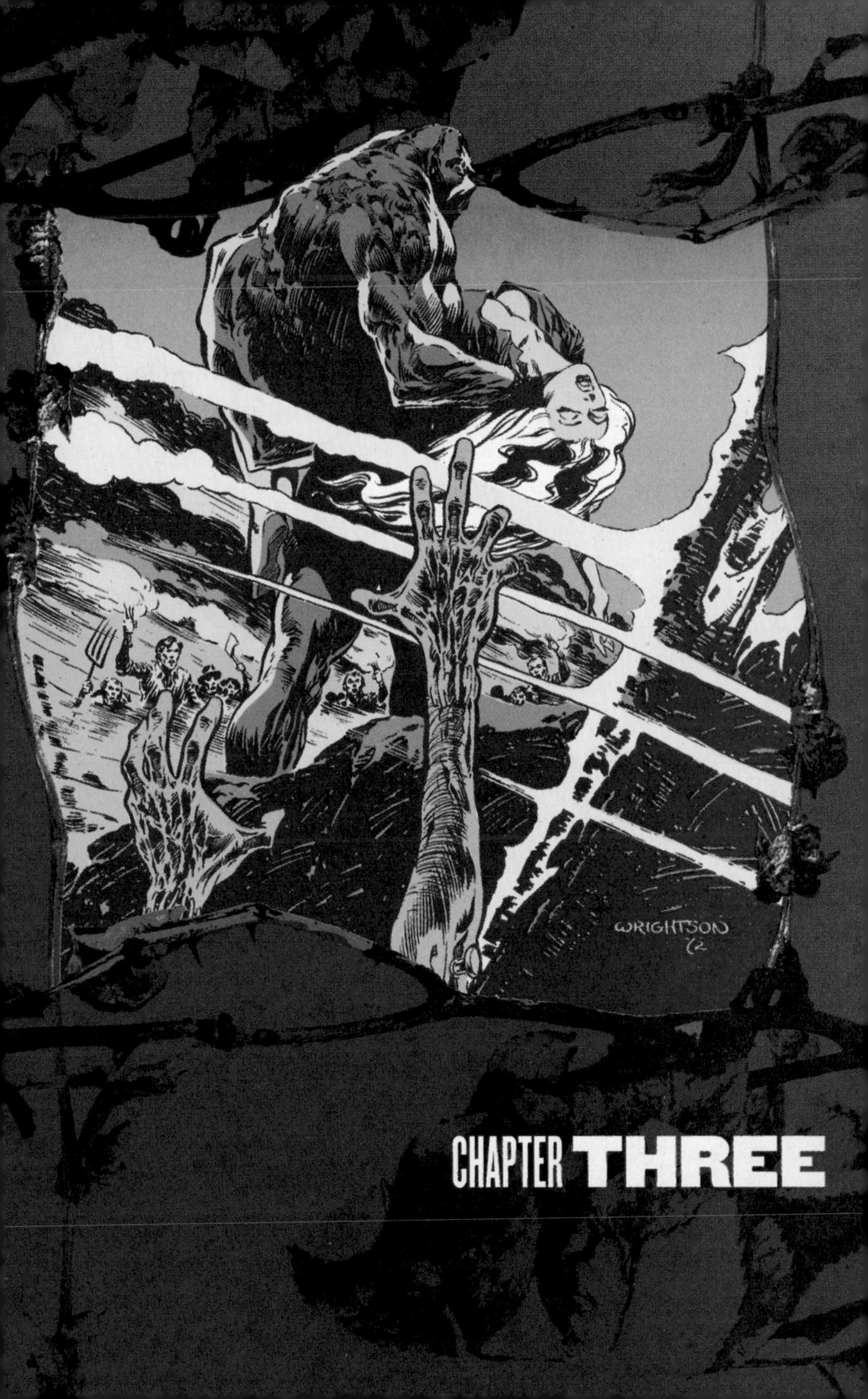
WRIGHTSON
'72

CHAPTER **THREE**

DAWN ROLLS IN WITH A WHIMPER, SPREADING SHIMMERING FINGERS OF SCARLET ACROSS THE SNOW-CAPPED BALKAN LANDSCAPE LIKE A BLIND MAN FEELING HIS WAY...

BELOW, IN THE VALLEY, THE *VILLAGE* IS COMING AWAKE-- SHUTTERS ARE THROWN OPEN, KETTLES ARE SET TO BOIL...

WHILE, MID-WAY UP THE MOUNTAINSIDE, AN INCREASINGLY FAMILIAR MOSS-CAKED FIGURE GAZES DOWN AT THOSE DAWN-TOUCHED ROOFTOPS WITH MORE THAN A TINGE OF *REGRET*...

HUMANITY... FRIENDSHIP... THEY WERE ALMOST *MINE* AGAIN...!

SO CLOSE... I CAME SO VERY CLOSE...!

WRIGHTSON '72

DAYLIGHT DANCES ON THE BATTLEMENTS AS THE MAN-MONSTER LOOKS OUT ACROSS THE MOUNTAINS-- AND *REMEMBERS* ...

THEN THE MUCK-ENCRUSTED MOCKERY OF A MAN TURNS -- AND SHAMBLES BACK THROUGH THE CASTLE'S TWISTING CORRIDORS ...

THAT *LIGHT*... COMING FROM...

...ARCANE'S *LABORATORY*... FILLED WITH *CHEMICALS*... *EQUIPMENT*...

...AND MAYBE... JUST *MAYBE*... A CHANCE TO FIND A *CURE* FOR MY... *CONDITION*...!

IT'S HIDDEN HERE *SOMEWHERE*... AMONG THE TUBES... AND VIALS... AND BEAKERS...

HE REMEMBERS THE GROTESQUE *UN-MEN*, WHO CARRIED HIM TO THIS DISTANT LAND AT THE COMMAND OF THE AGED WIZARD CALLED *ARCANE* ...

ARCANE, WHO TOOK THE FORM OF THE *SWAMP THING* AS HIS OWN, THUS TURNING *DOCTOR ALEC HOLLAND* HUMAN ONCE AGAIN ...

JUST A MATTER OF PUTTING THE MATERIALS TOGETHER... IN PRECISELY THE CORRECT RELATIONSHIP AND...

A HUMANITY VIOLENTLY *SACRIFICED* TO PROTECT THE UNKNOWING TOWNSFOLK FAR BELOW...

PLINK!

...NO GOOD...! HANDS TOO *THICK*... TOO *STRONG*...

DAMN--! ALL OF THIS *MATERIAL* AT HAND... AND ALL OF IT *USELESS*...!

THIS BODY IMPRISONS ME IN *MORE* WAYS THAN ONE... *REFUSES* TO HELP ME *RID* MYSELF OF IT...!

WELL...IF I CAN'T EFFECT A CURE *ALONE*...

...I'LL FIND SOMEONE WILLING TO WORK *WITH* ME...!

I'LL HEAD BACK TO THE *UNITED STATES*...AND BEGIN TO...

WHA..? THE FLAGSTONE *FLOOR*...GIVING WAY *BENEATH* ME...!

SLIPPING TOO *QUICKLY*... NOTHING TO GRAB *HOLD* OF...!

WHO?

HALTED IN MID-PLUNGE, THE MASSIVE MAN-MONSTER TURNS HIS BURNING EYES UPWARD--TO STARE IN ASTONISHMENT AT THE TWISTED FORM OF HIS UNEXPECTED *SAVIOR*...

UUHHNN... UUHHNN...

ONE OF ARCANE'S *CREATIONS*... BROKEN *FREE* OF HIS CHAINS...!

BUT IS HE *POWERFUL* ENOUGH...TO PULL ME *OUT* OF THIS HOLE...?

GNARLED FINGERS DIGGING FURROWS IN THE MOSSY FLESH, THE PATCHWORK FIGURE STRAINS TO PULL HIS AWESOME BURDEN OUT FROM THE YAWNING PIT...

SLOWLY... PONDEROUSLY... GAINING INCH AFTER PRECIOUS INCH, THE *SWAMP THING* RISES UPWARD...

...THEN, WITH FATAL SUDDENNESS, HE IS LOST AGAIN INTO THE DARKNESS -- LEAVING ONLY SCRAPS OF ROTTED VEGETATION BENEATH THE OTHER'S BROKEN FINGERNAILS TO ATTEST TO THE RESCUE'S *FAILURE*...

MY SKIN'S TOO *SLIPPERY*... HE COULDN'T MAINTAIN A *GRIP*...!

I'M FALLING... *FALLING*...!

LIKE AN OBSCENE BILLIARD BALL, THE MOSS-DAMP MONSTER PLUMMETS DOWNWARD...

...CAROMING FROM ONE AGED TIMBER TO ANOTHER...

...SHATTERING THEM WITH HIS WEIGHT...

FALLING...

FALLING...

FALLING...

...TO SMASH WITH SICKENING FINALITY ONTO THE SPRING-WET ROCKS BELOW...

KRWUMP

...THERE TO LIE SILENT AND STILL...

...AND TERRIBLY, TERRIBLY ALONE!

BUT THE STRANGE CREATURE THAT ONCE WAS *DOCTOR ALEC HOLLAND* HAS NO EXCLUSIVE CLAIM TO THAT SITUATION...

...AND WITHIN THAT PLANE, THERE SITS A MAN WHO'D BE *ALONE* IN THE HEART OF A CROWD...

MANY MILES AWAY, A MULTI-ENGINED SEAPLANE ARCS THROUGH THE AZURE SKY--FOLLOWING THE SELF-SAME PATH THE *SWAMP THING* HAD TAKEN A FEW BRIEF DAYS BEFORE...

A MAN WITH A DESPERATE *MISSION*...

WITHIN THAT SOARING SEAPLANE, LIEUTENANT *MATT CABLE* ENDURES THE FLIGHT--AND PONDERS...

EASY, POOCH-- *EASY!* IT WON'T BE MUCH LONGER!

ACCORDING TO OUR INFORMATION, THAT BLACK PLANE LANDED DEEP IN THE BALKAN MOUNTAINS...

...SO THAT'S WHERE *WE'RE* HEADING, TOO!

'CAUSE WHEREVER THAT *PLANE* WENT, THE *SWAMP THING* WENT AS WELL-- AND I HAVE A PERSONAL *SCORE* TO SETTLE WITH THAT MONSTER...

...THE *DEATHS* OF MY FRIENDS... *ALEC AND LINDA HOLLAND!*

THAT'S WHY I HAD MYSELF TRANSFERRED TO AN *INTERPOL* ASSIGNMENT...

...FOR, IF NEED BE, I'LL *FOLLOW* THAT KILLER-CREATURE TO THE ENDS OF THE EARTH!

EXCELLENT! OUR GOOD LIEUTENANT CABLE HAS *REACHED* HIS DESTINATION--

--AND WHEREVER HE TRAVELS, UNBEKNOWNST TO *HIM*--

--THE *CONCLAVE* WILL BE *WITH* HIM!

IT'S SAID 99% OF ALL POLICE WORK IS *INVESTIGATION*-- SO IT IS NOT UNUSUAL FOR THE ANXIOUS SECURITY AGENT TO BEGIN HIS RELENTLESS HUNT FOR THE *SWAMP THING* WITH THE RESIDENTS OF THE LOCAL TOWN...

DOORS ARE OPENED AND QUESTIONS ARE ASKED-- BUT THE ANSWER IS ALWAYS THE SAME...

SILENCE... COLD, UNAPPROACHABLE *SILENCE*...

AND FINALLY...

COME ON IN! SOMETHING I CAN *DO* FOR YOU, MISTER--?

CABLE-- *MATT CABLE*-- AND I'M *STUNNED!*

YOURS IS THE FIRST *FRIENDLY* FACE I'VE SEEN SINCE I ARRIVED IN THIS BURG, MISS--?

THE NAME IS *ARCANE*, MISTER CABLE--

--BUT YOU CAN CALL ME *ABIGAIL!*

ARCANE? THEN-- YOU'RE JUST THE PERSON I'M *LOOKING* FOR!

YOU DON'T HAPPEN TO OWN A *PLANE*, DO YOU?

ME? DON'T BE *SILLY!* THE SEA-PLANE BELONGS TO *MY UNCLE!*

CARE FOR A *LOLLI-POP?*

NO, MISS--ALL I'M INTERESTED IN IS *INFORMATION!*

WELL, I HAVE ALL THAT YOU'D *WANT*, MISTER CABLE--

--BELIEVE ME-- BEING THE ONLY *MEDIC* IN THIS TOWN, I KNOW *PLENTY!*

+CLINIC+

SIZZLING DROPLETS OF FLAME SPLATTER AGAINST A MOSS-ENSHROUDED CHEST--STIRRING A MASSIVE MAN-BRUTE TO CONSCIOUSNESS ONCE MORE...

WH-WHERE *AM I?* WHAT *HAPPENED* TO...?

HUH? BURNING *EMBERS*... RAINING ON ME...!

AND--AS HERCULEAN MUSCLES SHRUG THE RUBBLE ASIDE...

SOMETHING'S ON *FIRE* UP THERE...

...BUT *HOW*...?

NO!!

THAT CRAZY PATCHWORK CREATURE WHO TRIED TO STOP MY FALL ...*HE* IS RESPONSIBLE...!

...TURNED ARCANE'S *LABORATORY*... INTO AN *INFERNO*...!

GOT TO GET OUT OF HERE...FOLLOW THIS UNDERGROUND *STREAM*...?

PRAY IT LEADS *AWAY* FROM THE CASTLE...BEFORE...

FINGERS OF FLAME CURL LOVINGLY ABOUT THE AGED TURRETS OF *CASTLE ARCANE,* PASSION BUILDING TILL IT ERUPTS IN AN OUTBURST OF SHATTERED STONE AND WOOD...

FOR A MOMENT, THE RUPTURED BATTLEMENTS HANG SUSPENDED IN SPACE-- THEN FALL REMORSELESSLY TO THE VALLEY FAR BELOW...

HAUNTING THUNDER FADES INTO SILENCE--AS THE CLAMOR OF ANXIOUS FOOTSTEPS RISES TO TAKE ITS PLACE...

THE PEOPLE OF THE VILLAGE COME SCURRYING UP THE MOUNTAIN, BRINGING MORBID CURIOSITY...AND *DESPAIR*...

OUT OF MY *WAY*-- MY *UNCLE'S* IN THERE! HE *NEEDS* ME--!

IF HE *WAS* IN THERE, LADY-- HE'S *BEYOND* NEEDING *ANYTHING*! NOW CALM DOWN ABIGAIL--*CALM DOWN*!

Y-YOU...DON'T *UNDERSTAND*, CABLE! HE...WAS ALL THE FAMILY I HAD!

BUT I *DO* UNDER- STAND, ABIGAIL--

--MAYBE *MORE* THAN YOU COULD KNOW--!

YOU SEE--I LOST SOMETHING IN THAT *HOLOCAUST*, TOO--

SOMETHING I'VE *SEARCHED* FOR ACROSS THE FACE OF THIS *WORLD*--

--THE *KILLER*-- OF THE ONLY TWO *FRIENDS* I'VE EVER CARED FOR--

--A HEARTLESS, HIDEOUS *MONSTER*-- IN MANY *DIFFERENT* WAYS!

YEAH--WE *BOTH* LOST SOMETHING IN THAT FIRE, ABIGAIL!

--AND, GOD FORGIVE ME, I'M NOT SURE WHO'S LOST *MORE*!

HOW **LONG** HAS IT BEEN -- SINCE YOU **FELL** INTO THE WATER? HOW LONG HAVE YOU **DRIFTED** -- TOSSED BY THE GENTLE **TIDE?**

HOW **LONG?** IT DOES NOT **MATTER** -- FOR YOU FEEL **LAND** BE- NEATH YOUR MISSHAPEN FEET ONCE MORE -- RUPTURED ROCK AND SOD --

--AND YOU ARE **FREE** AGAIN -- TO **MOVE!**

FREE -- TO PICK YOUR WAY THROUGH THE WINDING FOREST PATHWAYS --

--TO RETRACE STEPS YOU SOMEHOW **KNOW** YOU HAVE TROD BEFORE...

YOU **WALK** -- AND SOMETHING TUGS AT YOUR BECLOUDED BRAIN --

--SOME- THING FLICKERS BEFORE YOUR HAZY EYES LIKE A DYING **FLAME** --

--SOMETHING THAT REKINDLES THE **MEMORIES**...

YOU REMEMBER *WALKING*-- A DIFFERENT *DAY*--THE *SAME* FOREST...

YOU WERE WALKING-- HURRYING *HOME!*

YOU HAD BEEN *AWAY* TOO LONG -- FROM YOUR VILLAGE--FROM YOUR *DAUGHTER*--

AND NOW THE PEOPLE FROM THE *GOVERNMENT* WERE COMING TO *TAKE* HER ...

BUT YOU WOULD NOT *LET* THEM STEAL THE ONE THING YOU *LOVED*--

YOU WOULD *FIGHT* THEM IF YOU MUST-- AND, FAILING THAT--

--YOU WOULD TAKE THE CHILD--AND *RUN!*

YOU MOVED SWIFTLY THROUGH THE FOREST, YOUR *HEART* POUNDING IN YOUR CHEST--

BOOM

--AND THEN YOUR *HEART* STOPPED--

--AND THE WORLD EXPLODED INTO *DARKNESS*...

YOU CAME TO *LOVE* THE DARKNESS--IT *NURTURED* YOU--KEPT YOU *SAFE*...

YOU EMBRACED THE *BLACK* FOR A TIME WITHOUT TIME...

--UNTIL AGONIZING SLIVERS OF *LIGHT* SLASHED THROUGH THE VELVET-- TO ROUSE YOU FROM YOUR *SLEEP*...

GREGORI--? AT LAST--YOU ARE *AWAKE*--!

GREGORI--MY *BROTHER!* I SHOULD HAVE *WARNED* YOU-- TO AVOID THE ANCIENT *MINE FIELD* HIDDEN IN THE FOREST--!

YOU COULD HAVE BEEN *KILLED!*

IT'S *FORTUNATE* I HEARD THE *EXPLOSION*-- AND DECIDED TO *INVESTIGATE*--

--OR YOUR--eh-- *BODY* MIGHT STILL BE *LYING* THERE-- AS *FODDER* FOR THE WOLVES!

THERE WASN'T MUCH *LEFT* OF YOU, YOU REALIZE--

I HAD TO *IMPROVISE* MY REPAIRS FROM THE MATERIALS AT HAND!

HERE-- I'LL *SHOW* YOU!

YOU REMEMBER THE *EXPRESSION* ON THE FACE OF THE MAN WHO SAID HE WAS YOUR *BROTHER*-- AS HE TURNED THE WEATHERED-LOOKING GLASS TOWARD YOU--

--AND YOU REMEMBER THE STARTLED *GASP* THAT ESCAPED YOUR CONSTRICTED THROAT--WHEN YOU SAW WHAT YOU HAD *BECOME*...

NOT EXACTLY A *FIRST-CLASS* JOB, BROTHER--

--BUT, UNDER THE CIRCUMSTANCES, IT WAS THE *BEST* THAT I COULD DO!

YOUR GNARLED HAND LASHED OUT BLINDLY, SEEKING TO *DESTROY* THE HIDEOUS IMAGE THAT MOCKED YOU SO...

GREGORI-- WHAT ARE YOU *DOING?*

MY EQUIPMENT-- MY EXPERI- MENTS--YOU'LL *RUIN* THEM!

FORGIVE ME, GREGORI-- BUT I CANNOT *PERMIT* YOU--!

THIS INJECTION WILL ONLY MAKE YOU *SLEEP!*

AND THE ARMS OF *DARKNESS* REACHED UP TO *COMFORT* YOU ONCE MORE...

YOU STAYED IN THAT MENTAL SHADOW- LAND, CHAINED IN YOUR BROTHER'S DUNGEON, REFUSING TO ACCEPT WHAT YOU'D BECOME --

--UNTIL THE DAY THE DOOR OPENED--AND A MORE AWE- SOME HORROR STOOD FRAMED IN THE LIGHT...

THE DOOR REMAINED OPEN WHEN THEY'D GONE--ONE BY ONE, THE OTHERS WAN- DERED MINDLESSLY AWAY...

SNAP!

... AND, AT LENGTH, YOU DECIDED TO *FOLLOW*...

WHEN YOU LOST THE MOSSY BEHEMOTH TO THE ANGRY CASTLE DEPTHS, YOU DISCOVERED YOUR BROTHER'S *LABORATORY*...

...AND YOUR CURIOUS MEDDLING TURNED THE OLD STRUCTURE INTO A BLAZING *HELL*...

NOW YOUR MIND IS MUDDLED, UNABLE TO FACE THE PAST...

YOU STUMBLE ALONG ON A HALF-FORGOTTEN QUEST--

--UNTIL A SUDDEN SOUND TURNS YOU FROM YOUR TASK...

THE MAN IS UNKNOWN TO YOU-- BUT THERE IS SOMETHING ABOUT THE GIRL--SOMETHING ACHINGLY FAMILIAR...

...AND A FRAGMENT OF YOUR JUMBLED MEMORY SNAPS FIRMLY INTO PLACE...

C-CABLE--! WHAT IN GOD'S NAME--?

IT'S THAT SWAMP--! NO--IT'S SOMETHING ELSE--

--BUT I WON'T LET IT TOUCH YOU!

SHE IS DIFFERENT SOMEHOW--BUT YOU CANNOT FORGET HER EYES-- OR THE IVORY IN HER HAIR...

SHE IS YOUR DAUGHTER-- THE ONE YOU'VE COME TO SAVE...

...AND YOU WILL NOT LET THEM KEEP HER FROM YOU...

THE GIRL GOES LIMP IN YOUR ARMS, SOFT, HELPLESS--

--AND YOU REMEMBER WHAT YOU SWORE...

YOU WILL TAKE THE CHILD--AND RUN!

A-ABIGAIL--?

BUT *WHERE* WILL YOU RUN? WHAT CONFUSED *DESTINATION* HIDES WITHIN YOUR MIND AS YOU SHAMBLE THROUGH THE *FOLIAGE*...

...AND FIND YOURSELF ONCE MORE ON THE BANK OF A FAMILIAR *STREAM?*

FOR A MOMENT YOU HESITATE-- THEN YOU STEP UPON THE *BRIDGE*...

BUT WOULD YOU BE SO QUICK TO *CROSS* THAT WOODEN SPAN IF YOU KNEW WHAT SLEEPS BELOW...

AND, HEARING YOUR PON-DEROUS FOOTFALLS, SUD-DENLY *AWAKENS*...?

HUH? SOMETHING *MOVING* ABOVE ME... *PEOPLE*...!

NO...NOT *PEOPLE*...! IT'S THE CREATURE FROM ARCANE'S CASTLE...! SOMEHOW, *HE* MAN-AGED TO SURVIVE THE EXPLOSION AS WELL...!

BUT... *WHAT* IS HE CARRYING...?

A *GIRL*... ONE OF THE LOCAL *VILLAGERS*... UNCONSCIOUS IN HIS ARMS...!

BETTER TAKE HER *AWAY* FROM HIM... BEFORE HE DOES HER *HARM*...

...AND I HAVE THE UNPLEASANT SUSPICION... HE WON'T BE TOO *FOND* OF THAT IDEA...!

YOU TURN AT THE NOISE BEHIND YOU--TO SEE THE MOSSY BEING WHOSE LIFE YOU SOUGHT TO SAVE *RISE* FROM THE WATER'S DEPTHS...

...AND YOU THINK THAT *HERE*, AT LAST, IS SOMEONE WHO'LL *UNDERSTAND*...

70

HE'S PUTTING THE GIRL *DOWN*....!

HAVE TO CHECK ON *HER* ... BEFORE I DO ANYTHING ABOUT *HIM* ...!

FEVERISHLY, YOUR BEFUDDLED BRAIN SEEKS A WAY TO *COMMUNICATE*-- TO TELL THIS NEWFOUND *FRIEND* ABOUT YOUR DESPERATE SITUATION...

SHE'S OUT *COLD*... *SHOCK*, PROBABLY...!

...THEN YOU SEE THAT HE'S NO *BETTER* THAN THE REST...

...AND DISCOVERING THIS--YOU *ACT!*

NO ONE--NO *THING*-- IS GOING TO STEAL THE ONE YOU LOVE...

...EVEN IF YOU MUST **KILL** TO MAKE CERTAIN...

HE'S GONE **CRAZY**...

...TRYING TO **STRANGLE** ME...FOR TOUCHING THE **GIRL**...

...AND, DESPITE HIS **LOOKS**... HE'S **STRONG** ENOUGH TO **SUCCEED**...!

GOT TO GET SOME **LEVERAGE**...PUT MY **WEIGHT** BEHIND IT...

...AND BREAK HIS **GRIP**...BEFORE HE BREAKS MY **NECK**...

YOU REEL BACK BENEATH THE THRUST OF A **MOSS-CAKED FOOT**--

--BUT SOMETHING **STOPS** YOU BEFORE THE BATTLE CAN BEGIN ANEW...

...THE ANGRY TUMULT OF AN APPROACHING **MOB!**

THERE HE IS, MEN! I TOLD YOU WE'D FIND HIM WITH--

--THE **SWAMP THING!**

THEN THAT MONSTER **DIDN'T** DIE IN THE CASTLE FIRE--!

IT COMES BACK TO YOU THEN-- THE REASON FOR ALL THIS SENSELESS FIGHTING...

YOU MUST SAVE THE GIRL--AT ANY COST...

...AND *NOTHING* MUST STAND IN YOUR WAY...

THWACK!

YOU RUN--BUT THEY ARE UPON YOU IN AN INSTANT--BAYING DOGS YAPPING AT THE HEELS OF A FAR-FROM-HELPLESS *"FOX"*...

THEY HAVE NOT *CHANGED* --THE PEOPLE OF YOUR VILLAGE--STILL THEY SEEK TO TAKE FROM YOU THE ONLY THING THAT GIVES *MEANING* TO YOUR HAUNTED LIFE...

IF NOT THROUGH *LEGAL* MEANS, THEN THROUGH SAVAGE, UNREASONING *VIOLENCE*...

...VIOLENCE THAT COULD *DESTROY* THE INNOCENT BURDEN YOU CARRY...

...AND YOU WILL NOT *PERMIT* THAT TO HAPPEN...

NO--YOU DEFINITELY WILL NOT PERMIT *THAT!*

KWARUNK!

BEFORE THE STARTLED CROWD CAN REGAIN ITS SENSES, YOU HAVE FLED INTO THE FOREST--

--LEAVING A CERTAIN ROOT-TANGLED MONSTER TO SUFFER THE CONSEQUENCES OF YOUR ACTIONS...

HE'S TAKEN THE GIRL... ESCAPED...

...AND IT SEEMS THE LOCAL FOLK... DON'T CARE *WHO* THEY BLAME... FOR THE *DAMAGE* TO THEIR BRIDGE..!

...AND I THINK *I* OUGHT TO FIND THAT... *PATCH-WORK MAN*... BEFORE *THEY* DO...!

IT WON'T TAKE THEM *LONG*... TO FIND ANOTHER WAY *ACROSS*...!

BUT THE HAPLESS *SWAMP THING* IS LONG FORGOTTEN WHEN YOU PAUSE BEFORE THE SMOLDERING *RUINS*...

THERE IS ONLY *ONE* SAFE HAVEN FOR YOU NOW--ONE PLACE YOU CAN CALL *HOME*...

YOU REST THE GIRL GENTLY ON THE ASH-DUSTED EARTH...

...AND YOU BEGIN TO DIG FOR THE *CASTLE*...

WH-WHERE AM I? WHAT *HAPPENED* TO...

NOW I REMEMBER--! THAT *MONSTER*-- KIDNAPPED ME--!

HAVE TO *STOP* HIM SOMEHOW--!

YOU HARDLY *FEEL* THE SMOKING TIMBER AS IT SLAMS AGAINST YOUR BACK...

...BUT YOU *ARE* ANGRY JUST THE SAME...

A CHILD--
HOWEVER
PRECIOUS
SHE IS--
MUST BE
DISCIPLINED
WHEN BAD...

YOU RAISE
YOUR
HAND
TO
STRIKE
HER...

...BUT THE
BLOW
NEVER
FALLS...

...FOR A MOSS--EN-
CRUSTED MONOLITH
STANDS ROOTED IN
YOUR PATH, HIS SAD
EYES BLAZING LIKE
UNHOLY EMBERS...

...AND, FOR THE
FIRST TIME
IN THIS
TWISTED,
MISMATCHED
BODY, YOU
KNOW WHAT
IT IS TO FEEL
PAIN...

THE SWAMP THING LIFTS
YOU, BATTERS YOU, SMASHES
YOU AGAINST THE BLACK-
CHARRED STRUCTURE...

...AND,
DEEP
WITHIN
THE
WRECKAGE,
SOMETHING
GIVES WAY...

HELP ME--
PLEASE--I'M--
FALLINNGGG...

75

SUSPEND *TIME* BY A THREAD AND LET IT SLOWLY UNRAVEL--AS IT STEALS AWAY THE MOMENTS OF A YOUNG WOMAN'S LIFE...

PLEASE-- *HELP*-- I CAN'T HOLD ON MUCH LONGER--!

TWO THEY CALL *MONSTER* STAND BY HELPLESSLY--AS *ABIGAIL'S* GRIP SLOWLY LOOSENS ON THE CHARRED WOODEN BEAM...

THEN THE RAGING TOWNSFOLK REACH THE CRUMBLING WRECKAGE--TO MAKE THE CAST *COMPLETE*...

GRIMLY, THE MAN-BRUTES PEER AT THE VILLAGERS...

THEN TURN TO THE HELPLESSLY HANGING GIRL...

...AND A *DECISION* IS REACHED...

IGNORING THE MOB, THE MONSTER-MEN CLAMBER DOWN THE WOODWORK-- CAREFUL NOT TO DISTURB *ABIGAIL'S* PRECARIOUS PERCH...

...BUT NOT QUITE CAREFUL ENOUGH...

NO-- *STOP*-- BEFORE THE WHOLE THING *COLLAPSES*--!

SLOWLY, CAUTIOUSLY, THE *PATCHWORK MAN* DESCENDS INTO THE ROUGH-HEWN ABYSS-- GRASPING HIS DAUGHTER WITH HANDS LIKE CHISELED STONE...

MISMATCHED MUSCLES BULGE AS THE GIRL IS LIFTED UPWARD-- INTO THE *SWAMP THING'S* POWERFUL HANDS...

THAT'S IT... GENTLY... GENTLY NOW...!

PLEADINGLY, THE CREATURE WHO WAS ONCE *GREGORI ARCANE* STARES INTO HIS DAUGHTER'S EYES--

--AND FROM THAT FLEETING GLANCE COMES A GLIMMER OF-- *RECOGNITION!*

THERE IS A HORRIBLE GROAN AS A TIMBER-SHANKED ARMS THRUST A FRAIL FORM UPWARD...

D-DADDY--?

...AND THE RUINED REMNANTS OF *CASTLE ARCANE* PLUNGE INTO THE BOWELS OF THE EARTH--CARRYING WITH THEM A LONE, MIS-SHAPEN FORM...

...A FORM THAT WEARS THE SEMBLANCE OF A *SMILE* ON ITS ONCE-HUMAN FACE...

THE RUMBLE FADES AND THE *SWAMP THING* TURNS-- TO CONFRONT AN ANTAGONISTIC AUDIENCE...

GET HIM, MEN-- BEFORE HE CAN *HURT* HER--!

THE MAN-BRUTE'S MOUTH BECOMES A TIGHT-LIPPED LINE, HIS DARK EYES NARROW--

--AND HE STRIDES DETERMINEDLY FORWARD...

...UNTIL HE STANDS FACE-TO-FACE WITH THE MAN WHO'S SWORN TO *KILL* HIM...

IF YOU WANT THE GIRL SO BADLY, CABLE...

YOU CAN **HAVE** HER...!

THEN THE MOSSY MONSTER SHAMBLES OFF INTO THE GROWING MOUNTAIN MIST...

...AND, CONTRARY TO EVERYTHING HE HAS SWORN, **MATT CABLE** DOES NOT LIFT A HAND TO **STOP** HIM...

EPILOGUE: LATE THE FOLLOWING AFTERNOON...

ARE YOU **SURE** ABOUT THIS, ABIGAIL?

QUITE SURE, MISTER CABLE--er--**MATT!**

WITH BOTH MY FATHER AND MY UNCLE **DEAD,** THERE'S NOTHING MORE TO **KEEP** ME HERE!

I'D RATHER GO WITH **YOU,** MATT! MAYBE YOUR ORGANIZATION CAN FIND A **USE** FOR ME SOMEWHERE?

POSSIBLY, ABIGAIL-- THOUGH **MEDICINE** IS A LITTLE **OUT** OF OUR LINE!

STILL-- IT COULDN'T HURT TO **ASK**--!

WHAT ABOUT **YOU,** MATT? WHAT WILL YOU **DO** NOW THAT THE **SWAMP THING** HAS VANISHED ONCE MORE?

TAKE UP THE **SEARCH** AGAIN! WHAT HE DID FOR YOU DOESN'T CHANGE A THING--!

HE'S **STILL** RESPONSIBLE FOR THE **DEATHS** OF MY FRIENDS--

--AND I'M GOING TO **FIND** HIM AGAIN-- IF IT TAKES THE REST OF MY **LIFE!**

THE END

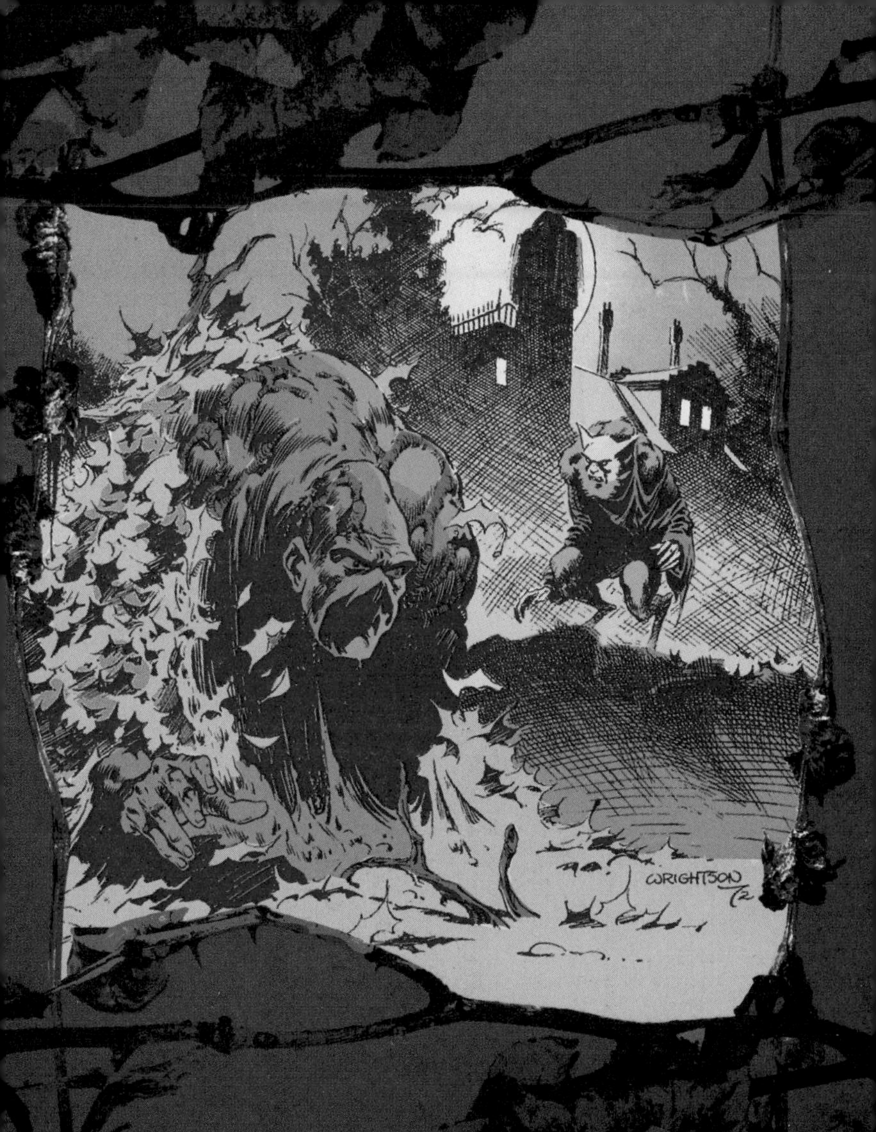
WRIGHTSON '72

CHAPTER FOUR

THE NIGHT IS MADE OF *FOG*: A MUSKY GRAY BLANKET THAT LIES UPON THE LAND-SCAPE LIKE A *SHROUD*, OPPRESSING ALL IT EMBRACES...

TREETOPS--HILLOCKS--EVERYTHING COVERED BY THE SAME PERVADING *MIST*... BUT THIS NIGHT, TWO *NEW* OBJECTS THRUST FROM THE *COLD* FEN FLOOR...

ONE, THE RUPTURED WRECKAGE OF WHAT ONCE HAD BEEN A SLEEK, FOUR-ENGINE *SEA-PLANE*...

THE OTHER, THE TWISTED RUIN OF WHAT ONCE HAD BEEN A *MAN*...

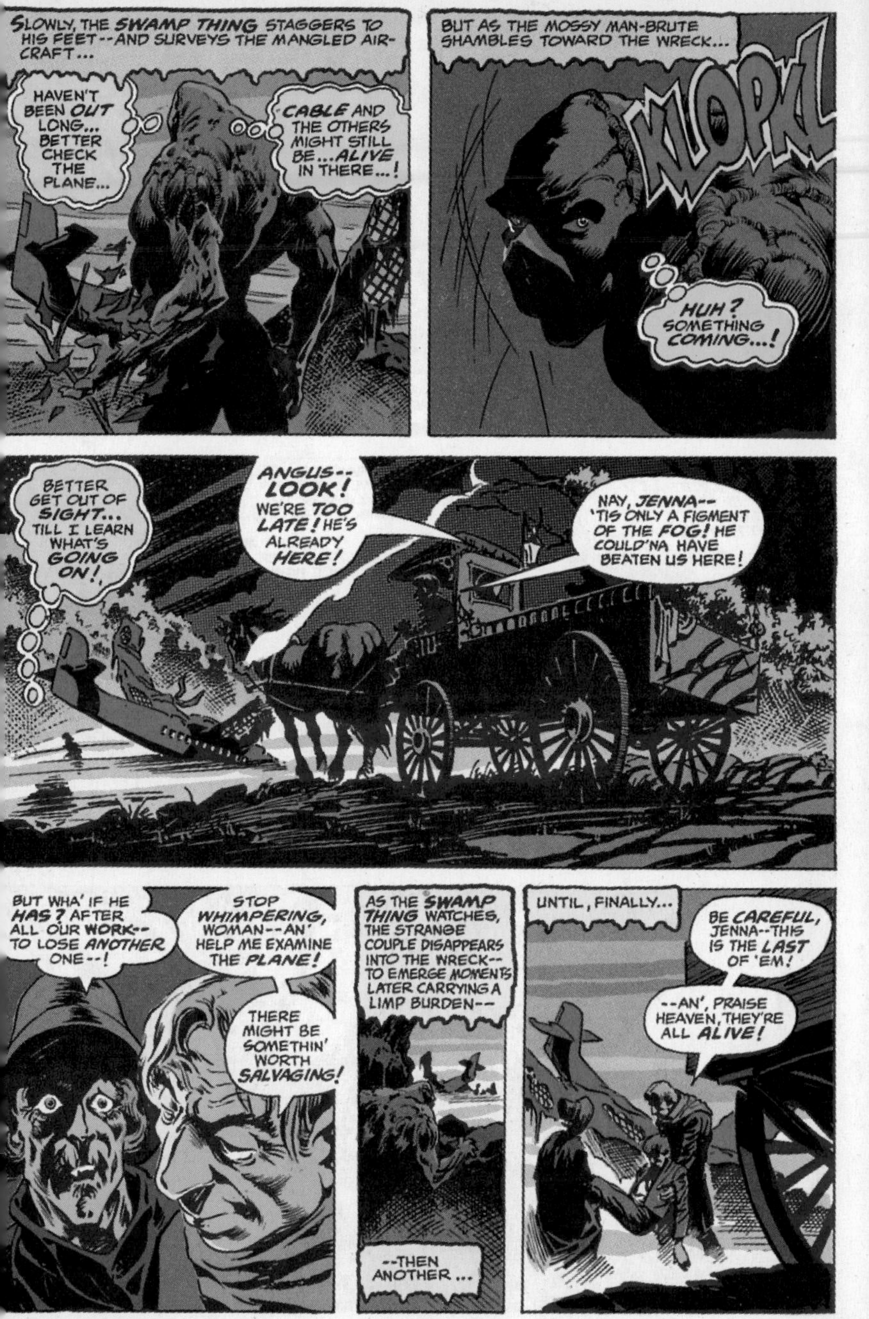

SLOWLY, THE SWAMP THING STAGGERS TO HIS FEET--AND SURVEYS THE MANGLED AIRCRAFT...
HAVEN'T BEEN OUT LONG... BETTER CHECK THE PLANE...
CABLE AND THE OTHERS MIGHT STILL BE...ALIVE IN THERE...!
BUT AS THE MOSSY MAN-BRUTE SHAMBLES TOWARD THE WRECK...
KLOPKL
HUH? SOMETHING COMING...!
BETTER GET OUT OF SIGHT... TILL I LEARN WHAT'S GOING ON!
ANGUS--LOOK! WE'RE TOO LATE! HE'S ALREADY HERE!
NAY, JENNA--'TIS ONLY A FIGMENT OF THE FOG! HE COULD'NA HAVE BEATEN US HERE!
BUT WHA' IF HE HAS? AFTER ALL OUR WORK--TO LOSE ANOTHER ONE--!
STOP WHIMPERING, WOMAN--AN' HELP ME EXAMINE THE PLANE!
THERE MIGHT BE SOMETHIN' WORTH SALVAGING!
AS THE SWAMP THING WATCHES, THE STRANGE COUPLE DISAPPEARS INTO THE WRECK--TO EMERGE MOMENTS LATER CARRYING A LIMP BURDEN--
--THEN ANOTHER...
UNTIL, FINALLY...
BE CAREFUL, JENNA--THIS IS THE LAST OF 'EM!
--AN', PRAISE HEAVEN, THEY'RE ALL ALIVE!

AYE--AND 'TIS NO WONDER *THIS* ONE IS--BEIN' SUCH A FINE, STRONG BROTH OF A LAD! NOT AT ALL LIKE--!

ENOUGH, JENNA-- I'LL HAVE NO MORE OF YER *WEEPIN'* FOR WHAT *CAN'NA* BE CHANGED!

BUT WE *CAN* CHANGE IT, ANGUS--I *KNOW* WE CAN!

WHERE D'YE SUPPOSE THEY WERE *GOIN'?*

WHO CAN *SAY?* IT MAKES NO DIFFERENCE-- *NOW!*

FROM THE *SOUND* OF THEIR VOICES...I'D GUESS WE CRASHED... SOMEWHERE ON THE *SCOTTISH MOORS...*

...BUT FROM THE *TONE* OF THEIR VOICES...I *DON'T* THINK CABLE AND COMPANY HAVE... FALLEN INTO *SAFE* HANDS...!

SCOTLAND OR NOT... I'VE NEVER SEEN AN *AMBULANCE* TO RESEMBLE *THAT* ONE...

I DOUBT IF MY *FRIENDS...* ARE BEING TAKEN TO A *HOSPITAL...*

...BUT *WHEREVER* THEY'RE GOING...

...I'M GOING WITH THEM!

TIME PASSES : A RUTTED, MIST-SWEPT ROAD ECHOES TO THE SQUEAL OF RUSTED SPRINGS AS THE ANTIQUE CARRIAGE ROLLS ON...

ABOVE, AN ANGRY AMBER MOON CLAWS AWAY ITS CLOUDY COVERING TO RULE A STAR-STREAKED SKY...

AND, AT LAST--AT VERY LONG LAST--A MOSS-ENCRUSTED MOCKERY FINDS HIMSELF STANDING BEFORE A BUILDING--THE ONLY STRUCTURE TO DEFY THE FOG FOR COUNTLESS MILES 'ROUND...

THE SWAMP THING STUDIES THE AGING MANOR--ITS MUSTY, GRIM FACADE--AND HE KNOWS THAT THE WAGON HAS COME--HOME!

83

SPIN THE HANDS OF THE CLOCK--AND IT IS LATER THAT SAME NIGHT--AS A REVIVED MATT CABLE--HIS COMPANION, ABIGAIL ARCANE--AND THEIR PILOT, PAUL RODMAN, SHARE TEA WITH THEIR NEWFOUND HOSTS...

CALL ME ANGUS, MR. CABLE--AN' YE OWE US NOTHING! 'TWAS ONLY THE DECENT THING TO DO! WE COULD'NA HAVE LEFT YE LYIN' THERE!

BUT TELL ME, MAN-- HOW CAME YE TO BE THERE IN THE FIRST PLACE?

GUESS WE OWE YOU OUR LIVES, SQUIRE MacCOBB! IF YOU HADN'T PULLED US FROM THE PLANE...

"TO TELL THE TRUTH, ANGUS-- I'M STILL NOT ENTIRELY CERTAIN...

"I KNOW THE BEGINNING WELL ENOUGH--BUT THE ENDING IS PRETTY BLURRED...

"WE WERE FLYING THROUGH A STORM, THAT MUCH I REMEMBER--A BAD STORM GETTING WORSE...

"PAUL WAS DOING HIS BEST, BUCKING THAT WIND--WHEN..."

MATT--WHAT'S HAPPENING?

SOMETHING WRONG WITH THE ENGINES, ABIGAIL!

IT FEELS LIKE WE'RE FALLING!

STRAP YOURSELF IN! I'M GOING FORWARD TO TALK TO PAUL!

"TWO OF OUR ENGINES WERE OUT--NOT A CHANCE OF MAKING IT TO AN AIRPORT. WE DESCENDED, LOOKING FOR A FLAT STRETCH TO USE FOR AN EMERGENCY LANDING, WHEN SUDDENLY WE SPOTTED..."

--RUNWAY LIGHTS! THERE MUST BE A PRIVATE AIRSTRIP DOWN THERE!

THIS BABY'S NOT EXACTLY BUILT FOR TOUCHING DOWN ON LAND, BUT--!

--BEGGARS CAN'T BE CHOOSERS-- TO COIN A PHRASE!

JUST SET HER DOWN EASY, PAUL--

--AND PRAY!

WE WENT DOWN FOR THAT LANDING-- AND THE NEXT THING I REMEMBER IS-- WAKING UP *HERE*!

WE COULD HAVE BEEN *KILLED*!

AYE--AN' 'TIS A *MIRACLE* YE WEREN'T!

NO, SQUIRE... IT WASN'T A *MIRACLE*... IT WAS *MUSCLE*...!

I AM THE *REASON*... YOUR GUESTS ARE STILL AMONG THE *LIVING*...!

I SAW WHAT THE OTHERS DID *NOT*... THAT THERE *WAS* NO RUNWAY... ONLY THE STRINGS OF *LIGHTS*...

YOU SEE... *I* WAS A PASSENGER ON THAT PLANE, TOO... *OUT-SIDE* THE PLANE... RIDING ONE OF THE *PONTOONS*...

...AND WHEN THAT GREAT BIRD CAME SCREAMING IN FOR A NON-EXISTENT LANDING... IT WAS *I* WHO CUSHIONED THE CRASH... USING MY OWN DEFORMED *BODY* AS A BRAKE...

IT WOULD BE SO *SIMPLE* FOR ME TO WALK IN THERE... AND EXPLAIN IT ALL TO YOU...

...JUST BURST IN AND SHOUT... THAT I'M *DOCTOR ALEC HOLLAND*...

...BUT ALEC HOLLAND IS *DEAD* IN MATT CABLE'S EYES...

...AND HE *MUST REMAIN* THAT *WAY*...

...FOR ALEC HOLLAND *ALONE* KNOWS THE SECRET OF THE *BIO-RESTORATIVE FORMULA*... THE CHEMICAL THAT MADE ME WHAT I'VE BE- COME...

...AND NOBODY *ELSE* MUST EVER BE TEMPTED TO DISCOVER IT *AGAIN*...!

WHILE, WITHIN THE CRUMBLING OLD MANOR...

WELL, IF YOU'LL *EXCUSE* ME-- I'M GONNA CHECK THE DAMAGE TO MY PLANE!

I WOULD'NA *DO* THAT IF I WERE YE, MISTER RODMAN...

I STILL HAVE A *REPORT* TO MAKE OUT!

...THE MOORS ARE A *DANGEROUS* PLACE AT NIGHT--PROWLED BY WILD ANIMALS--WOLVES--DOGS-- HEAVEN KNOWS WHAT ELSE--!

AYE, MAN-- YE'D BE WELL-ADVISED TO STAY *IN-DOORS* TONIGHT!

ADVICE NOTED, SQUIRE-- BUT MY *PLANE* TAKES PRIORITY! THERE MAY STILL BE A CHANCE THAT THE *RADIO* IS WORKING!

BE BACK SHORTLY!

PAY *HEED*, MAN--OR YE MAY'NA BE BACK AT ALL!

THE NIGHT IS MADE OF *FOG*--AND SHAPED BY *SHADOWS*: KALEIDO- SCOPIC PATTERNS SPILL AT RAN- DOM ACROSS THE MARSH--CREATING *LIFE* WHERE NONE EXISTS...

...AND SOMETIMES *HIDING* LIFE THAT DOES...

FEEL A *CHILL* DOWN MY SPINE! EITHER I'M NOT *DRESSED* WARMLY ENOUGH FOR THIS COLD, DAMP *WEATHER*...

...OR SOMETHING IS *FOLLOWING* ME!

MY GOD-- I'M *RIGHT!*

SOMETHING IS FOLLOWING ME--!

SOMETHING... **INHUMAN!**

SOMEHOW, THE FEAR-FILLED *SCREAM* THAT DRIFTS IN FROM THE BOG IS NOT TOTALLY UNEXPECTED BY THOSE IN THE ANCIENT MANOR--BUT ALL HEADS TURN AT THE SOUND JUST THE SAME...

SOME ARE ALARMED AND FRIGHTENED...

...OTHERS ONLY *CURIOUS*...

THAT SHRIEK... *NOT* THE HOWL OF THE WIND...!

OUGHT TO FIND OUT WHAT IT WAS...!

WAS: PAST TENSE OF THE VERB *IS*... AND APPROPRIATE, INDEED-- FOR PAUL RODMAN *WAS* ALIVE...

BUT *IS* NO LONGER...

HOW HORRIBLE-- HIS *THROAT*--!

--LIKE IT WAS *TORN OUT* BY SOME WILD *DOG*--!

AYE-- 'TIS WILD A'RIGHT--

--BUT 'TIS *NOT* A *DOG!*

AND WHAT IS *THAT* SUPPOSED TO MEAN?

WHA' IT SAYS, MAN! THE *CREATURE* THAT STALKS THIS FEN BY NIGHT...

...IS NOT A *NATURAL* BEAST!

IT'S STRUCK *BEFORE*, IT HAS--KILLED SOME SHEEP-- HORSES--

--AN' TONIGHT IT'S KILLED A *MAN!*

SEEMS I'M NOT THE *ONLY* MONSTER... WALKING THE MOORS THIS EVE...!

THINK I'LL STICK AROUND AWHILE... TO MEET THE *OTHER* ONE...!

AND AFTER THE REMAINS OF THE HAPLESS PILOT ARE BUNDLED UP AND CARRIED INSIDE...

I'M SORRY ABOUT YER FRIEND, MISTER CABLE-- BUT HE SHOULD'NA HAVE IGNORED MY *WARNIN'*--!

SCOTLAND IS AN *ANCIENT* COUNTRY-- WITH A HERITAGE OF *LEGENDS* AND *MYSTERIES*--

--AND MORE THAN ITS SHARE OF *MONSTERS!*

THAT'S A CROCK OF *CLAPTRAP*, SQUIRE!

IF YOU EXPECT ME TO BELIEVE THE *LOCH NESS MONSTER* IS GONNA COME SCRATCHING AT YOUR DOOR, YOU'RE WASTING YOUR...

WHAT IN THE NAME OF--?

SCRATCH SCRATCH SCRATCH

MATT--BE *CAREFUL!* YOU'VE *NO* IDEA WHAT'S *OUT* THERE!

MAYBE NOT--BUT IF IT *IS* THE *LOCH NESS MONSTER,* I WANT TO *SEE* IT FOR MYSELF!

NOW KEEP *BACK*, EVERY- ONE-- I MAY HAVE TO COME OUT SHOOT- ING!

THERE IS THE FAINTEST HINT OF A TREMBLE IN MATT CABLE'S HAND AS HE THROWS OPEN THE OLD OAKEN DOOR TO REVEAL ...

THE POOR *MUTT!* IN THE CONFUSION, I *FORGOT* ALL ABOUT HIM!

C'MERE, BOY-- COME ON *IN!* I WOULDN'T WANT YOU TO SPEND THE NIGHT *ALONE!*

MATT--IT'S YOUR *DOG!* HE FOLLOWED US ALL THE WAY FROM THE PLANE--!

THE SUN RISES EARLY THE NEXT MORNING AND THE TWO TRAVELING COMPANIONS RISE WITH IT! A BRIEF JOURNEY IS MADE TO RETRIEVE SOME LUGGAGE FROM THE SHATTERED AIRCRAFT-- THEN...

I'M AFRAID WE *MUST* LEAVE, LADY MAC COBB!

AS SOON AS YOUR HUSBAND HAS THE *HORSES* HARNESSED, WE'LL BE ON OUR...

WHAT--? Y-YE CAN'NA BE *LEAVIN'* ALREADY!? WHY-- YE HARDLY *GOT* HERE!

MOTHER--WHY DID YE NOT *TELL* ME WE HAD *COMPANY?*

HOPE I DID'NA *STARTLE* YE-- BUT 'TIS NOT OFTEN WE HAVE *GUESTS* HERE!

I'M IAN MAC COBB-- AND 'TIS A PLEASURE TO *MEET* YE, MISTER--?

MATT CABLE, IAN-- AND THE PLEASURE IS *MUTUAL!*

WITNESS: TWO HANDS EXTENDED TO SEAL A BOND THAT TRANS- CENDS ALL THEOLOGIES AND NATIONALITIES-- THE BOND OF *FRIENDSHIP...*

THEN...

HERE--LET ME CARRY YER BAGS OUT TO THE *CARRIAGE* FOR YE!

DON'T BOTHER! OUR GUESTS ARE GOIN' *NOWHERE!*

SORRY IF I *STARTLED* YE--BUT I HAVE *BAD* NEWS!

IN ALL THE *EXCITEMENT* LAST NIGHT, I'M AFRAID I DID'NA STABLE THE *HORSE* PROPERLY--

--AN' NOW SHE SEEMS TO HAVE *RUN OFF!*

WE'RE *ISOLATED* OUT HERE--NO USE FOR *AUTO-MOBILES* AND SUCH--

--SO BECKY WAS THE ONLY *TRANSPORTATION* AROUND FER MILES!

IT'LL TAKE A DAY OR SO TO HAVE *SOMETHIN'* SENT UP HERE FER YE--

--SO YE'RE WELCOME TO SPEND ANOTHER *NIGHT!*

SUNSET, THE RIBBON-LIKE CURTAIN OF CLOUDS GROWS WILDER, DARKER--AS THE STRUGGLING SUN IS TORN APART AND PULLED INTO THE SEA ...

AND WITHIN THE *SOLITARY MANOR,* THE CONQUEST OF *DARKNESS* GOES ALL BUT *UNNOTICED...*

...BY ALL SAVE ONE...

HEY--WHAT'S *WRONG* WITH THE DOG?

GROWLING LIKE SOMEONE WAS *STEALING* HIS LAST *BONE!*

RROWRRR

MATT--SOME-THING'S *FRIGHTEN-ING* HIM!

I *KNOW* IT, ABIGAIL--

--AND I THINK I'LL FIND OUT *WHAT!*

Matt--wait! I'm coming with you!

No, Abigail-- stay inside! You'll...

On second thought, maybe you'd better stay with me--!

The last time I made the mistake of leaving someone alone, I had to bury her next to her husband--

--and I swore I'd never have to live through that again!

Stay close, Abbie-- and we'll...

Déjà vu: the persistent feeling you've experienced a situation once before...

Matt--!

What in the--?

Example: Interpol agent Matt Cable whirling at the sound of a low, throaty growl--to find himself confronting his mind's darkest nightmare...

And as the creature lopes forward...

The slug-- went right through him-- harmlessly--!

BLAM!

He's between us and the house, Abbie-- run for the moors!

Maybe we can lose him in the fog!

THE FUR-TUFTED CREATURE WATCHES AS THE TWO FLEEING FIGURES FADE INTO THE MIST...

...AND WHAT IS ALMOST A *SMILE* CROSSES ITS *SLAVERING* LIPS...

IT HAS PLAYED THIS GAME BEFORE--ENJOYING THE THRILL OF THE *HUNT*--

--HERDING ITS VICTIMS BREATHLESSLY BEFORE IT --

--UNTIL THEY HAD NO PLACE LEFT TO *RUN*...

THE CREATURE SQUATS ON ITS HAUNCHES, MUSCLES BUNCHING, STUDYING ITS DESPERATE PREY FOR THE POINT OF GREATEST *WEAKNESS*--

--TOO INVOLVED IN THE MOMENT TO NOTICE--

--THAT THE HUNTER HAS SUDDENLY BECOME THE *HUNTED!*

THE MIST CLEARS EVER SO SLIGHTLY AS A MOSSY MONOLITH BURSTS FROM THE SHADOWS, PULL-ING THE SHAGGY STALKER INTO THE AIR AS A MOTHER LIFTS HER CHILD--

--BUT *WITHOUT* A MOTHER'S *TENDERNESS*...

DON'T KNOW *WHAT* THIS CREATURE IS... BUT IT HAS ALREADY KILLED *ONCE...!*

CAN'T GIVE IT... A *SECOND* CHANCE...!

ABIGAIL-- *QUICK!* LET'S GET *OUT* OF HERE!

THE **SWAMP THING** PEERS AT HIS OPPONENT ANXIOUSLY, TRYING TO IDENTIFY IT THROUGH THE ALL-PERVADING **MIST**...

FOG TOO **THICK**... CAN'T SEE WHAT I'M FIGHTING...!

FOR AN INSTANT, TIME STANDS STILL...

...AND THE SHAGGY BEAST-THING CHOOSES THAT INSTANT--TO **ACT**!

UHH... CAN'T KEEP A **GRIP** ON IT...

A BLUR OF MOTION--AND THE CREATURE IS UPON THE **SWAMP THING'S** BACK-- CLAWING--TEARING--SPITTING OUT GREAT CLOTS OF FOUL-TASTING **SAP**...

IT'S... RIPPING ME TO **PIECES**! GOT TO GET HIM...

--**OFF**!

ACTION--**REACTION**--A MOSSY FOOT SLIPS ON WET STONE AND...

LOST MY BALANCE... FALLING INTO...

...**QUICKSAND**!!

THE BEAST-CREATURE WATCHES WITH INTEREST-- AS THE MUCK-ENCRUSTED MONSTROSITY SINKS LOWER AND LOWER IN-TO THE OOZE..

MY **WEIGHT**... PULLING ME **DOWN**...!

...UNTIL THE MINGLING OF MONSTER AND MIRE IS COMPLETE....

...AND THERE IS NOTHING LEFT TO **WATCH**...

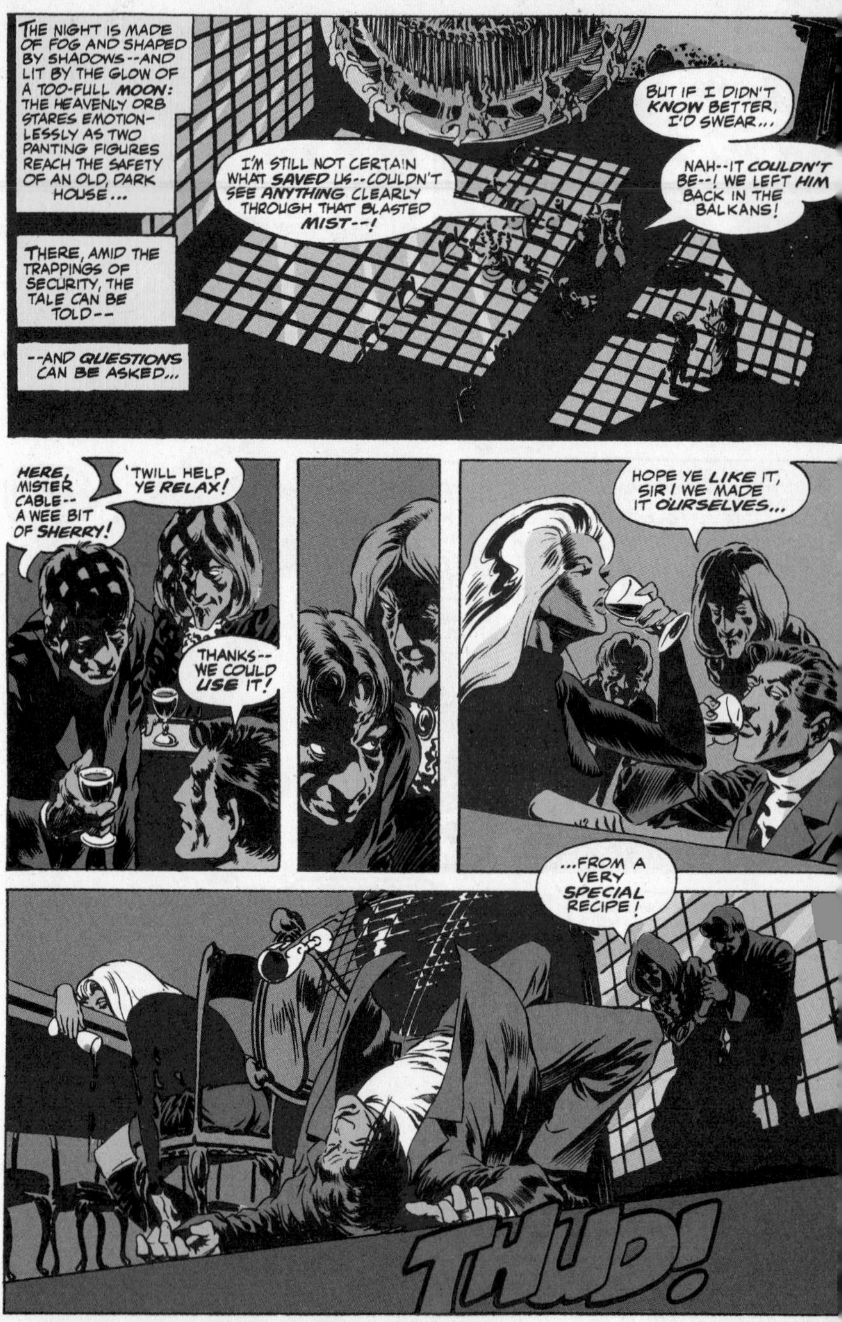
THE NIGHT IS MADE OF FOG AND SHAPED BY SHADOWS--AND LIT BY THE GLOW OF A TOO-FULL MOON: THE HEAVENLY ORB STARES EMOTIONLESSLY AS TWO PANTING FIGURES REACH THE SAFETY OF AN OLD, DARK HOUSE...
THERE, AMID THE TRAPPINGS OF SECURITY, THE TALE CAN BE TOLD--
--AND QUESTIONS CAN BE ASKED...
I'M STILL NOT CERTAIN WHAT SAVED US--COULDN'T SEE ANYTHING CLEARLY THROUGH THAT BLASTED MIST--!
BUT IF I DIDN'T KNOW BETTER, I'D SWEAR...
NAH--IT COULDN'T BE--! WE LEFT HIM BACK IN THE BALKANS!
HERE, MISTER CABLE-- A WEE BIT OF SHERRY!
'TWILL HELP YE RELAX!
THANKS-- WE COULD USE IT!
HOPE YE LIKE IT, SIR! WE MADE IT OURSELVES...
...FROM A VERY SPECIAL RECIPE!
THUD!

FOR A TIME OUT OF TIME, MATT CABLE KNOWS NOTHING--THEN THERE COMES THE SENSATION OF *MOVEMENT*--OF STRAPS BEING FASTENED--TAPE BEING PRESSED AGAINST STILL LIPS-- AND AT LAST...

WELCOME BACK, MISTER CABLE--YE'VE BEEN *SLEEPIN'* FER ALMOST A *DAY!*

PLEASE--DON'T *STRUGGLE!* I ASSURE YE-- YER BONDS'RE QUITE *TIGHT!*

S-STRUGGLE--? WHA--WHERE *AM I?*

WHAT'S *HAPPENIN'?*

WHY AM I *STRAPPED DOWN?*

EASY NOW, LADDIE-- YE'VE BEEN *SLEEPIN'*..

--BUT 'TIS GOIN' TO BE A'RIGHT-- *NOW!*

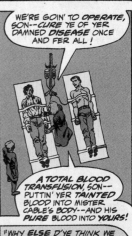

WE'RE GOIN' TO *OPERATE,* SON--*CURE* YE OF YER DAMNED *DISEASE* ONCE AND FER ALL!

A TOTAL BLOOD *TRANSFUSION,* SON-- PUTTIN' YER *TAINTED* BLOOD INTO MISTER CABLE'S BODY--AND HIS *PURE* BLOOD INTO *YOURS!*

MOTHER--NO! YE CAN'NA DO IT! IT'S *HORRIBLE--* INSANE!

EVEN IF HE *SURVIVES,* D'YE REALIZE WHAT'LL *HAPPEN* TO HIM?

I DON'T CARE ABOUT HIM, SON... I CARE ABOUT *YOU!*

WHY ELSE D'YE THINK WE STRUNG THOSE LANTERNS IN THE STORM...

...TO GIVE THE APPEARANCE OF A *RUNWAY BELOW...*

95

"D'YE KNOW HOW MANY PLANES BELIEVED THOSE GLOWING LIES...

"...AND PAID THE PRICE OF THEIR BELIEF ON THE COLD AND FOGGY FEN...?

"WE'D HAVE PERFORMED THE TRANSFUSION LONG AGO, SON--BUT NOBODY EVER SURVIVED THOSE DREADFUL WRECKS...

"...UNTIL NOW...

"WE BURIED THE POOR UNFORTUNATES--AND THE PIECES OF THEIR PLANES-- DEEP IN THE BOG...AN'KEPT WAITING...WAITING...!"

AND NOW OUR WAITIN'S DONE!

NO-- YOU CAN'T--!

SNAP!

SON--YE DO'NA UNDERSTAND--!

NO-- IT'S YOU WHO DO'NA UNDERSTAND--!

HOW COULD YOU?

YOU'VE NEVER FELT THE MOONLIGHT-- BURNIN' DEEP IN YER FLESH--!

NEVER FELT YER BODY CHANGE-- MUSCLES TWISTING-- PULLING--!

NEVER FELT THE BLOOD- LUST-- AARRGH-- RAGIN' INSIDE YE-- LIKE A FIRE OUT OF CONTROL--!

PLEASE-- AARRGHH-- YE CAN'NA DO IT--! YE CANNA INFECT AN INNOCENT-- ARRGHH-- WITH THE CURSE THAT TURNS ME INTO...

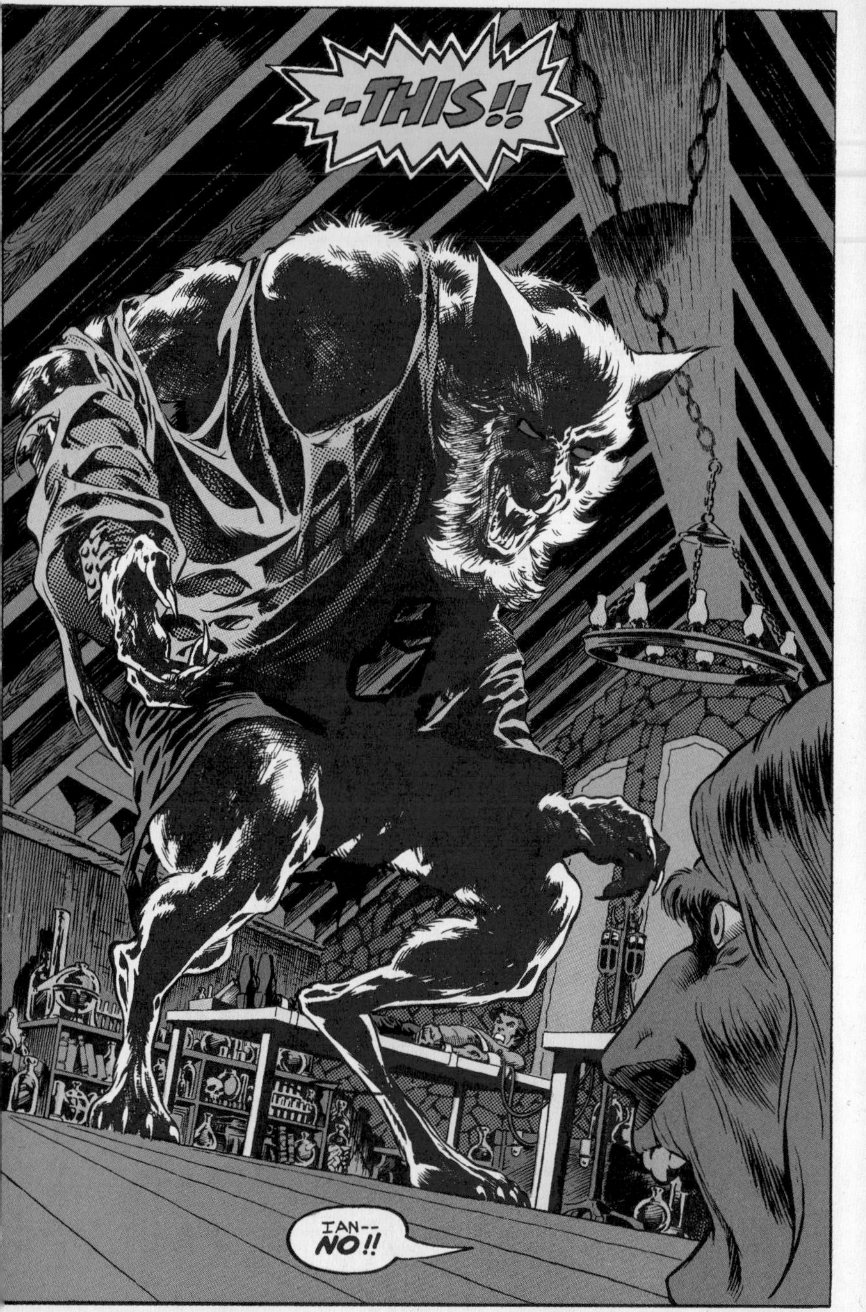
--THIS!!
IAN--
NO!!

ABIGAIL'S EYES GROW WIDE WITH *FEAR* AS SHE WATCHES THE LAST VESTIGES OF *HUMANITY* DRAIN FROM THE FACE OF THE SHAGGY HORROR THAT CONFRONTS HER...

TO BE REPLACED BY THE GLEAM OF PURE ANIMAL *LUST*...

...AND *HUNGER*...

...A HUNGER THAT WILL NOT BE *DENIED*...

IAN--*NO!!* NOT *HERE*... NOT *NOW!!*

STOP HIM, ANGUS! FER PITY'S SAKE--*STOP* HIM!!

THE QUESTION IS-- *HOW?*

AND THE *ANSWER* COMES LOOMING THROUGH THE ATTIC'S OLD TRAPDOOR...

...A PORTAL FAR TOO *SMALL* TO CONTAIN SUCH MONSTROUS *BULK*...

SPENT ALMOST A *DAY*... CLAWING FREE OF THE *QUICKSAND*...

...THEN FOLLOWING THE BEAST'S *TRACKS*... *HERE*...!

...BUT HAVE I ARRIVED... *TOO LATE*...?

RRRGHHH

WHAT IN--? THE *SWAMP THING!?!*

RRRAGGHH!

IAN--*NO!!*

CABLE AND THE GIRL... STILL *ALIVE...!*

GOT TO *FINISH* THIS CREATURE BEFORE IT FINISHES *THEM...!*

BUT *HOW...?* HOW DO YOU *KILL.... A WEREWOLF...?*

UUNNHH... FORCE OF HIS *LUNGE...* CARRYING US BOTH *DOWN-STAIRS...!*

HE'S *STRONG... INCREDIBLY* STRONG... AND IF THE WEREWOLF LEGENDS ARE *TRUE...*

...HE'S ALSO... *IMMORTAL...!*

ONLY *ONE* THING CAN DESTROY A WEREWOLF... *SILVER...* BUT THERE'S *NONE* WITHIN REACH...!

HIS PARENTS HAVE GOTTEN... *RID* OF IT ALL...!

HAVE TO GET HIM *OFF* ME... BEFORE HE TEARS ME TO *PIECES...*

...BUT THE BEAST HAS A GRIP... LIKE *STEEL...!*

MUST PRY HIM *LOOSE* OR...

NO...! IS IT *POSSIBLE..?*

HIS PARENTS REMOVED ALL THE *SILVER...* FROM THE *CUPBOARDS...* THE *WALLS...*

...FROM EVERY PLACE *BUT...*

99

THEY MUST HAVE *FOR-GOTTEN* ABOUT IT...

...OR FIGURED THAT NO ONE COULD POSSIBLY... USE IT AS A *WEAPON*...

...BUT THEY FIGURED... *WRONG*...

...THE *CEILING*...!

UNLESS MY *MOSSY* CONDITION HAS AFFECTED MY *EYESIGHT*... THIS CHANDELIER IS TRIMMED WITH... *SILVER*...!

THIS SHOULD HOLD HIM *BACK*...TILL I CAN THINK OF SOMETHING... MORE *EFFECTIVE*...!

PLEASE-- *NO!* DO'NA HURT MY *BOY*--!

THE ANXIOUS *JENNA MacCOBB* REACHES HER TRANSFORMED SON--AS THE ALREADY--WEAKENED CHANDELIER CHAIN DECIDES TO...

SNAP!

THERE IS TIME FOR ONLY ONE MOTION...

...BUT IS IT THE *WEREWOLF*-- OR THE *MAN* WITHIN-- WHO PUSHES THE OLD WOMAN OUT OF HARM'S WAY...?

...THEN EXPLODES INTO THE NIGHT...

WARASH

IAN? IAN--SON--WHY'D YE DO IT?

WHY DESTROY YERSELF TO SAVE ME--?

M-MOTHER--?

OH, IAN--I'M AN OLD LADY--MY TIME IS ALMOST DONE--

--BUT YOU HAD...

I HAD NOTHING--BUT AN ETERNAL HELL--LIVING IN FEAR OF THE MOON--

--ALWAYS DREADING THE MOMENT THE BEAST THAT I AM WOULD TURN ON SOMEONE I LOVE--!

NO, MOTHER, BELIEVE ME--IT'S BETTER THIS WAY...

...MUCH... BETTER...

IAN--? OH, IAN--!

SLEEP WELL, MY SON--SLEEP, WELL!

101

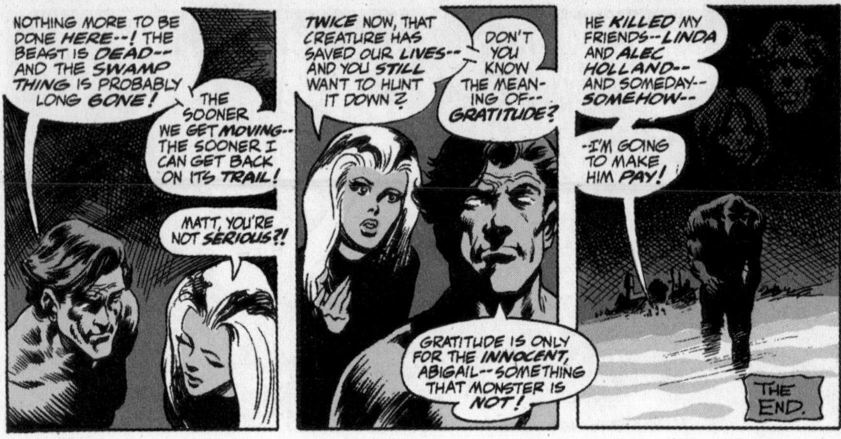
NOTHING MORE TO BE DONE HERE--! THE BEAST IS DEAD-- AND THE SWAMP THING IS PROBABLY LONG GONE!
THE SOONER WE GET MOVING-- THE SOONER I CAN GET BACK ON ITS TRAIL!
MATT, YOU'RE NOT SERIOUS?!
TWICE NOW, THAT CREATURE HAS SAVED OUR LIVES-- AND YOU STILL WANT TO HUNT IT DOWN?
DON'T YOU KNOW THE MEANING OF-- GRATITUDE?
GRATITUDE IS ONLY FOR THE INNOCENT, ABIGAIL--SOMETHING THAT MONSTER IS NOT!
HE KILLED MY FRIENDS--LINDA AND ALEC HOLLAND-- AND SOMEDAY-- SOMEHOW--
-I'M GOING TO MAKE HIM PAY!
THE END.

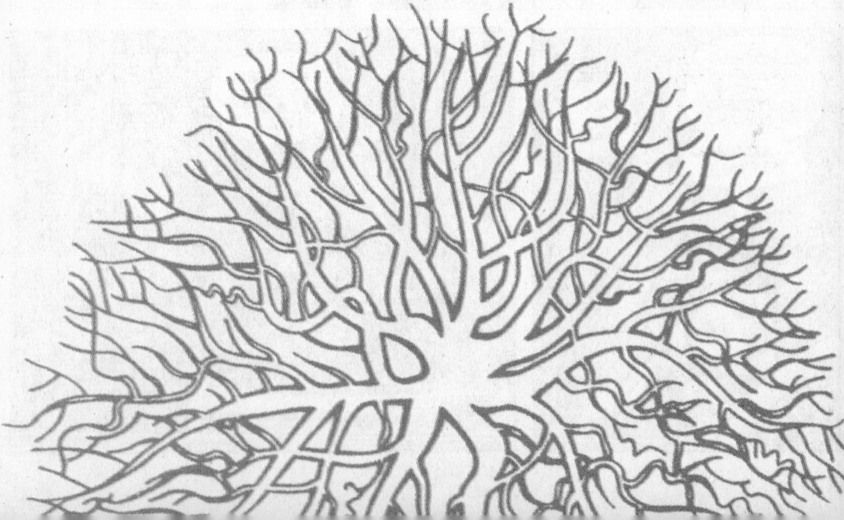

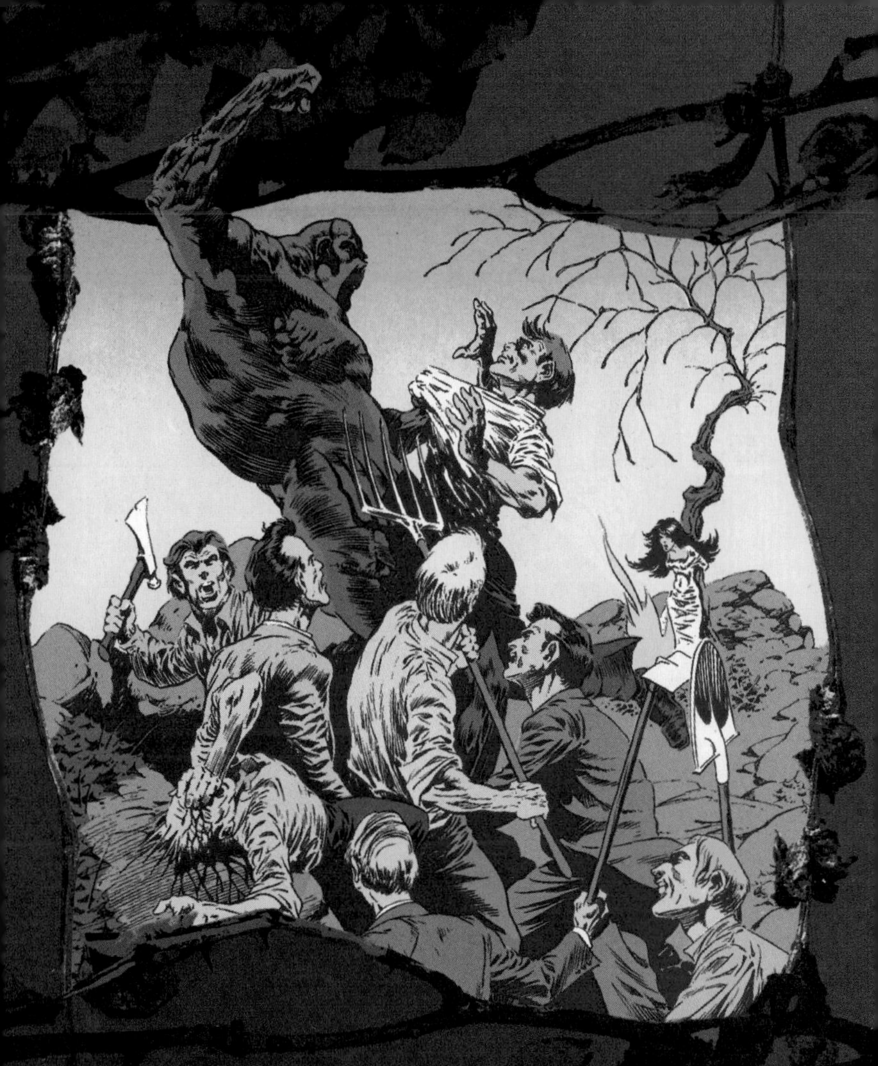

CHAPTER FIVE

IT WAS LARABEE ON NIGHT WATCH WHO FIRST NOTICED THE *STOW-AWAY* LEANING ON THE GUARD-RAIL, HIS TOPCOAT BUNDLED TIGHTLY AGAINST THE BRISK PRE-DAWN *CHILL*...

"*A BIG 'UN*," THOUGHT LARABEE AS HE QUIETLY GATHERED THE CREW. "*HE'S LIABLE TO GIVE US TROUBLE!*"

LARABEE WAS A MASTER OF *UNDER-STATEMENT!*

THEY'VE *DISCOVERED* ME...! TOPCOAT WON'T HELP ME... *NOW*..!

HELP! *HELP!* WE GOT A *MONSTER* ON DECK!

104

IT WAS *FOOLISH*...TO COME OUT OF *HIDING*...! IF ONLY THAT *HOLD*...HADN'T BEEN...SO *CRAMPED*...!

NOW I'LL HAVE TO *PAY*...FOR WANTING TO *STRETCH* MY LIMBS...!

DON'T KNOW WHERE YE *CAME* FROM, MONSTER-- BUT YE'LL NOT *JINX THIS* SHIP--!

WE'LL SEND YE BACK TO THE ARMS OF *NEPTUNE* FIRST!

CHUK!

ME *SAINTED MOTHER*--! TH-THE *GAFF* DID'NA EVEN *BOTHER* HIM--!

YOU'RE *WRONG*, MY FRIEND...IT *BOTHERED* ME, ALL RIGHT...

...IN FACT... *YOU* BOTHER ME...

...BUT YOU'RE *NOT* WORTH...BOTHERING ABOUT IN TURN...!

SO WHY NOT JUST...LEAVE ME *ALONE*...?

BUT THEY *WON'T* LEAVE ME ALONE... NOT *NOW*...

MY CHANCES OF *SURVIVAL*... ARE BETTER IF... I *SWIM* THE REST OF THE WAY...

...BUT *NOT MUCH* BETTER...!

THESE WATERS ARE COLD... *FREEZING*... THEY'RE *NUMBING* MY REFLEXES...!

...BUT NOT YOUR MEMORIES, SWAMP THING-- NO, THE BITING COLD ONLY STRENGTHENS THEM...

COLD HAD FOLLOWED YOU THAT NIGHT-- AS YOU SHAMBLED THROUGH THE WOODLAND SURROUNDING MANOR MAC COBB--

--TO DISCOVER THE SQUIRE'S SUPPOSEDLY "MISSING" HORSE AND WAGON SECURELY HIDDEN IN THE MISTS...

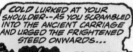

COLD LURKED AT YOUR SHOULDER--AS YOU SCRAMBLED INTO THE ANCIENT CARRIAGE AND URGED THE FRIGHTENED STEED ONWARDS...

--TOWARDS CIVILIZATION...

COLD WHIPPED WILDLY ABOUT YOU--WHEN, AT LAST, YOU REACHED YOUR DESTINATION--AND STOOD ATOP A WINDSWEPT HILLOCK IN THE HOURS BEFORE DAWN..

COLD RIPPLED IN ON THE TIDE--WHEN YOU LOCATED TRANSPORTATION AWAY FROM THAT SMALL SCOTTISH PORT TOWN...

COLD STOOD LAUGHING AT YOUR SIDE-- AS YOU ASSUMED THE GUISE OF A MAN ONCE MORE--TO GAIN PASSAGE ABOARD THAT BATTERED OLD CARGO SHIP...

...AND COLD HAD TREMBLED UP YOUR SPINE--AS YOU SILENTLY ACCOMPLISHED YOUR CHARADE...

106

COLD HAS BEEN YOUR FOND *COMPANION*, SWAMP THING...

EVEN NOW, IT STAYS FAITHFULLY *WITH* YOU--AS YOUR SEMI-CONSCIOUS MOSS-CAKED FORM DRIFTS WITH THE RANDOM TIDES...

...UNTIL A HAUNTINGLY-FAMILIAR *TUMULT* DISTURBS YOUR MOCK SERENITY...

SURF...!? THE TIDE HAS CARRIED ME TO A *SHORE...!*

MUST START *SWIMMING* AGAIN BEFORE...

TOO LATE...! I'M *CAUGHT* IN THE CURRENT...!

THESE *BREAKERS* WILL...*SMASH* ME AGAINST THE ROCKS...LIKE A *BRITTLE...*

NO HOPE OF *FIGHTING* IT...!

NO HOPE AT ALL...

BUT THE ETERNAL POUNDING OF NATURE'S BRINY WONDER IS ONLY A RUMBLING *WHISPER* TO THE TWO BREATHLESS FIGURES WHO RACE DESPERATELY THROUGH THE NEARBY SHADOWED WOODS...

FASTER, BROTHER-- *FASTER!* GIDEON AND THE OTHERS WILL SOON BE *UPON* US!

BUT I'M SO *TIRED* OF RUNNING, SISTER-- AND MY FEET ARE BEGINNING TO HURT--!

OH, *LOOK*-- A SECRET *CAVE!*

WE CAN *HIDE* THERE-- AND THE BAD MEN WILL *NEVER* FIND US!

PERHAPS... IT'S A *CHANCE!*

SEE, SISTER-- I *TOLD* YOU--!

THEY'LL *NEVER* FIND US-- *NEVER*--!

HUSH, CHILD-- NOT A *SOUND!* IF THEY *HEAR* US...

...WE'RE *DOOMED!*

UUHHNNNNNNNN

THE *ROCKS*... THE *SURF*... *BATTER* ME MERCILESSLY...

...AND NOW I'M SEEING... *VISIONS*...!

...BUT VISIONS CAN'T... *HELP* ME...

TWUDD

VISIONS--A BALANCE BETWEEN DARKNESS AND LIGHT--TUMBLE THROUGH THE MAN-MONSTER'S MIND WHILE HE LIES SPRAWLED ON THE COLD CAVE FLOOR...

THE *LIGHT* THINGS COME FIRST--VISIONS OF THE MAN HE USED TO BE--

--VISIONS OF *DOCTOR ALEC HOLLAND*-- AND HIS LOVELY WIFE, *LINDA*...

THEY WERE *MORE* THAN LOVERS, THE VISIONS RECALL--THEY WERE *PARTNERS*--CO-WORKERS--TOGETHER TO SHARE THE BITTER STING OF *FAILURE*...

...AND THE SWEET KISS OF *SUCCESS*...

SUCCESS THAT TURNS TO *TRAGEDY* AS THE BALANCE SHIFTS...

...IN THE HEAT AND FLAME OF A SHATTERING *EXPLOSION*...

NOW THE VISIONS OF *DARK* THINGS--OF ALEC HOLLAND'S MUTILATED BODY SINKING INTO THE DEPTHS OF A LOUISIANA SWAMP...

...THERE TO BE NURTURED AND FED LIKE SOME MISSHAPEN EMBRYO WITHIN A DARK AND MUDDY *WOMB*...

...UNTIL, IN THE FURY OF A RAGING STORM, THE FETID BOG GIVES *"BIRTH"*--TO A CREATURE *LESS* THAN HUMAN--

--BUT *MORE* THAN MAN...

AND SUCH THOUGHTS ARE ENOUGH TO AWAKEN *ANYONE*...

WHA...THE *GIRL*...! THEN SHE *WASN'T* A VISION...!

I CAN SEE *BEWILDERMENT* IN YOUR EYES, MY STRANGE FRIEND--BUT YOU NEEDN'T BE *ALARMED*--!

WE'RE REALLY QUITE *SAFE* HERE!

MY NAME IS *REBECCA RAVEN-WIND*! MY BROTHER IS CALLED *TIMOTHY*!

WE'VE BEEN HIDING HERE TO ESCAPE A MAN NAMED *GIDEON* AND HIS FOLLOWERS!

YOU SEE-- THEY SAY I'M A *WITCH*!

THAT ISN'T *TRUE,* OF *COURSE*! I REALLY ONLY TEND A SMALL *FARM*--AND *CARE* FOR MY *BROTHER*!

HE'S A LITTLE-- er--*SIMPLE,* YOU MIGHT SAY!

GIDEON SHOULD BE *GONE* BY NOW-- AND TIMOTHY AND I MUST FIND OUR WAY *AWAY* FROM HERE!

GOOD-BYE, MY STRANGE, SILENT *FRIEND*-- MAY IT BE *WELL* WITH YOU!

NO, REBECCA... NOT *GOODBYE*...!

NOT UNTIL I REPAY THE *DEBT*... I OWE YOU...!

YOU LOOKED AFTER *ME*... WHEN I NEEDED *HELP*...

...NOW IT'S *MY* TURN... TO LOOK AFTER *YOU*...!

THE MOSS-WET MONSTROSITY SHAMBLES INTO STEP BEHIND THE FUGITIVE SIBLINGS-- BUT THEY HARDLY SEEM TO *NOTICE*--

YET THEIR *PACE* SLOWS SLIGHTLY TILL THE CREATURE HAS GAINED THEIR SIDE--

--AND A SUDDEN *SPARKLE* LIGHTS A FIRE IN REBECCA'S EYES...

THEY MOVE THROUGH THE UNDERBRUSH SILENTLY, THIS STARTLING TRIO-- FOR THEY KNOW ANY SHARP *SOUND* MAY ALERT THEIR PURSUERS...

...ANY SOUND AT ALL !

SNAP!

OVER *THERE*, LADS--WE'VE *FOUND* THEM !

THE CLAMOR OF THE APPROACHING MOB REACHES MOSS-ENCRUSTED EARS-- AS THE *SWAMP THING* THRUSTS HIS COMPANIONS BEFORE HIM--AND *RUNS*--

BLEW IT...! NO PLACE TO GO FROM HERE...

...BUT *DOWN*...!

--RUNS DESPERATELY THROUGH AN UNKNOWN WOODLAND--UNTIL THERE IS NOWHERE *LEFT* TO RUN...

THERE THEY BE, LADS! WE'VE GOT THEM NOW !

LOOK FOR YOURSELVES, LADS ! SHE BE A *WITCH* BY THUNDER--!

SHE'S SUMMONED UP A THING FROM *HELL* TO PROTECT HER FROM OUR RIGHTEOUS *WRATH!*

WELL, NO SPAWN OF SATAN WILL PROTECT THAT LITTLE VIXEN FROM *JOCKO*, BOYS !

I DON'T WANT TO... HURT YOU, JOCKO... BUT IF YOU DON'T... PUT DOWN THAT SCYTHE... I'M GOING TO...

NO, DEMON-- YOU WON'T LAY YOUR FILTHY HANDS ON JOCKO!

KRAK!

IN FACT, I'LL FIX IT SO YOU DON'T LAY THOSE HANDS ON ANYBODY EVER AGAIN--!

SWAC

DEAR LORD...! HE CUT OFF MY ARM... AND I DIDN'T EVEN FEEL IT...!

THERE, DEMON-- HOW WILL YOU SPREAD YOUR EVIL, NOW?

EVIL...? I'LL SHOW YOU EVIL, JOCKO...!

WHEN YOU WAKE UP... TAKE A GOOD LOOK... IN THE MIRROR...!

YOU'LL SEE... ALL THE EVIL YOU CAN STAND...!

JOCKO HAS *FAILED* US, LADS-- BUT DO NOT LOSE *HEART!* WE ARE NOT BEATEN *YET!*

NOW, SMITH-- THROW YOUR *LAN-TERN*--

--AND WE WILL CONSIGN THE DEMON TO THE *FLAMES* FROM WHENCE IT WAS SUMMONED!

FOOLS... WHAT ARE THEY *DOING...?*

CRASH!

THE MAN-MONSTER'S *ANSWER* IS A RAGING WALL OF *FIRE* THAT SPRINGS TO LIFE BEFORE HIM...

FILLING THE AIR WITH ACRID SMOKE--BLISTERING HEAT--AND *MORE*--

--MUCH MORE...

MEMORIES: THE PAINFUL IMAGE OF A TORTURED *ALEC HOLLAND* RIPPLES IN THE SWIFTLY-MOVING FLAMES...

--AND IN THAT INSTANT, THE *SWAMP THING* RECALLS THE AGONY OF UNCLASSIFIED CHEMICALS SEEPING INTO HIS FLESH--

--AND IN HORROR, TAKES A SINGLE STEP *BACKWARDS*--

A SINGLE-- *FATAL*-- STEP...

HUH...? CLIFF EDGE... *CRUMBLING* UNDER MY WEIGHT...!

FALLING INTO THE *SEA* AGAIN...

...AND *THIS* TIME... I MAY NOT *SUR-VIVE*...!

AND THE CRASHING WAVES ECHO THE *SWAMP THING'S* THOUGHT...

YOUR HELL-BORN SERVANT IS *GONE*, REBECCA RAVEN- WIND--THERE IS NOTHING TO KEEP YOU FROM US NOW!

TAKE THEM TO THE VILLAGE, LADS-- AND LET *JUSTICE* BE DONE!

113

DIVINITY, MAINE -- FOUNDED CIRCA 1648 -- POPULATION: 97 GOOD, GOD-FEARING PEOPLE: PRINCIPAL INDUSTRY: SCRAMBLING FOR AN EXISTENCE -- PRINCIPAL PRODUCE: IGNORANCE... AND *FEAR*...

STOP *STRUGGLING,* WITCH -- IT WILL DO YOU NO GOOD!

THERE IS NO PLACE YOU CAN RUN -- NO PLACE YOU CAN *HIDE* -- THAT WE'D NOT *FIND* YOU AGAIN!

SMITH, PUT THE *BOY* IN A GOOD, STRONG *CELL! HE* CAN BE DEALT WITH LATER!

IT'S HIS ACCURSED *SISTER* WHO IS OUR *PROBLEM!*

TIMOTHY --?

IT'S ALL RIGHT, *REBECCA* -- DON'T *WORRY!* OUR FRIEND WILL HELP US!

YOU'LL SEE... EVERYTHING WILL BE *FINE* AGAIN... JUST *FINE!*

AND WHEN THE YOUNGSTER'S INNOCENT REASSURANCES HAVE FADED DOWN THE STREET...

COME ON, LADS -- LET'S GET THE WITCH TO *COURT!*

SHE'S ENTITLED TO A *TRIAL* --

-- BEFORE WE *BURN* HER AT THE *STAKE!*

114

COURT: ANOTHER WORD FOR A DUST-STREWN OLD CHAMBER THAT HAS NOT BEEN PUT TO USE IN TWICE A SCORE OF YEARS...

FOR CRIME IS NO PROBLEM TO THE PEOPLE OF DIVINITY--

--NO ORDINARY CRIME, AT LEAST!

THIS WOMAN STANDS ACCUSED OF UNHOLY ACTS-- OF CRIMES AGAINST MAN--AND GOD!

IS THERE ANY AMONG YOU WHO'LL TAKE THE STAND TO PUT THE LIE TO THESE CHARGES--OR TO SUPPORT THEM?

CITIZENS, YOU SEE BEFORE YOU, REBECCA RAVENWIND-- LAST OF A FAMILY OF HELLISH NECROMANCERS WHO'VE TROUBLED OUR VILLAGE SINCE FIRST IT WAS SETTLED!

I PRESENT HER TO YOU--TO BE JUDGED AS YOU SEE FIT!

SHE'S A STRANGE ONE, A'RIGHT-- NEVER JOINS IN COMMUNITY FUNCTIONS-- KEEPS TO HERSELF--LIKE SHE WAS TOO GOOD FER US!

AND YOU SAY YOU'VE SEEN HER TALK TO ANIMALS-- ACTUALLY CONVERSE WITH THEM?

DOESN'T THAT SEEM A TRIFLE ODD TO YOU?

IT'S HER BLASTED GARDEN-- GROWS LIKE 'TWAS EDEN ITSELF!

AND ME UNABLE TO RAISE EVEN A WEED! 'TIS WITCHCRAFT, I TELL YOU!

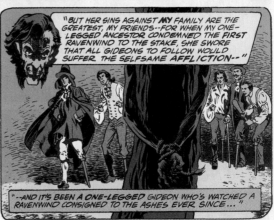

"BUT HER SINS AGAINST MY FAMILY ARE THE GREATEST, MY FRIENDS--FOR WHEN MY ONE-LEGGED ANCESTOR CONDEMNED THE FIRST RAVENWIND TO THE STAKE, SHE SWORE THAT ALL GIDEONS TO FOLLOW WOULD SUFFER THE SELFSAME AFFLICTION--"

"--AND IT'S BEEN A ONE-LEGGED GIDEON WHO'S WATCHED A RAVENWIND CONSIGNED TO THE ASHES EVER SINCE..."

I STAND BEFORE YOU NOW ON A LIMB OF WHITTLED *WOOD* BECAUSE OF HER FAMILY'S *SORCERY*--

--AND I SAY TO YOU THERE MUST BE AN *END* TO IT--NOW AND FOR-EVER!

THE *CURSE* LAID UPON US MUST BE PUT TO *REST* BEFORE--!

GIVE ME THE *CHILD,* WOMAN!

NO--YOU *MUSTN'T*--!

CONFOUND YOU, WOMAN-- I SAID *HAND* ME THE *CHILD!*

NO-- PLEASE-- *NO!*

THERE, PEOPLE OF DIVINITY-- NEED YOU ANY FURTHER *PROOF?*

DO YOU *SEE* WHAT THE RAVENWINDS' WITCHCRAFT HAS DONE TO MY SON--?

--WHAT IT WILL DO TO MY *SON'S* SON--AND *HIS* SON THEREAFTER-- UNLESS WE PUT A *STOP* TO IT!

WITH THE DEATH OF *REBECCA,* THE *RAVENWIND* LINE IS FINISHED-- ITS CURSE FOR-EVER *BROKEN!*

WITH THE *EVIDENCE* BEFORE YOU, IS THERE ANY OTHER *VERDICT* YOU CAN GIVE?

GUILTY! BURN HER! GUILTY!

BURN THE WITCH!

WHILE, BY THE TURBULENT SEACOAST, A MOSSY CHUNK OF UNWANTED *FLOTSAM* IS CAST VIOLENTLY UPON THE SHORE...

FEEL LIKE A... USED *SPONGE*...! SO *WEAK* MY ARMS... CAN BARELY *SUPPORT* ME...!

MY *ARMS*...?

DEAR LORD... MY SEVERED *ARM*... HAS BEGUN TO GROW *BACK*...!

THE *BIO-RESTORATIVE FORMULA*...IN MY SYSTEM... IN THE LAB... IT CAUSES RAPID *REGENERATION*... OF PLANT-LIFE...

...AND *PLANT-LIFE* IS EXACTLY... WHAT I'VE *BECOME*...!

AMAZING...! MY ARM IS *REFORMING*... EVEN AS I WATCH...!

...THICKER... STRONGER... *DUPLICATING* WHAT I'D *LOST*...

...ROOTS... MOSS... MINGLING TOGETHER...

...*EVERYTHING* JUST AS IT WAS *BEFORE*!

...I'M *WHOLE* AGAIN... IN A MATTER OF *MINUTES*...

...AND, *GOD*, IT FEELS *GOOD*...! *STRENGTH* SURGING THROUGH MY BODY...

...STRENGTH TO BE... PUT TO *USE*...

...FOR, UNLESS I MISS MY GUESS... THERE'S A *TOWN* NEARBY...

...AND I HAVE SOME... *UN-FINISHED BUSINESS*... TO ATTEND TO...!

"BOYS WILL BE BOYS," THE TIRED OLD ADAGE GOES. THE FACES CHANGE FROM YEAR TO YEAR-- BUT THE ATTITUDES ARE CONSTANT. BOYS ARE ENERGETIC...IMPRESSION-ABLE...MISCHIEVOUS...

HEY, MY DAD WAS RIGHT! THIS GUY IS A DOPE!

JUST LOOK'A HIS FACE--! HE'S OFF IN DREAMLAND SOMEWHERE!

THERE IS ALSO A PROVERB ABOUT "THE SINS OF THE FATHER..." BUT WE NEED NOT GO INTO THAT HERE...

MY DAD TOLD ME ALL ABOUT YOU AND YOUR SISTER, PANSY-FACE--

--AND WE'RE GONNA SHOW YA WHAT HAPPENS TO WITCHES IN THIS TOWN!

WON'T WE, FELLAS?

WON'T WE...

⸘GULP!⸘

CRASH

IT'S ALL RIGHT, TIMOTHY... I'M HERE NOW...!

I'LL TAKE CARE OF YOU...!

I'LL TAKE CARE OF... EVERY-THING...!

NOW STAND AWAY FROM... THE WALL...

...AND I'LL GET YOU... OUT OF THAT STINKING HOLE...!

RRRAKKKUMPH!

YOUR *SISTER*, TIMOTHY...TELL ME... WHERE HAVE THEY...*TAKEN* HER...?

THANK YOU, FRIEND-- I *KNEW* YOU'D COME BACK TO *HELP* US!

IF WE *HURRY*, WE CAN STILL SAVE *REBECCA!* THEY'VE TAKEN HER TO THE HILLS BEYOND TOWN TO *BURN* HER!

WITHOUT AN INSTANT'S HESITATION, THE MOSSY MAN-BRUTE TURNS AND SHAMBLES TOWARDS THE EDGE OF TOWN...

IN HIS ANXIOUSNESS, ALMOST FORGETTING...

HEY, FRIEND, WAIT FOR ME!

ALL RIGHT, BOY... I WON'T GO *WITHOUT* YOU...! SHE *IS* YOUR SISTER...!

HUH...? TIMOTHY...!

CLIMB ABOARD... AND HANG ON *TIGHT...!*

YOU'RE IN FOR THE *PIGGYBACK* RIDE... OF YOUR LIFE...!

THE RAGGED HILLTOP STANDS A GOODLY DISTANCE *AWAY* FROM FAIR DIVINITY-- FAR ENOUGH THAT THE VILLAGE AIR WILL NOT BE TAINTED BY CRUDE THREATS AND OBSCENITIES--

--OR THE ODOR OF BURNING *FLESH*...

REBECCA RAVENWIND, YOU HAVE BEEN TRIED AND FOUND GUILTY OF THE UNHOLY CRIME OF--*WITCHCRAFT*--

--AND SO, HAVE BEEN SENTENCED TO THE *STAKE!* HAVE YOU ANYTHING TO *SAY?*

PLEASE-- THIS IS *INSANITY!*

I'M *INNOCENT*, GIDEON-- I'VE DONE *NOTHING* TO YOU!

YOU *CAN'T* BLAME ME FOR YOUR FAMILY'S *GENETIC DEFORMITY*--!

CAN'T I, WOMAN? THE FORCE THAT CRIPPLES THE GIDEONS COMES *NOT* FROM OUR MAKER BUT FROM *YOU*--

--AND *YOU* ARE THE ONE WHO SHALL *PAY* FOR--!

EH? THAT COMMOTION--! WHAT IS--?

FOUND HER... AND JUST IN *TIME*...IT APPEARS...!

GO AHEAD, WOMAN-- DENY YOUR WITCHHOOD *NOW*--

--NOW THAT YOU'VE SUMMONED YOUR *DEMON SPAWN* ONCE MORE!

GET THE BEAST, LADS-- *DESTROY* IT!

THE RAVENWINDS'LL *NOT* ESCAPE OUR JUSTICE THIS TIME!

PAUSE FOR A MOMENT AND CONSIDER THIS SCENE: A GREAT MOSS-ENCRUSTED BEHEMOTH STRUGGLING SILENTLY AGAINST HALF A SCORE OF WILDLY FANATIC MEN...

A GHASTLY-LOOKING *SWAMP THING* BATTLING TO *SAVE* A LIFE THE FINE AND HANDSOME TOWNSFOLK ARE DESPERATE TO *TAKE*...

CONSIDER THIS SCENE--AND DECIDE FOR YOURSELF: WHO REALLY IS THE *MONSTER*?

AND, ACROSS THE BARREN FIELD, THE *OBJECT* OF THIS CONFLICT STARES MUTELY AT THE SEARING FLAMES THAT LICK HIGHER AND HIGHER ABOUT HER...

121

AND THE *SWAMP THING* BATTLES ON, UNAWARE OF THE DIRE IMMEDIACY OF REBECCA'S PLIGHT...

...UNTIL A SCREAM LIKE SHATTERED CRYSTAL LANCES THE EVENING AIR...

...CATCHING THE ATTENTION OF *OTHERS* AS WELL...

HAVE TO GET TO HER QUICKLY BEFORE THE FIRE CAN *SPREAD*...!

NO, MY FRIEND-- GO *BACK!* IT'S TOO LATE TO SAVE *ME*--!

THAT REMAINS... TO BE *SEEN,* REBECCA...! IF I CAN'T... GO *THROUGH* THE FLAMES...

...MAYBE I CAN GO... *AROUND* THEM...!

WITH REMARKABLE SPEED FOR ONE WHO SEEMS SO PONDEROUS, THE MIS-SHAPEN MAN-BRUTE SKIRTS THE ROARING FIRE AND...

THERE'LL BE TIME...TO *EXTINGUISH* THE BLAZE... *AFTER I GET...* REBECCA TO *SAFETY...!*

WHHA-RACKK!

NOW...ANY-ONE WHO WANTS TO GET TO *REBECCA...* WILL HAVE TO...GO *THROUGH* ME...!

AND I'LL *BREAK* ANY-ONE WHO... *HUH?*

IT'S *ALL RIGHT,* MY *FAITHFUL, SILENT FRIEND--*

--I'LL TAKE OVER NOW!

HOLD, WITCH--YOUR EVIL MUST NOT *ESCAPE* THIS PLACE!

MY EVIL? NO, GIDEON-- *YOU* ARE THE ONE WHO IS *TRULY* EVIL HERE!

YOURS IS THE *WORST* KIND OF EVIL--THE KIND THAT HOLDS PEOPLE IN *IGNORANCE* SO THAT YOU CAN MAINTAIN *POWER!*

YOU'VE *SMOTHERED* DIVINITY, GIDEON--AS YOUR FAMILY HAS FOR *300 YEARS!*

NO, GIDEON-- THERE'S BEEN *ENOUGH* DEATH IN DIVINITY--

LIAR! YOU'LL *DIE* FOR THAT!

--IT'S TIME THERE WAS AN *END* TO IT!

REBECCA RAVENWIND CLOSES HER LIMPID EYES--AND THE SKY IS FILLED WITH *STORM!* GREAT GOUTS OF ELECTRICAL FIRE LEAP ACROSS THE BLACK--THE DEAFENING PEAL OF UNEARTHLY THUNDER SHAKES THE VERY GROUND--

--AND AMID THE TUMULT OF THAT ACCURSED MADNESS, GIDEON AND HIS FOLLOWERS SUDDENLY BEGIN TO-- *SCREAM!*

THE SCREAMS FADE TO A WHIMPER--THEN A SIGH--AND FINALLY TO SILENCE--AND THE STORM-TOSSED CLOUDS SEEM TO QUIET IN TURN...

SEE, SISTER--I *TOLD* YOU EVERYTHING WOULD BE *FINE*! THOSE BAD MEN WILL NEVER *BOTHER* US AGAIN!

I'VE HEARD OF...SUDDEN *STORMS* BEFORE...BUT THIS ONE... WAS *RIDICULOUS*...!

GOOD LORD... THEY'VE ALL BEEN...TURNED INTO *FLOWERS*...! THEN REBECCA IS...

--A *WITCH*! THAT'S WHAT YOU'RE THINKING I *AM*, ISN'T IT, MY FRIEND?

WELL, I'M *NOT*, YOU KNOW! I DIDN'T *LIE* TO YOU!

THE POWER'S NOT *MINE*-- IT'S *TIMOTHY'S*!

I'M WHAT YOU WOULD CALL-- HIS *FAMILIAR*--THE OBJECT HE FOCUSES HIS POWER THROUGH! HE'S SO *HARMLESS*, I DON'T *MIND* IT, REALLY!

ALL HE EVER CONJURES UP IS--*FLOWERS*!

NOW, MY DEAR FRIEND, I'M AFRAID WE MUST *LEAVE* YOU!

WE HAVE FRIENDS IN *BOSTON* WHO'LL TAKE CARE OF US! WE NEED NOT BURDEN *YOU*!

GOODBYE-- AND *GOD* BE WITH YOU!

AND MAY HE... BE WITH *YOU*, REBECCA...! YOUR TRIALS ARE *OVER*...!

NOBODY EVER SAID... THE LAST OF THE *RAVENWIND* WITCHES... HAD TO BE...A *GIRL*...!

GIDEON WAS A *FANATIC*... SHORT-SIGHTED...NARROW-MINDED...AND HE HAS PAID... THE *PRICE*...!

125

ADDENDUM: Countless miles away on a moonlit New England porch...

THE AIR IS SO *CRISP*, YOU CAN ALMOST HEAR IT *CRACKLE*!

I DIDN'T THINK THEY *MADE* NIGHTS LIKE THIS ANYMORE!

THEY *DON'T!* WHAT YOU'RE EXPERIENCING IS A *MANIFESTATION* OF YOUR MOST *SECRET DESIRES*!

HONEY, MY MOST *SECRET DESIRES* HAVE ABSOLUTELY *NOTHING* TO DO WITH THE *WEATHER*!

IF YOU MEAN WHAT I *THINK* YOU MEAN, SIR--

--YOU SHOULD BE *ASHAMED*!

BUT I *AM*, LINDA DARLING-- I MOST CERTAINLY *AM*!

OH, YOU *SILLY*--! I JUST *DON'T* KNOW WHAT I'M GOING TO DO WITH YOU... *DOCTOR ALEC HOLLAND*!

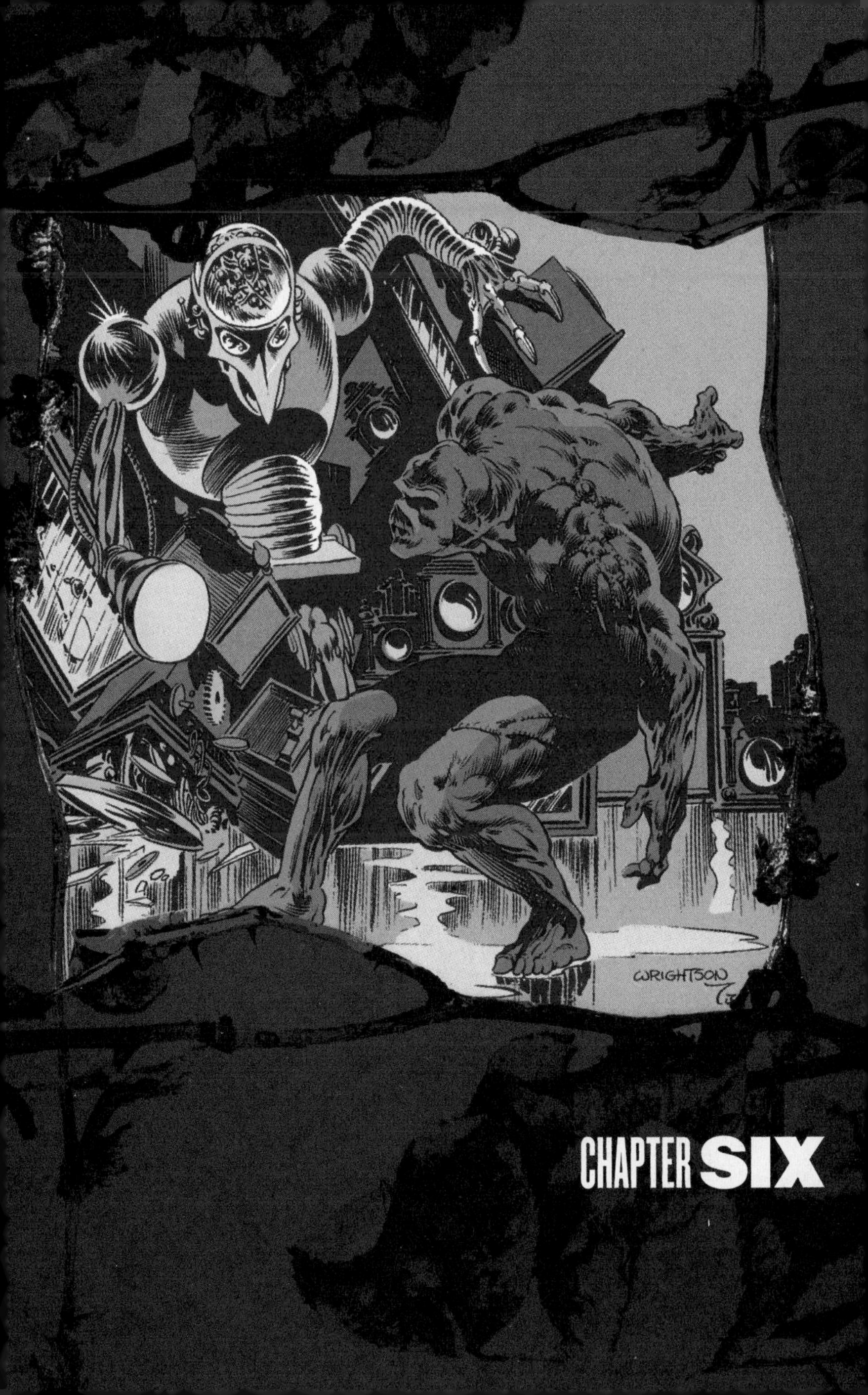
WRIGHTSON

CHAPTER SIX

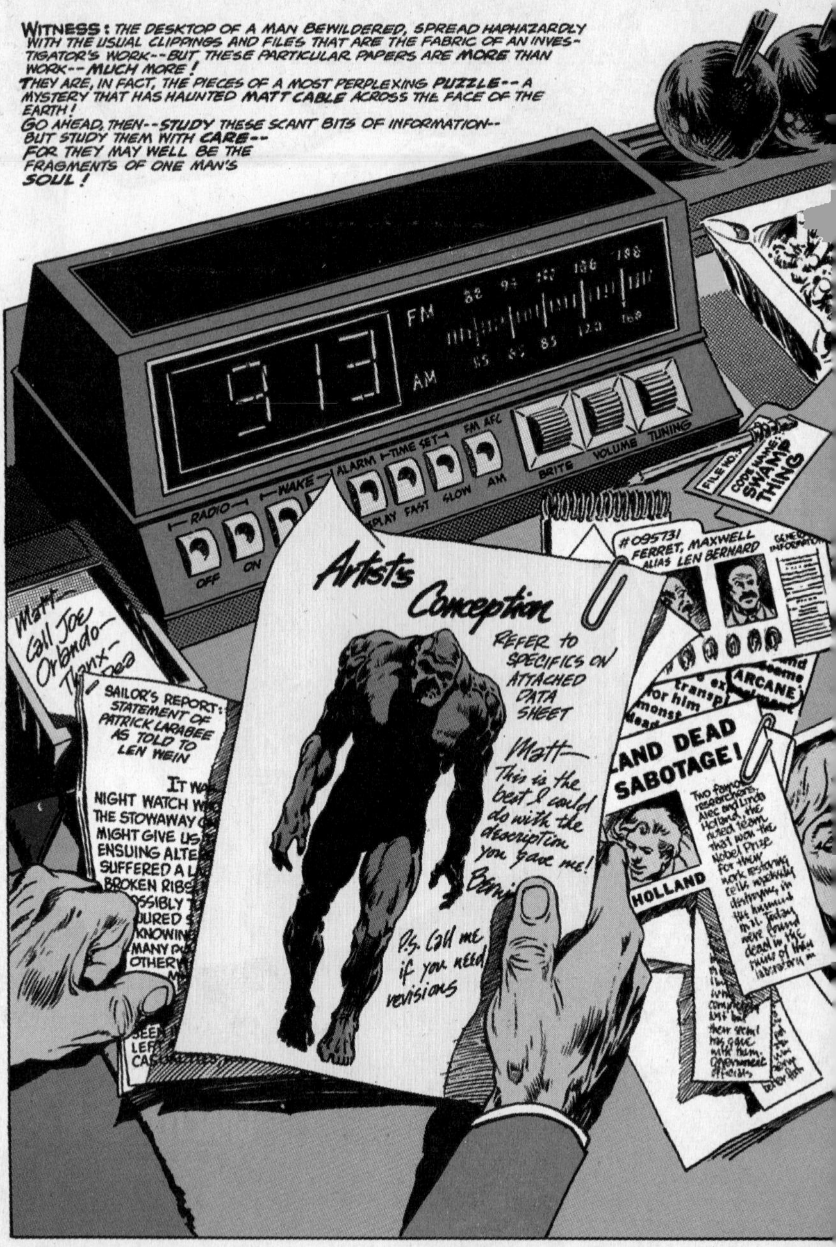
WITNESS: THE DESKTOP OF A MAN BEWILDERED, SPREAD HAPHAZARDLY WITH THE USUAL CLIPPINGS AND FILES THAT ARE THE FABRIC OF AN INVESTIGATOR'S WORK--BUT THESE PARTICULAR PAPERS ARE MORE THAN WORK--MUCH MORE!
THEY ARE, IN FACT, THE PIECES OF A MOST PERPLEXING PUZZLE--A MYSTERY THAT HAS HAUNTED MATT CABLE ACROSS THE FACE OF THE EARTH!
GO AHEAD, THEN--STUDY THESE SCANT BITS OF INFORMATION--BUT STUDY THEM WITH CARE--FOR THEY MAY WELL BE THE FRAGMENTS OF ONE MAN'S SOUL!
FM AM
RADIO OFF ON WAKE ALARM TIME SET FAST SLOW FM AFC AM
BRITE VOLUME TUNING
FILE NO.
CODE NAME: SWAMP THING
#095731
FERRET, MAXWELL
ALIAS LEN BERNARD
Matt-- Call Joe Orlando-- Thanx--
SAILOR'S REPORT: STATEMENT OF PATRICK LARABEE AS TOLD TO LEN WEIN
Artist's Conception
REFER to SPECIFICS ON ATTACHED DATA SHEET
Matt-- This is the best I could do with the description you gave me!
P.S. Call me if you need revisions
ARCANE
SABOTAGE!
HOLLAND
Two famous researchers, Alec and Linda Holland, the husband team that won the Nobel Prize

BLAST! THE ANSWER IS IN THESE PAPERS *SOMEWHERE,* ABIGAIL-- I *KNOW* IT IS!

WHAT I DON'T KNOW IS HOW IN HELL TO *FIND* IT!

DON'T *UNDER-ESTIMATE* YOURSELF, MATT! YOU'RE THE *BEST* INVESTIGATOR YOUR GOVERNMENT *HAS!*

'SCUSE ME, FOLKS-- HOPE I'M NOT *INTERRUPTIN'* ANYTHIN'!

AND IF *ANYONE* CAN SOLVE THE RIDDLE OF THAT *SWAMP THING,* YOU--

HEY, JACK! C'MON IN-- AND PULL UP A *CHAIR!*

I BETTER NOT, MATT--'CAUSE IN SIX SECONDS YOU MAY NOT EVEN WANNA *LOOK* AT ME!

IT'S *BAD* NEWS, MATT! THEY'RE TAKIN' YOU *OFF* THAT "HOLLAND/SWAMP THING" ASSIGNMENT--'CAUSE YOU'RE TOO "PERSONALLY *INVOLVED*," THEY SAY!

THEY GOT SOMETHIN' *NEW* FOR YOU-- SOME STRANGE LITTLE TOWN IN *VERMONT* THEY WANT CHECKED OUT!

I'M *SORRY,* MATT--

--I KNOW HOW YOU *FELT* ABOUT THE HOLLAND COUPLE--

--BUT THERE'S *NOTHIN'* TO BE DONE!

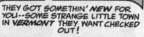

INVOLVED? THEY'RE DAMNED *RIGHT* I'M INVOLVED!

THAT INHUMAN MONSTER *MURDERED* MY BEST FRIENDS-- AND ASSIGNMENT OR *NO* ASSIGNMENT, I'M NOT GONNA QUIT UNTIL I *FIND* IT--

--AND MAKE IT *PAY!*

ALEC AND LINDA HOLLAND DEAD!

--WHICH MIGHT NOT BE AS *DIFFICULT* AS MATT CABLE THINKS...

OBSERVE; A TWISTING TWO-LANE *ROADWAY* IN THE MOUNTAINS OF *VERMONT*--

--A *VEGETABLE TRUCK* OWNED BY ONE GUIDO ROSELLI, ITINERANT FARMER...

--AN UNREPAIRED *POTHOLE* OVER WHICH SAID VEGETABLE TRUCK JOUNCES--

--AND A MOSS-ENCRUSTED *MOCKERY* OF A MAN--

--WHO HAD CHANCED TO STEAL A RIDE IN THE *REAR* OF THE AFOREMENTIONED VEHICLE--

--AND, IN SO DOING, LEARNS THAT--

--THERE AIN'T NO SUCH THING AS A *FREE RIDE!*

UUHHNN... WHAT... HAPPENED...?

FEELS LIKE... I WAS PUT THROUGH... A *CEMENT MIXER...!*

FALL KNOCKED EVERYTHING... *OUT* OF ME...! HAVEN'T THE *STRENGTH* TO...

...*HUH*...?

A...*BOOT...* A *GIRL'S BOOT...!*

HI--NEED ANY *HELP?*

NO... IT CAN'T *BE...!*

I'M SO GLAD YOU FINALLY CAME TO YOUR *SENSES,* MATT!

YOU REALLY *DO* NEED A BREAK FROM THAT *SWAMP THING* CASE--TO HELP CLEAR UP YOUR *THINKING* ON IT!

LOOK, ABIGAIL-- I'M ONLY HERE BECAUSE I'M A *PROFESSIONAL*--

--AND BECAUSE THE SOONER I'M *FINISHED* WITH THIS ASSIGNMENT, THE SOONER I CAN GET *BACK* TO THAT MONSTER!

SITUATION *UNDERSTOOD?*

PLEASE, MATT--GIVE YOURSELF A *CHANCE!* THIS SOUNDS LIKE SUCH AN *INTERESTING* CASE--!

DOES IT, ABIGAIL? WHAT'S SO INTERESTING ABOUT A DESERTED *MINING TOWN* SPRINGING BACK TO LIFE?

IF IT WASN'T FOR THE FACT THAT NONE OF THE TOWN'S NEW *RESIDENTS* HAS EVER REGISTERED WITH THE GOVERNMENT OR PAID ANY *TAXES*--

--WE'D NEVER HAVE EVEN *HEARD* OF IT!

...*HEARD* OF IT!

--WERE IT NOT FOR THE SECRET *TRANSMITTER* IMPLANTED IN THE SKULL OF YOUR CANINE *PET!*

NOR WOULD I, MR. CABLE--

A TOWNFUL OF *ANONYMOUS* PEOPLE, *eh?* IT WILL INDEED PROVE INTERESTING TO DISCOVER THE REASONS BEHIND IT!

PERHAPS THERE MIGHT EVEN BE A WAY FOR THE *CONCLAVE* AND I TO *PROFIT* FROM IT!

HEY, FELLA--GLAD YOU'RE AWAKE! HAD US *WORRIED* THERE FOR A MINUTE!

THE NAME'S *ALEC HOLLAND*--THIS IS MY WIFE, *LINDA!*

NO...THIS IS A... *NIGHTMARE*....! LINDA IS ...*DEAD* AND...AND...I WAS ALEC HOLLAND...!

C'MON, FELLA-- *CAT* GOT YOUR TONGUE?

WE TOLD YOU *OUR NAMES*-- WHAT'S *YOURS?*

I MUST BE... *DELIRIOUS*... IMAGINING THINGS...!

OH, YOU POOR THING! YOU *CAN'T* SPEAK, CAN YOU? YOU WERE *HURT* IN THE FALL!

FALL...? YES... *THAT'S* IT...! I'M STILL... *UNCONSCIOUS*... DREAMING ALL THIS...!

HERE-- LET ME HELP YOU *UP!*

NOW LITTLE LINDA... IS LIFTING ME ... *OFF* THE GROUND.. AND I WEIGH... OVER 500 POUNDS..!

I'VE GOT TO... SNAP *OUT* OF THIS...!

GO AWAY...*BOTH* OF YOU...! YOU'RE ONLY...*FIGMENTS* OF...A FEVERED MIND...!

AWWW, YOU POOR DEAR--YOU'RE *CONFUSED,* AREN'T YOU?

COME ON--WE'LL TAKE YOU INTO TOWN TO MEET THE *MAYOR!* HE'LL EXPLAIN *EVERY-THING* TO YOU!

HE'S *GOOD* AT THAT!

SURE... WHY *NOT*...? TAKE ME TO...YOUR MAYOR ...!

AT *THIS* POINT... I'D BELIEVE JUST ABOUT... *ANYTHING*...!

132

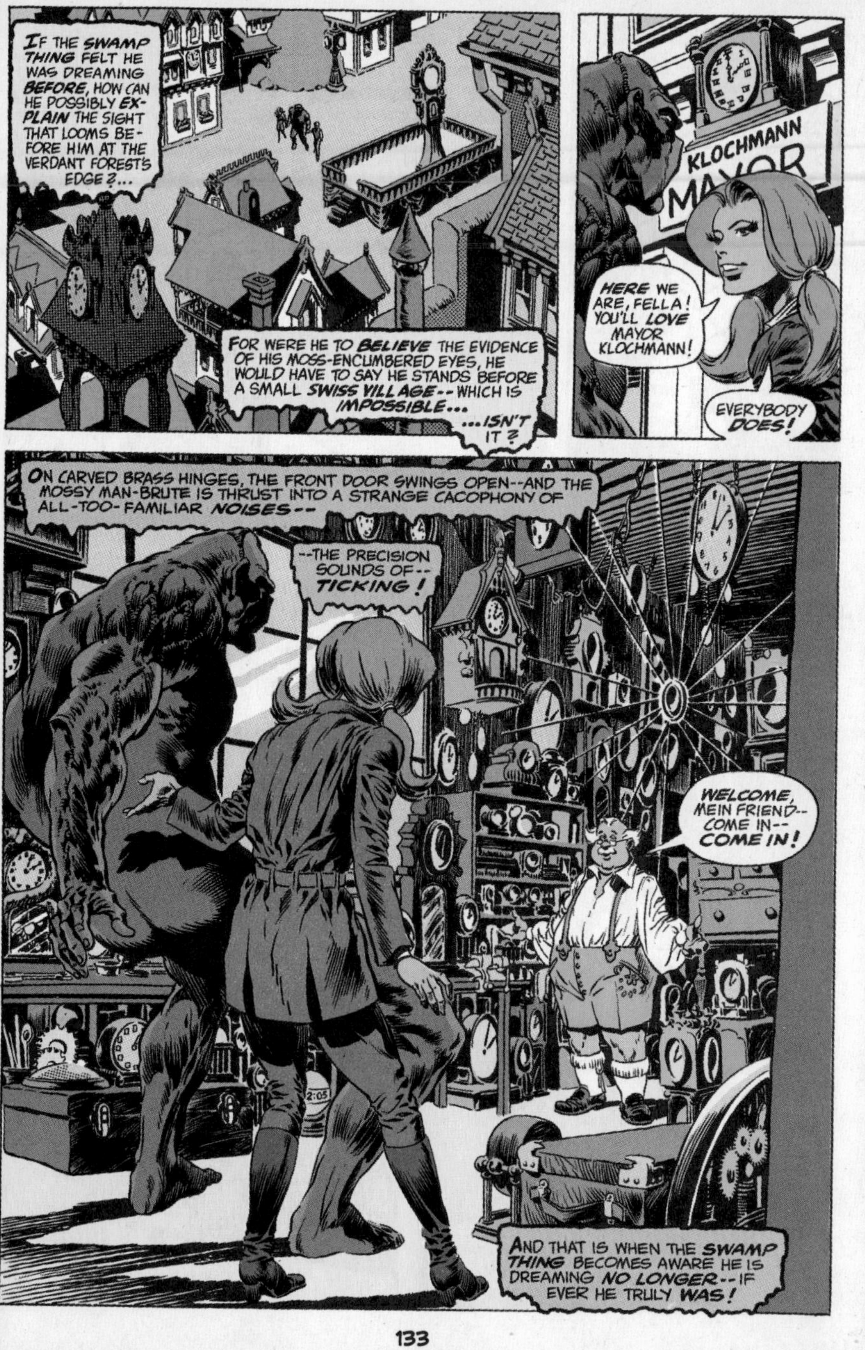
IF THE SWAMP THING FELT HE WAS DREAMING BEFORE, HOW CAN HE POSSIBLY EXPLAIN THE SIGHT THAT LOOMS BEFORE HIM AT THE VERDANT FOREST'S EDGE?...
FOR WERE HE TO BELIEVE THE EVIDENCE OF HIS MOSS-ENCUMBERED EYES, HE WOULD HAVE TO SAY HE STANDS BEFORE A SMALL SWISS VILLAGE--WHICH IS IMPOSSIBLE...
...ISN'T IT?
KLOCHMANN
MAYOR
HERE WE ARE, FELLA! YOU'LL LOVE MAYOR KLOCHMANN!
EVERYBODY DOES!
ON CARVED BRASS HINGES, THE FRONT DOOR SWINGS OPEN--AND THE MOSSY MAN-BRUTE IS THRUST INTO A STRANGE CACOPHONY OF ALL-TOO-FAMILIAR NOISES--
--THE PRECISION SOUNDS OF--TICKING!
WELCOME, MEIN FRIEND--COME IN--COME IN!
AND THAT IS WHEN THE SWAMP THING BECOMES AWARE HE IS DREAMING NO LONGER--IF EVER HE TRULY WAS!

I TRUST HERR ALEC AND FRAU LINDA HAF SHOWN YOU THROUGH OUR LITTLE *VILLAGE*? VE ARE ALL QUITE *PROUD* OF IT, YOU KNOW-- THOUGH *I*, PERHAPS, AM *PROUDER* ZAN THE REST!

BUT, AS USUAL, I FORGET MEIN *MANNERS*--! I TALK AND *TALK*--AND DO NOT EVEN *INTRODUCE* MYSELF--!

I AM *HANS KLOCHMANN*--CARPENTER, WATCH-MAKER, AND LATELY, *MAYOR* OF *BÜRGESS* TOWN--AT YOUR MOST WILLING SERVICE!

YOU VOULD CARE, PERHAPS, FOR SOME *COOKIES*--A GLASS OF *MILK*--?

NO--I SUPPOSE *NOT*--!

I *DESIGNED* THE TOWN, YOU SEE-- *BUILT* MOST OF IT WIZ MEIN OWN TWO *HANDS*--!

I CAN SEE FROM YOUR *EYES*, YOU DESIRE NO REFRESHMENTS--ONLY *ANSWERS*!

THEN ANSWERS YOU SHALL *HAVE*, MEIN STRANGE, SILENT FRIEND!

MAKE YOURSELF *COMFORTABLE*--IF ZAT IS *POSSIBLE*--AND I VILL TELL YOU *EVERYTHING* YOU VANT TO--

BBBRRRINNGG!

ACH--LOOK AT ZER *TIME*! FORGIVE ME, MEIN FRIEND--

--BUT I AM AFRAID MEIN TALE MUST *VAIT*!

AS MAYOR, ZERE ARE CERTAIN *DUTIES* I MUST PERFORM!

THE VILLAGERS VILL EXPECT ME IN THE *TOWN SQUARE* MOMENTARILY--AND I MUST NOT *DISAPPOINT* ZEM!

ZEY ARE ALL LIKE SUCH *CHILDREN*--AND ZEY SHOULD NOT BE KEPT *VAITING*!

BUT PLEASE, MEIN FRIEND--*JOIN* ME!

MOST OF THE TOWNSFOLK HAVE ALREADY *ARRIVED* WHEN THE SWAMP THING AND HIS CHERUBIC HOST AT LAST MOUNT THE STAIRS TO THE HAND-CARVED *PLATFORM...*

THERE, THE MOSSY MAN-BRUTE STANDS SILENTLY, HIS DARK-HOODED EYES CURIOUSLY STUDYING THE EXULTANT MULTITUDE GATHERED BEFORE HIM--AND HE CANNOT REMEMBER WHEN HE LAST SAW SO MANY PEOPLE SO SIMPLY, OUTRAGEOUSLY *HAPPY*--

BUT, STILL, SOMETHING *NAGS* AT THE BACK OF THE MAN-MONSTER'S MIND--AN UNCOMFORTABLE, ALMOST UNDEFINABLE *FEELING*--

HELLO, MEIN FRIENDS! EVERYTHING IS *FINE!* I'M STILL *HERE!*

--ARE THE SWAMP THING'S SENSES STILL AFFECTED BY HIS FALL--OR ARE MOST OF THE FACES IN THIS CROWD REALLY THAT *FAMILIAR* TO HIM?

WONDERFUL PEOPLE, ARE THEY *NOT*, MEIN FRIEND?

SMILING--CAREFREE--TOTALLY *UNABLE* TO FEEL JEALOUSY--GREED--HATRED--OR ANY OF THE BILLION *OTHER* SINS THE SOUL OF MAN IS HEIR TO!

HAH! YOU STARE AT ME IN *DISBELIEF* --BUT I *ASSURE* YOU, MEIN FRIEND, I *KNOW* WHAT I SAY!

AFTER ALL, WHO COULD KNOW THE CITIZENS OF *BURGESS BETTER*--

--THAN THE FAT OLD MAN WHO *BUILT* THEM?

COME--IT IS TIME TO *CONTINUE* MY INTERRUPTED TALE!

135

IN SWITZERLAND, I VAS AN *ARTISAN*-- A MAKER OF CLOCKWORK *TOYS*-- BUT WHEN THE *SECOND GREAT WAR* BEGAN, I FLED MY HOMELAND IN *FEAR*--

--AND CAME TO *AMERICA*-- WHERE I STUMBLED UPON ZIS DESERTED *MINING TOWN*--

--AND KNEW I'D *FOUND* VHAT I VAS SEARCHING FOR!

I RECONSTRUCTED THE RUINS IN THE STYLE OF MEIN HOMELAND--THEN BUILT *CLOCKWORK PEOPLE* TO BRING THE TOWN TO *LIFE!*

VHY I GAVE MEIN CREATIONS FACES FROM THE NEWSPAPER *OBITUARY* COLUMNS I DO NOT *KNOW*--

--EXCEPT, PERHAPS, TO OFFER ZOSE POOR UNFORTUNATES A *SECOND* CHANCE--

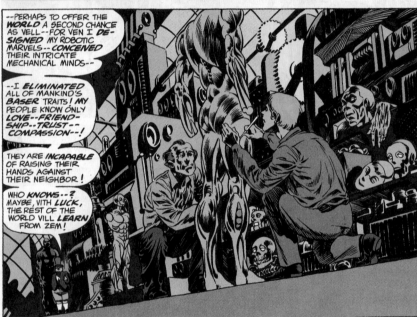

--PERHAPS TO OFFER THE *WORLD* A SECOND CHANCE AS VELL--FOR VEN I *DESIGNED* MY ROBOTIC MARVELS--*CONCEIVED* THEIR INTRICATE MECHANICAL MINDS--

--I *ELIMINATED* ALL OF MANKIND'S *BASER* TRAITS! MY PEOPLE KNOW ONLY *LOVE*-- *FRIENDSHIP*-- *TRUST*-- *COMPASSION*--!

THEY ARE *INCAPABLE* OF RAISING THEIR HANDS AGAINST THEIR NEIGHBOR!

WHO *KNOWS*--? MAYBE, WITH *LUCK*, THE REST OF THE WORLD VILL *LEARN* FROM ZEM!

BUT *ENOUGH* OF SUCH MAUDLIN MATTERS!

LINDA, I'M CERTAIN OUR GUEST VOULD ENJOY A TOUR OF THE SURROUNDING *COUNTRYSIDE!*

YOUR--er-- *HUSBAND* AND I HAVE THINGS TO ATTEND TO *HERE!*

OKAY, MAYOR KLOCHMANN--I'LL GIVE *"TALL, DARK, AND SILENT"* HERE A LESSON IN *FORESTRY* HE'LL NEVER FORGET!

AN ALMOST-FORGOTTEN SENSATION RIPPLES ALONG THE *SWAMP THING'S* SPINE AS HE WRAPS HIS MISSHAPEN, MOSS-ENCRUSTED *HAND* AROUND LINDA'S FAR MORE *DELICATE* FINGERS...

FACTORY BLDG. NO. 16

THEN, SMILING, THE TWO *STROLL* CASUALLY AWAY TO DISCOVER THE NEARBY *FOREST*--

--NEVER KNOWING HOW *NARROWLY* THEY HAVE MISSED AN ENCOUNTER WITH AN OLD--AND *DETERMINED*--FRIEND!

SOUNDS LIKE PEOPLE *WORKING* INSIDE, ABIGAIL!

C'MON--MAYBE SOMEBODY *HERE* CAN TELL US WHERE TO FIND THE *HEAD MAN* IN THIS LOONEY TUNES TOWN!

WELCOME, MEIN FRIENDS-- *COME IN!* I AM MAYOR KLOCHMANN!

IN *THAT* CASE, PAL-- I'VE GOT SOME *QUESTIONS* FOR YOU!

AND WHEN MATT CABLE'S MANY QUESTIONS HAVE BEEN ANSWERED--AND THE TALE RETOLD FOR THE *SECOND* TIME THIS DAY...

A TOWN PEOPLED WITH *MECHANICAL MEN* WHO MOVE AND SPEAK EXACTLY LIKE *HUMANS*--AND AN OLD MAN CAPABLE OF CREATING *MORE*--?!?

THIS *IS* A FIND INDEED--AND SOMETHING TO BE DEALT WITH *PROMPTLY!*

TASK FORCE *FOUR*-- *IMMEDIATE SCRAMBLE!*

I HAVE A MOST IMPORTANT *JOB* FOR YOU!

BEAUTIFUL, ISN'T IT? THE MAYOR CALLS THIS LAND "GOD'S COUNTRY"--

--BUT IF THAT'S TRUE, I CAN'T IMAGINE WHY GOD WOULD EVER WANT TO PART WITH IT!

STILL--I'M GLAD THAT HE DID-- VERY GLAD!

WHAT A SHAME IT WOULD BE TO HAVE LIVED --WITHOUT EVER SEEING SOMETHING LIKE THIS! IT'S SIMPLY--!

HEY-- WHAT'D I SAY?

IT'S STARTED-- RAINING!

WELL, DON'T JUST STAND THERE, SILLY-- HUNT COVER!

DO YOU WANT TO RUST?

RUST...? WHAT AN APT... CHOICE OF WORDS...!

THERE-- ALL SAFE AND SOUND! NOW-- WHAT WOULD YOU LIKE TO TALK ABOUT?

TALK...? IF ONLY I COULD...! SHE'S JUST A ROBOT... I KNOW THAT...

...BUT SHE LOOKS...SO MUCH LIKE LINDA... ACTS SO MUCH LIKE HER...

...THAT I WANT... TO TAKE HER IN MY ARMS AND...

NO!!

BY ALL THAT'S HOLY... WHAT AM I DOING...?

SHE'S A ROBOT... ONLY A ROBOT... WITH PROGRAMMED EMOTIONS...

...BUT HOW COULD I EXPECT... EVEN A MACHINE... TO RESPOND TO A... TO A...

...TO A WHAT...? IN GOD'S NAME... WHAT AM I?

WOW--LISTEN TO THAT *RAIN*!

SOUNDS LIKE THE STORM IS GETTING *WORSE*!

I'D *AGREE*--EXCEPT FOR *ONE* THING, ABIGAIL--

--IT'S *STOPPED* RAINING!

NO--SOMETHING *ELSE* IS HOWLING UP THAT *RACKET* OUT THERE--

--AND I THINK I'D BETTER *FIND OUT* WHAT IT *IS*!

AND WHAT IT *IS* IS...

--A HELI-COPTER!

BUT LIKE NO CHOPPER I'VE EVER SEEN!

WELL, IF YOU THINK THE *HELICOPTER* IS BIZARRE, MATT CABLE--WAIT TILL YOU GET A LOOK AT ITS *PASSENGERS*...

FOR WITH A *ROAR* LIKE A HURRICANE IN A WIND-TUNNEL, THE MASSIVE DEVICE SETTLES SOFTLY TO EARTH--AND A HUGE, GLEAMING *PORTAL* IN ITS SIDE HISSES OPEN TO REVEAL...

TASK FORCE FOUR--DEPLOY YOURSELVES IN THE PREDESIGNATED PATTERN!

COMPLETE CONTROL OF THE IMMEDIATE AREA MUST BE EFFECTED AT ONCE!

WELCOME, MEIN FRIENDS! I AM HANS KLOCHMANN-- THE MAYOR!

IS THERE SOME WAY I CAN BE OF SERVICE TO YOU?

KLOCHMANN? YES--YOU CAN BE OF GREAT SERVICE TO US-- AND YOU ALONE! I REPRESENT AN ORGANIZATION KNOWN AS THE CONCLAVE--

--AND WE DESIRE EXCLUSIVE CONTROL-- OF YOU AND YOUR MECHANICAL CREATIONS!

YOU WHAT? BUT THAT IS IMPOSSIBLE-- QUITE IMPOSSIBLE!

NOTHING IS IMPOSSIBLE, MISTER KLOCHMANN-- AS YOU WILL SOON LEARN!

AS YOU CAN SEE, THE CONCLAVE HAS HAD SOME SMALL SUCCESS IN THE FIELD OF ROBOTICS-- NOTHING CLOSE TO YOUR OWN, OF COURSE--

--AND WE INTEND TO MAKE USE OF YOUR KNOWLEDGE ONE WAY OR--

OVER MY DEAD BODY, YOU WILL!

THAT CAN BE MOST EASILY ARRANGED, YOU IMPULSIVE IDIOT--

--IF YOU DARE ATTEMPT ANYTHING SO FOOLISH AGAIN!

BR-R-R-RITT!

MATT-- YOUR ARM--!

PLEASE, MISS ARCANE-- YOU NEED NOT CONCERN YOURSELF SO OVER A MINOR FLESH WOUND!

MATTHEW CABLE HAS SUFFERED MUCH WORSE IN HIS TIME, I ASSURE YOU!

COME NOW, MR. CABLE-- YOU NEEDN'T LOOK SO *ASTONISHED!* I'VE KEPT A CLOSE *WATCH* ON YOU FOR SEVERAL *MONTHS* NOW!

INDEED--I KNOW ALL *ABOUT* YOU-- AND YOUR *HUNT* FOR THE CREATURE CALLED THE *SWAMP THING!*

YES, MATTHEW-- YOU'VE BEEN MOST *IN-VALUABLE* TO US OF LATE--

--BUT I'M AFRAID THAT VALUE HAS COME TO AN *END!*

I DON'T KNOW WHAT YOU'RE *TALKING* ABOUT, TIN-MAN--BUT THAT *LAST* COMMENT DOESN'T EXACTLY *BREAK* MY HEART!

WE HAVE *NO* INTEREST IN BREAKING YOUR *HEART,* MR. CABLE--

--ONLY YOUR *WILL!*

THERE IS MUCH WE WISH TO *KNOW* ABOUT THE OPERATION OF YOUR SECURITY ORGANIZATION--

--BUT I AM QUITE CERTAIN THAT ALL SUCH *INFORMATION* MUST BE GLEANED FROM YOU BY *FORCE*--

--AND *THOSE* ACTIVITIES CAN BEST BE CONDUCTED IN OUR *HOME OFFICE!*

GOODBYE, MR. CABLE-- I WILL *REJOIN* YOU WHEN I'VE CONCLUDED MY BUSINESS *HERE!*

BUT YOU HAF *NO* BUSINESS HERE, YOU VILE MONSTER!

EVEN IF YOU *KILL* ME, I VOULD *NEVER* WORK FOR SUCH AS YOU!

KILL YOU, MAYOR KLOCHMANN? WE WOULD NEVER *DREAM* OF SUCH A THING--

--BUT YOUR *MECHANICAL* CONSTITUENTS ARE *ANOTHER* THING ENTIRELY!

SQUEE-RANG

NO!

AND, FROM THE EDGE OF THE NEARBY CLEARING, THE CRY IS *ECHOED* IN TONES VERY FAR FROM *MECHANICAL*..

ALEC--? OH, NO-- NO!!

ANGUISHED, THE GIRL RACES FORWARD-- STARTLING A JUMP-SUITED GUNMAN--

--WHOSE STILL-SMOKING WEAPON DESCRIBES A SHORT HORIZONTAL ARC--

--AND ONCE MORE, IN LESS TIME THAT IT TAKES TO *TELL* IT, THE FRAGMENTS OF AN AUTOMATED LIFE ARE SCATTERED ACROSS THE TOWN SQUARE...

PLEASE--NO! I LOVE HIM-- LOVE-- *SQUEEE*

LINDA...? GOD, NO... NOT *AGAIN*...!

THERE'S NOTHING... I CAN *DO* FOR HER... NOW...!

--LOVE HIM-- LOVE HIM--

--LOVE HIM-- LOVE HIM--

OH, LINDA... HAVE I *FOUND* YOU...ONLY TO *LOSE* YOU... FOR A *SECOND* TIME...?

NO, LINDA... IT'S ME YOU LOVE ...THE ME I *USED* BE...!

--LOVE HIM-- LOVE HIM--

PLEASE, LINDA... *STOP* THAT...! IT'S *ME* YOU LOVE, *ME*...!

STOP IT, LINDA... YOU *DON'T* LOVE HIM, YOU *DON'T*...!

--LOVE HIM-- LOVE HIM--

STOP IT, LINDA... STOP IT... *STOP* IT... *STOP* IT...!

KRUMP

SQUEEE

--LOVE HIM-- LOVE HIM--

HIS HYSTERICAL FURY SPENT, THE MOSSY MAN-BRUTE STARES SHAMEFULLY FOR A MOMENT AT THE SHATTERED IMAGE OF THE WOMAN HE *LOVED*--

OUT OF MY *WAY*, SCUM... OR YOU'LL GET... JUST A *TASTE*... OF WHAT I PLAN... FOR YOUR *MASTER*...!

SO--OUR LITTLE COMPANY IS *COMPLETE*! AT LONG LAST, THE *SWAMP THING* ENTERS THE SCENE!

--THEN THE *RAGE* THAT WELLS WITHIN HIM CAN SCARCELY BE *CONTAINED*!

YES, MONSTER--WE *KNOW* OF YOU! IN FACT, WE'VE *HUNTED* YOU FOR QUITE A *TIME* NOW!

THANK YOU VERY MUCH FOR BRINGING OUR SEARCH TO AN *END*!

THWUMP!

I'M CERTAIN OUR PEOPLE IN *GOTHAM* CAN GAIN EASILY AS MUCH FROM *YOU* AS THEY CAN FROM *MATT CABLE*!

CABLE...? THEY HAVE *HIM* TOO...?

NOW JUST SIT THERE QUIETLY UNTIL WE ARE READY TO *LEAVE*--

--AND MY MIGHTY *HYDRAULIC ARM* WILL NOT BE PUT TO *USE* AGAIN!

SIT HERE QUIETLY... AFTER WHAT *YOU* HAVE DONE...?

THOOM!

ROBOT... YOU MUST BE... *JOKING*..!

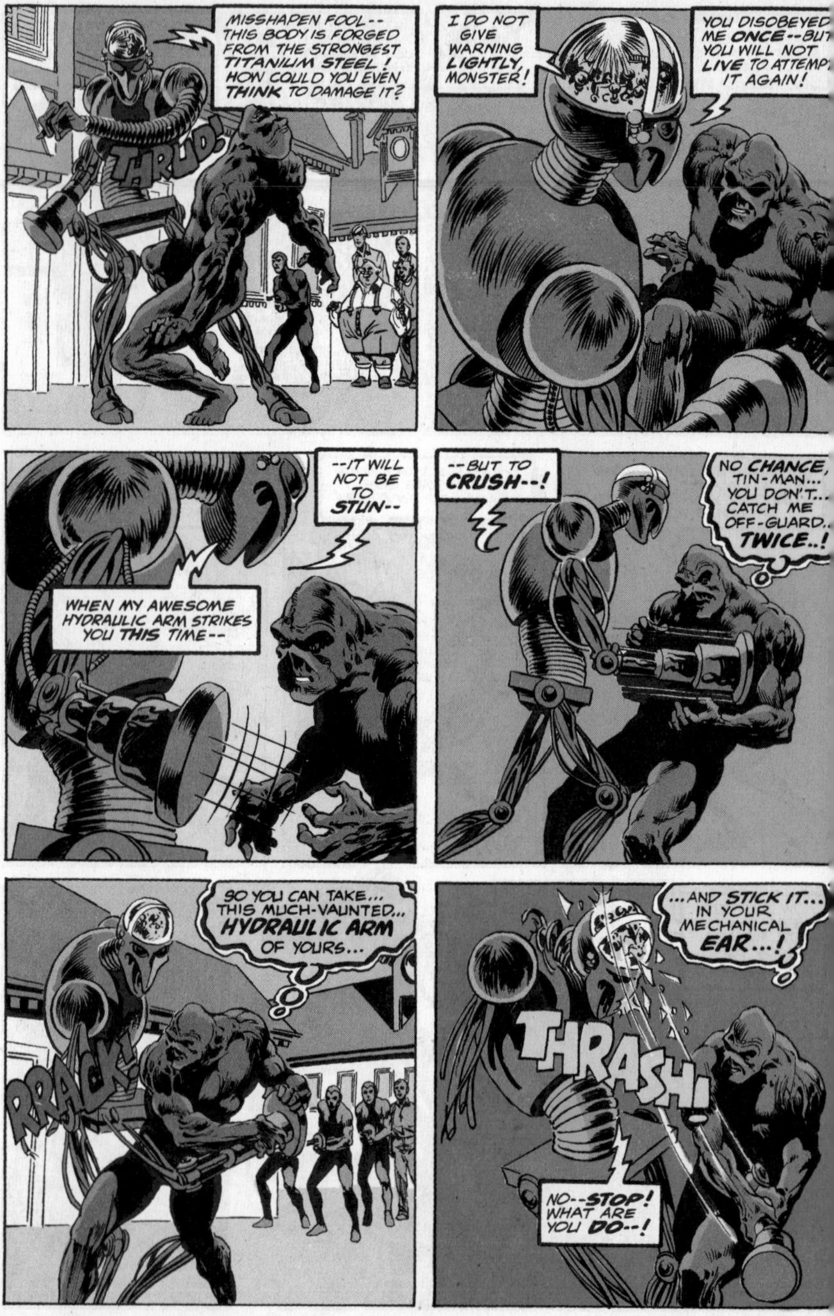
MISSHAPEN FOOL-- THIS BODY IS FORGED FROM THE STRONGEST TITANIUM STEEL! HOW COULD YOU EVEN THINK TO DAMAGE IT?
THRUD!
I DO NOT GIVE WARNING LIGHTLY, MONSTER!
YOU DISOBEYED ME ONCE--BUT YOU WILL NOT LIVE TO ATTEMPT IT AGAIN!
--IT WILL NOT BE TO STUN--
WHEN MY AWESOME HYDRAULIC ARM STRIKES YOU THIS TIME--
--BUT TO CRUSH--!
NO CHANCE, TIN-MAN... YOU DON'T... CATCH ME OFF-GUARD... TWICE..!
SO YOU CAN TAKE... THIS MUCH-VAUNTED... HYDRAULIC ARM OF YOURS...
RRACK!
...AND STICK IT... IN YOUR MECHANICAL EAR...!
THRASH!
NO--STOP! WHAT ARE YOU DO--!

WHAT DO WE DO *NOW*, PETE? SHOULD WE *TAKE* HIM?

YOU *CRAZY?* YOU SAW WHÁT THAT MONSTER DID TO THE *BOSS'S ROBOT!*

WANT HIM TO DO THE SAME TO *US?*

SPINELESS FOOLS! THE *SWAMP THING'S* WRATH WILL BE *NOTHING* COMPARED TO THE CONCLAVE'S *VENGEANCE* IF YOU *DISOBEY* MY ORDERS!

DESTROY THE-- MONSTER-- I-- COMMAND-- *SQUEEEE*

YOU *HEARD* THE MAN, FELLAS!

NO--I *BEG* OF YOU--DO NOT *DO* THIS THING--!

GUN HIM-- *NOW!*

THERE HAS BEEN *ENOUGH* VIOLENCE HERE TODAY! DO NOT MAKE A *MOCKERY* OF ALL THAT I HAF *LIVED*--

UUNNGH!

BRATAT

NO...! KLOCHMANN STEPPED INTO... THE LINE OF FIRE...BEFORE I COULD *MOVE*..!

THEY'VE... *KILLED* HIM...!

FOR A SEEMING ETERNITY, *SILENCE* HANGS HEAVILY UPON THE SCENE--

--AS THE STUNNED ASSEMBLAGE GAZES MUTELY AT THE SPRAWLED FORM OF A MAN WHO WAS WILLING TO *DIE* FOR HIS DREAM...

...AND A HARSH *CHILL* RIPPLES THROUGH THE COSTUMED GUNMEN AS THEY STARE UP AT THE MECHANICAL BEINGS WHO SURROUND THEM...

--FOR THE *EXPRESSIONS* CARVED UPON THOSE HUMANOID FACES COULD NEVER HAVE BEEN PLACED THERE BY THE LATE *HANS KLOCHMANN.*

"*THEY ARE INCAPABLE OF RAISING THEIR HANDS AGAINST THEIR NEIGHBORS.*" THOSE WERE THE LITTLE CLOCKMAKER'S *WORDS*--

IF HANS KLOCHMANN HAD LIVED TO *WITNESS* THIS ATROCITY, HE WOULD SURELY HAVE BEEN *HEARTBROKEN*--

--PERHAPS HE WOULD HAVE *CRIED*--

--FOR THE RING OF TORN AND TWISTED MECHANICAL BODIES THAT PRESSES INEXORABLY *IN* UPON THE FOUR TERRIFIED HENCHMEN IS A CIRCLE BORN OF THE BURNING NEED FOR *VENGEANCE*--

--AND THOUGH THAT VENGEANCE IS NOT SO MUCH SOUGHT OUT OF *HATRED* FOR THE GUNMEN AS IT IS OUT OF *LOVE* FOR THE OLD MAN THEY HAD SLAIN--

--BUT THEIR *MEANING* IS SOON DROWNED OUT BY THE FURIOUS CHATTER OF *MACHINE GUN FIRE* THAT ECHOES ACROSS THE SQUARE...

--BUT THEN, IF THE JOVIAL MAYOR OF BURGESS *HAD* LIVED, THIS SPECTACLE WOULD *NEVER* HAVE COME TO PASS--

--ITS RESULT IS HORRIBLY, PITIABLY, THE *SAME*!

WHEN THE CLAMOR OF BULLETS RENDING METAL--AND OF METAL CRUSHING FLESH--AT LAST FADES INTO SILENCE--

--THERE IS ONLY THE SOLEMN *SWAMP THING* LEFT STANDING IN THE VILLAGE SQUARE!

146

POOR *KLOCHMANN*...! IN THE END... HIS *NEW* RACE OF MEN... WAS NOT SO TERRIBLY *DIFFERENT*... FROM THE *OLD*..!

WHAT A *SHAME* THAT...

BONG! BONG! BONG! BONG!

BONG! BONG! BONG! BONG!

BONG! Bo...KWA WRAM!

COME ON, MUTT...! THERE ARE *THINGS* WE HAVE TO DO... BEFORE TIME RUNS OUT... FOR *US*...!

ADDENDUM: THREE HOURS LATER, ON A SLOW-MOVING FREIGHT TRAIN...

GOTHAM CITY...! THAT'S WHERE THE TIN-MAN... WANTED TO *SEND* ME...

...AND... I'LL WAGER... WHERE HE SENT... *MATT CABLE*, TOO...!

WELL, LITTLE ONE... IF CABLE IS *THERE*... WE'RE GOING TO *FIND* HIM...

...AND MAKE HIS CAPTORS... *PAY*...!

GOTHAM CITY 213 miles

147

CHAPTER SEVEN

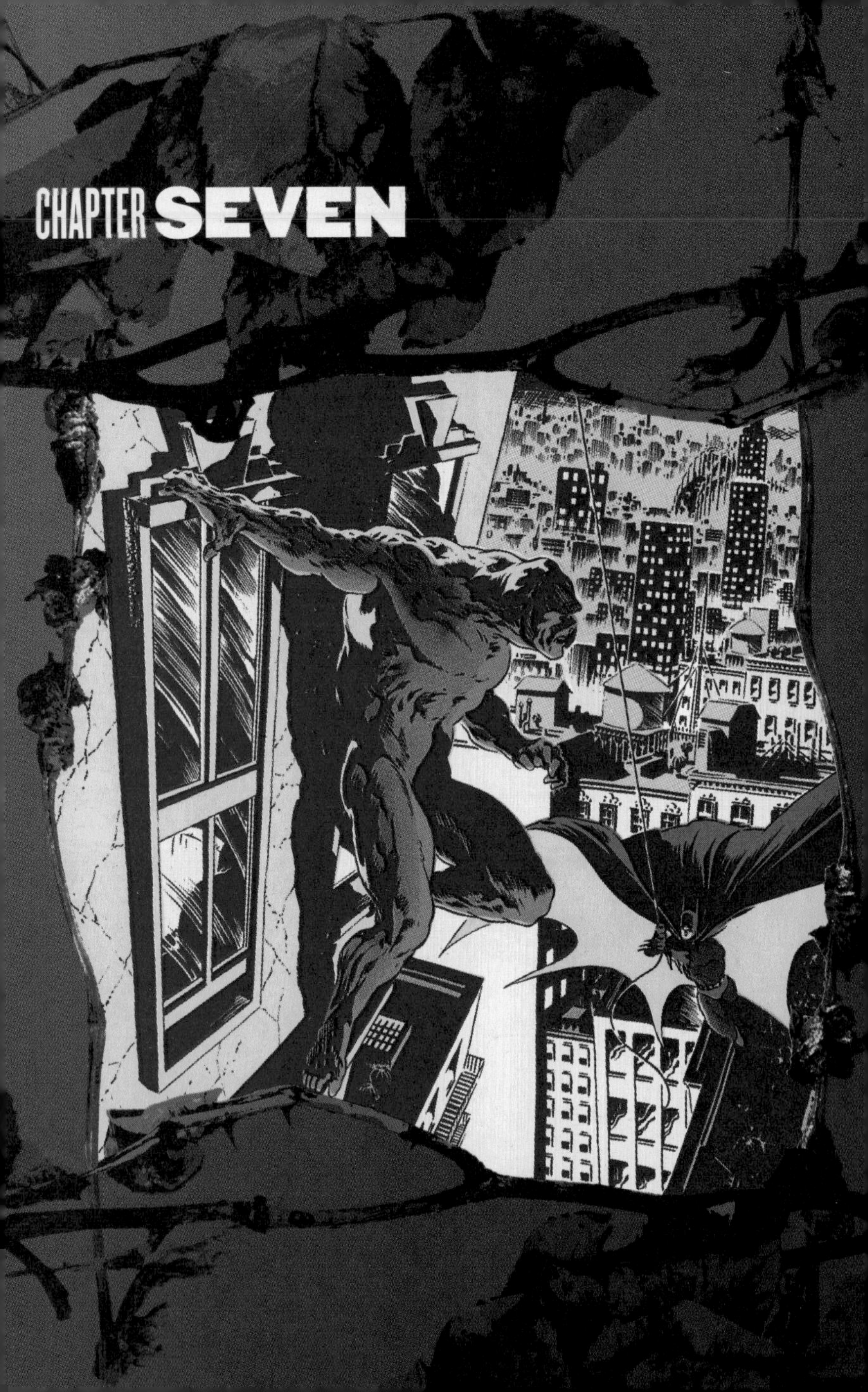

Like one that on a lonesome road
Doth walk in fear and dread,

And, having once turned round, walks on,
And turns no more his head;

Because he knows a frightful fiend
Doth close behind him tread.

SAMUEL TAYLOR COLERIDGE SAID THAT IN THE "RIME OF THE ANCIENT MARINER".

"AND I SWEAR BY THE SPIRITS OF MY PARENTS TO AVENGE THEIR DEATHS BY SPENDING THE REST OF MY LIFE WARRING ON ALL CRIMINALS."

BRUCE WAYNE SAID THAT BY A GOTHAM CITY GRAVE-SIDE.

THERE IS MOST DEFINITELY A CONNECTION BETWEEN THE TWO--AND WE SHALL ALL SOON DISCOVER EXACTLY WHAT IT IS!

HOPE SEEING *ME*... DIDN'T GIVE THAT POOR GUY... A *HEART ATTACK*...

...BUT SEEING *HIM*... GAVE ME AN IDEA...

...CLOTHES..!

CAN'T REALLY... GET AROUND THE BIG BAD CITY... *WITHOUT* THEM...

USED ITEM FURNITURE CLOTHING BOOKS-A

YEAH, O'HARA-- I SAID A *MONSTER*-- WITH A *DOG*, YET! IT'S...

...AND IT APPEARS... I'VE *LOCATED* JUST THE PLACE... TO *ACQUIRE* SOME...!

C'MON, O'HARA-- I HAVEN'T TOUCHED A *DROP* OF THE STUFF! NOW GET ME A FEW *SQUAD CARS* OVER HERE-- *PRONTO*--

--AND, FER HEAVEN'S SAKE, NO *SIRENS*! THE *LAST* THING I WANNA DO IS *IRRITATE* HIM!

SEVERAL MOMENTS LATER...

OKAY, MEN--SPREAD OUT--AND STAY *UNDER COVER*!

WE'RE DEALIN' WITH A *MONSTER*, ALL RIGHT, CHIEF!

ANYTHING THAT CAN TEAR APART STEEL GATES WITH HIS *BARE HANDS*...

"...HAS GOTTA BE THE *GRAND-DADDY* MONSTER OF 'EM ALL!"

THERE, MUTT...!

PRESENTING THE *NEW ALEC HOLLAND*... STAR OF STAGE... SCREEN... AND *SUMP-HOLE*...!

WELL.... AT LEAST *THIS* WAY... NOBODY WILL BE QUICK TO NOTICE... SEVEN-PLUS FEET OF SHAMBLING SWAMP GUNK...!

COME ON, MUTT...! LET'S GET...?

THIS IS THE POLICE! YOU ARE UNDER *ARREST*!

COME FORWARD *PEACEFULLY*-- HANDS ABOVE YOUR HEAD--AND YOU WILL NOT BE *HURT*!

MISTER... YOU HAVE GOT TO BE *KIDD*...

UHNN!

BLAM!

SARGE, H-HE'S *ATTACKING* US!

150

!OOK, FELLAS... *PLEASE*... I REALLY DON'T WANT...TO *HURT* YOU...!

FUTT SPAK FAKK

TH-THE *SLUGS*-- THEY'RE GOIN' *THROUGH* HIM!

I'M IN GOTHAM CITY...ON *PERSONAL* BUSINESS...

...AND IF YOU TRY... TO MAKE MY BUSINESS... *YOUR* BUSINESS...

...YOU ARE *ALMOST CERTAINLY*... GOING TO *REGRET* IT...!

KWAROOMM!

OH, MY *LORD*-- IT'S NOT *POSSIBLE*--!

COME ON, MUTT...WHILE THEY'RE STILL *DISTRACTED*... LET'S GET *OUT* OF HERE...!

LOOK! WE'VE GOT THE MON- STER *NOW,* MEN!

HE'S RUNNING INTO A...

...DEAD... END... ALLEY!

KWAM

AT LEAST-- IT *WAS* A DEAD END ALLEY!

BETTER GET OUT AN "*ALL POINTS*" ON HIM--AND *QUICK*!

... AND THE *TRANS-EUROPEAN HOMES FOR THE AGED AND INFIRM* HAVE INCREASED RESIDENCY BY 23.8 PERCENT!

THAT'S JUST ABOUT *EVERYTHING*, BRUCE!

THANK YOU, NATHAN! WELL -- I BELIEVE THAT TAKES CARE OF ALL OUR *BUSINESS* HERE TONIGHT!

I'D LIKE TO THANK YOU *ALL* FOR STAYING SO *LATE* AND GIVING THESE MATTERS THE ATTENTION THEY DESERVE!

NO THANKS *NECESSARY*, BRUCE, MY BOY-- *EVER!* ANYTHING NATHAN ELLERY CAN DO TO HELP THE *NEEDY* OF THE WORLD--

I *KNOW*, NATHAN -- AND I *APPRECIATE* IT! I REALLY *DO!*

YES, WELL -- er -- I'LL SEE YOU *NEXT WEEK*, MY BOY!

GOOD NIGHT, NATHAN -- AND THANKS *AGAIN*, ANYWAY!

MOMENTS LATER, AS BRUCE WAYNE'S PRIVATE ELEVATOR HUMS TOWARDS HIS PENTHOUSE APARTMENT...

THE MEETING RAN A TRIFLE *OVERLONG* THIS EVENING, SIR!

YES, ALFRED -- BUSINESS BEFORE *PLEASURE!*

HAVE MY "*WORK-CLOTHES*" READY WHEN I ARRIVE!

WILL YOU BE GONE *LONG*, SIR?

ONLY AS LONG AS *NECESSARY* -- ALFRED -- HOWEVER LONG IT *TAKES!*

SHORTLY -- AN EERIE, BLACK-CLAD FIGURE HURTLES FROM THE PENTHOUSE WINDOW -- AND ARCS OVER THE CITY HE CALLS *HOME*...

TONIGHT -- AS ON SO MANY *OTHER NIGHTS* --

-- THE BATMAN PROWLS THE STREETS OF GOTHAM ONCE AGAIN...

BUT THE CAPED CRUSADER IS NOT THE *ONLY* CREATURE MOVING THROUGH THE DARKNESS THIS NIGHT...

FOR AT THE DOCKYARDS ON GOTHAM'S LOWER WEST SIDE, A GANG OF *WHARF RATS* GOES ABOUT ITS BUSINESS... -- *SMUGGLING,* TO BE EXACT!

C'MON, YA IDJITS-- *MOVE IT!* WE AIN'T GOT *FEREVER,* YA KNOW!

THE LOCAL COP CAR'LL BE COMIN' AROUND ON *PATROL* SOON, YA KNOW--

--AN' WE *DON'T* NEED ANY KIND'A *GRIEF,* YA KNOW!

THAT'S *TOO BAD,* FRIEND-- BECAUSE YOU'VE JUST BOUGHT ALL THE *GRIEF* YOU CAN HANDLE... "YA KNOW"?

WHO--?

OH... *NO!*

DON'T GO *AWAY,* LITTLE MAN!

I WANT TO HAVE *WORDS* WITH YOU!

I--I DON'T KNOW *NUTHIN',* BATMAN-- I *SWEAR* I DON'T--!

THEN SUPPOSE WE *RATTLE* YOUR LITTLE *HEAD* AROUND--

--AND SEE IF WE CAN'T *SHAKE* SOMETHING *FREE?*

CHUDD!

WE'LL SHAKE SOMETHIN' *FREE,* ALL RIGHT, BATMAN!

WE'RE GONNA SHAKE *YOU* FREE-- FROM YER *LIFE!*

HIT 'IM, BOYS!

WELL, WELL-- I'VE BEEN *WAITING* FOR THE REST OF YOU PUNKS TO CRAWL OUT OF YOUR *HOLES*--

153

--BUT AFTER I'M *THROUGH* WITH YOU--

WAK!

SPLAT

--IF YOU HAVE ANY *BRAINS* LEFT AT ALL--

THRACK!

--YOU'LL CRAWL *BACK* INTO THOSE HOLES--

WHAOKK

--AND PULL THE *DIRT* IN AFTER YOU!

GET THE *POINT?*

THUDD!

THEY'RE ALL *OUT* OF IT-- BUT I FOUND WHAT I WAS *LOOKING* FOR--

--THE NEXT CLUE TO THE IDENTITY OF *MR. E--*

--THE *MYSTERIOUS* LEADER OF THE UNDER-WORLD COM-BINE CALLED *THE CON-CLAVE!*

THIS SMUGGLING OPERATION WAS JUST AN INFINI-TESIMAL *FRACTION* OF THE CONCLAVE'S TOTAL ACTION AND...

UH-OH--LOOKS LIKE THE *CONCLAVE* WILL HAVE TO *WAIT!*

COMMISSIONER GORDON DOESN'T USE THE *BAT-SIGNAL* ANY-MORE--UNLESS IT'S AN *EMERGENCY!*

154

RECALL THE MOMENT--AS BRUCE WAYNE SAUNTERS AWAY DOWN A STERILE CORRIDOR TO BECOME THE DREADED *BATMAN*--

--AND HIS ASSOCIATE, NATHAN ELLERY, TAKES THE PUBLIC ELEVATOR DOWN TO THE TWILIT *STREET*--

--WHERE HE IS GREETED BY A SHINING, WHITE LIMOUSINE --

EVENING, MR. ELLERY!

GOOD EVENING, DRISCOLL!

--AND A FRIGHTENINGLY *FAMILIAR* PET...

WHERE TO *TONIGHT*, MR. E.?

TO THE *POTTER'S STREET WAREHOUSE*, DRISCOLL! I HAVE SOME *UNFINISHED BUSINESS* AWAITING ME THERE!

ALONG GOTHAM'S MAIN BOULEVARDS, THE IVORY VEHICLE CHURNS--THEN THROUGH A DARKER, QUIETER PART OF TOWN--AND, FINALLY, DOWN A GRIMY ALLEYWAY--

--WHERE A SPECIAL SEQUENCE OF BLINKING *HEADLIGHTS* ROLLS BACK A THICK TITANIUM STEEL DOOR--

--TO REVEAL ...

GOOD EVENING, DR. HAMMERSCHMIDT! AND HOW ARE OUR *RELUCTANT GUESTS* DOING THIS FINE NIGHT?

ACH--HERR E. VHAT A PLEASANT *ZURPRISE* TO SEE YOU!

HERR *CABLE* UND FRAULEIN *ARCANE* ARE DOINK *SPLENDIDLY*--

--BUT THEY STILL REFUSE TO *TALK!*

YOU **STILL** REFUSE 2 IN GOD'S NAME -- **WHY?**

YOU **KNOW** WE WILL EVENTUALLY LEARN **EVERYTHING** -- ONE WAY OR **ANOTHER!**

SUCK A **PEACH,** FAT MAN!

TSK TSK -- SUCH **VEHEMENCE,** MATTHEW!

DR. HAMMER-SCHMIDT -- GIVE MR. CABLE ANOTHER TASTE OF THE **ELECTRON-CHAIR!**

JA, HERR E. -- MIT DER UTMOST **PLEASURE!** HEE HEE HEE!

DIE **EFFECTS** OF DER MACHINE NEFER CEASE TO **FASCINATE** ME!

TORTURE ME ALL YOU WANT, FAT MAN -- BUT YOU WON'T GET ME TO **TALK** --

AARRGGHH!

LET US AVERT OUR EYES FROM THIS UNPLEASANT **SCENE** -- AND FOCUS INSTEAD UPON A CERTAIN OFFICE IN THE HEART OF GOTHAM CITY...

YOU **CALLED,** COMMIS-SIONER?

WHO --? OH, BATMAN -- YOU **STARTLED** ME!

WELL, WHAT I AM ABOUT TO SAY MAY STARTLE **YOU!**

THERE'S A **MONSTER** LOOSE IN GOTHAM, **BATMAN** --

NO JOKE -- NO **DELUSION** -- A DOZEN OF OUR BEST MEN HAVE **SEEN** HIM --

-- AND THE GOVERNMENT **CONFIRMS** HIS EXISTENCE!

IN FACT, I WAS JUST GOING OVER THE GOVERNMENT'S SECRET **FILE** ON THE CREATURE WHEN YOU ARRIVED!

THE FILE'S CODE **NAME** IS -- "**SWAMP THING**"!

IF THE PUBLIC WAS TO **DISCOVER** A **SWAMP THING** LURKING IN THEIR MIDST, IT COULD CREATE A CITY-WIDE **PANIC!**

THAT'S WHY I CALLED **YOU,** BATMAN --

-- TO ASK YOU TO TRACK THAT MONSTER **DOWN** BEFORE THE PEOPLE BE-COME **AWARE!**

THE MONSTER IS NOW **DISGUISED,** I'M TOLD -- AND TRAVELLING IN THE COMPANY OF A SMALL BROWN **DOG!**

SO THE SOONER YOU GET **STARTED,** BATMAN -- THE BETTER IT WILL -- **BATMAN?**

OH!

WHILE, IN A GRIMY ALLEYWAY ON GOTHAM'S LOWER EAST SIDE...

OKAY, MUTT... YOU WAIT *HERE*...!

THIS IS SOMETHING I HAVE TO DO... *ALONE*...!

PECK'S WATER'S EDGE *Bar Grille*

UGH...! THIS PLACE IS *GRUBBIER* THAN I AM...

...BUT IF I'M EVER...GOING TO FIND A *LEAD*... TO CABLE'S WHERE-ABOUTS...

IT'S IN A JOINT... LIKE *THIS* ONE...!

ALL I'VE GOT TO DO... IS SIT *QUIETLY*...

STAY OUT OF *SIGHT*...

...AND KEEP MY *EARS* OPEN FOR...

WHAT'LL IT *BE*, PAL-- *BEER*?

UH-OH... BETTER JUST *NOD*...!

YEAH-- UH-- OKAY, PAL-- WHATEVER YA *SAY*--!

LORD, WHEN HE NODDED HIS *HEAD*, I THOUGHT IT WAS GONNA *FALL OFF*!

FOR A WHILE, THE *SWAMP THING* SITS, HIS BEER GROWING WARM IN HIS GREAT, MOSSY HAND--

UNTIL, AT LAST, HIS SILENT VIGIL BEARS *FRUIT*...

YEAH--IMAGINE-- *THE CONCLAVE* HIRIN' ME!

AIN'T *MUCH* TA START--JEST RE-PLACIN' SOME GUYS WHAT USED TA RUN A *SMUGGLIN'* OPER-ATION--BUT IT'LL *GROW*!

I'M S'POSED TA MEET MY *CONTACT* AT DE ADDRESS ON DIS PAPER--

--BUT I FIGURED FIRST I'D HAVE ME A *BEER* WIT' ME PALS AN'--

NO... HE'S KNOCKED MY... *HAT* OFF...!

'EY--GIMME BACK DAT *PAPER*, YA LOUSY--!

OH...MY... *GOD*...!

DON'T KNOW **WHAT** YA ARE, UGLY--

--BUT I'M GONNA HAVE DAT **PAPER** BACK!

FRIEND... ALL **YOU** ARE GOING TO HAVE...

...IS A **SPLITTING** HEADACHE...!

'EY--DAT'S ME **PAL** YOU'RE BEATIN' ON!

THRUNCH!

THAT'S **NICE**...

WITH ANY **LUCK**...THEY'LL GIVE YOU... **ADJOINING** BEDS... IN THE HOSPITAL...!

PAF!

AND MOMENTS LATER...

I DIDN'T MEAN... TO **START** THIS SORT OF **RUCKUS**...

...BUT THESE DRUNKEN **IDIOTS**... JUST WON'T QUIT **COMING**...!

WELL...WHETHER I **STARTED** IT... OR NOT...

...I'M DEFINITELY GOING TO... **FINISH** IT...!

BAR

DECK'S
R'S EDGE

CRASSHH!

GOTHAM'S *YOUR* CITY KEEP IT CLEAN

OKAY, MUTT... LET'S GET **MOVING**...!

WE'VE **FOUND** OUR FIRST **CLUE**...! NOW LET'S FIND... **MATT CABLE**...!

IT DOES NOT TAKE THE MOSSY MAN-BRUTE LONG TO LEARN THE BASIC RUDIMENTS OF THE UNDER-WORLD'S INFORMATIONAL STRUCTURE: ONE CLUE LEADS TO ANOTHER--THEN ANOTHER-- AND ANOTHER AFTER THAT--

--SOME GARNERED IN SHADOWED DOORWAYS--

--OTHERS FROM HASTILY-SCRAWLED NOTES--

--AND STILL OTHERS SPEWED FROM BE-TWEEN BLOODIED LIPS--

TIME TO *TIE UP* LOOSE ENDS, MY PET!

CABLE AND THE GIRL ARE *OURS*-- AND THE *SWAMP THING* HAS DISAPPEARED!

ONLY THE *DOG* REMAINS--

--AND THIS RADIO FREQUENCY SHOULD REACT MOST INTERESTINGLY UPON THE *TRANSMITTER* WE PLANTED INSIDE THE *MONGREL'S HEAD!*

...POTTER'S STREET... WAREHOUSE...!

IF THIS PUNK... DIDN'T *LIE* TO US, MUTT...

...THAT'S WHERE WE'LL FIND... *MATT CABLE*...!

BUT AS THE SWAMP THING TURNS, HIS FURRY COMPANION SQUIRMS FROM HIS GRASP AND...

HEY...! WHERE ARE YOU... GOING, MUTT...?

HEY...! WHAT'S *WRONG*... WITH YOU...?

COME BACK HERE... COME...

YIP!

YIP!

YIP!

WHILE, ACROSS THE SPRAWLING CITY, THE METHODS EMPLOYED BY THE SWAMP THING ARE IN TURN EMPLOYED BY THE GRIM BAT-COWLED BEING WHO PURSUES HIM--

--BUT WITH FAR LESS *SUCCESSFUL* RESULTS--

--UNTIL, AT LAST...

THAT *DOG*-- FITS THE COMMISSIONER'S *DESCRIPTION!*

NO *MONSTER* WITH HIM--

--BUT HE'S STILL *CHECKING OUT!*

YIP! YP! YIP!

HOLD ON, LITTLE FELLA--

--I THINK I HAVE SOME *BUSINESS* WITH YOU!

YICK--HE'S THE *SWAMP THING'S* DOG, ALL RIGHT!

TRACES OF DECAYING *MOSS* STILL CLING TO HIS *FUR!*

DON'T KNOW WHERE YOU'RE *RUNNING*--

--BUT I'LL BET IT'S TO YOUR *SWAMPY MASTER!*

YIP! YP!

SO I'LL *TAG ALONG* FOR THE *RIDE!*

BLAST... MUTT'S GONE...

...AND I HAVEN'T GOT... TIME NOW TO CHASE... AFTER HIM...!

GOT TO GET... TO CABLE QUICKLY... OR IT MAY BE... TOO LATE...!

AND SO, WHILE THE BATMAN FOLLOWS A SMALL MONGREL DOG THROUGH THE DARKENED STREETS OF GOTHAM, ANOTHER, BURLIER FIGURE FOLLOWS A DESPERATE COURSE OF ACTION...

--A COURSE THAT LEADS HIM TO A DECIDEDLY FAMILIAR BUILDING...

THIS IS... THE PLACE... ALL RIGHT...

...BUT I OUGHT TO... KNOW WHAT I'M... GETTING MYSELF INTO... BEFORE I MAKE... MY MOVE...!

THERE...! THIS CRATE SHOULD... PUT ME JUST HIGH ENOUGH... TO GET A LOOK... THROUGH THAT GRIMY WINDOW...!

A MOSS-ENCRUSTED HAND BRUSHES AWAY CRUST OF A DIFFERENT KIND TO FIND...

CABLE AND THE GIRL... ARE HERE...!

ACH-- IT VILL BE INTERESTINK TO SEE IF YOU CAN RESIST ZIS NEXT ELECTRONIC INDUCEMENT, HERR CABLE!

NO-- PLEASE DON'T--!

EASY, ABIGAIL-- SOMEHOW WE'LL TAKE HIS WORST!

PERHAPS... CABLE, OLD FRIEND... BUT HIS WORST IS NOTHING...

...COMPARED TO WHAT... I CAN DO TO HIM...!

LIEBER GOTT! DER MONSTER TEARS THROUGH STEEL PLATE-- AS IF IT VERE PAPER!

BE THANKFUL... I DON'T DO THE SAME...TO *YOU*, DOCTOR...

...BUT IF YOU'VE DONE... ANY PERMANENT *DAMAGE*... TO CABLE OR THE GIRL... I MIGHT JUST... *CHANGE* MY MIND...!

THE *SWAMP THING*-- *HERE?*

I DON'T GET IT-- I DON'T *UNDERSTAND...!*

FIRST YOU HELP *MURDER* MY TWO BEST FRIENDS-- THEN YOU KEEP POPPING UP TO SAVE MY *LIFE!*

WHY, MONSTER-- *WHY?*

SNAKT!

EVEN IF I *COULD...* TELL YOU, MATTHEW... YOU'D NEVER... *BELIEVE* ME...!

HAMMERSCHMIDT TO MR. E-- EMERGENCY-- CONDITION *RED!*

DIE CREATURE YOU *VARNED* US ABOUT--*DIE* CREATURE WHO KILLED *FERRETT*-- IS *HERE!* HE'S *HERE!*

FERRETT!?!

AT THE NAME, THE SWAMP THING TURNS-- AND, FOR AN INSTANT, HIS MIND IS AWASH WITH *MEMORIES*...

FERRETT, WHO, REPRESENTING A *MYSTERIOUS COMBINE,* ATTEMPTED TO *BUY* DR. ALEC HOLLAND'S *BIO-RESTORATIVE* FORMULA

--AND, FAILING *THAT,* ARRANGED AN *EXPLOSION* THAT TORE HOLLAND'S *MARSHLAND LAB APART*--

--AND HURLED THE DOCTOR'S CHEMICAL-SEARED BODY DEEP INTO THE CLUTCHING *MUCK*--

--TO RISE FROM THE BOG SOMETIME LATER AS A *TWISTED,* SHAMBLING *MOCKERY* OF LIFE...

--ONLY TO *DISCOVER* THAT *DEATH* HAD CLAIMED HIS *LOVING WIFE, LINDA,* AT FERRETT'S TAINTED HAND!

IN THE LONG WEEKS SINCE, THIS THING THAT WAS ONCE DR. ALEC HOLLAND HAS SEARCHED FOR FERRETT'S *EMPLOYER*--THE MAN RESPONSIBLE FOR IT ALL--

--BUT HE HAS SEARCHED THE WORLD IN *VAIN*--

--UNTIL *NOW!*

BUT WHILE **ONE** SEARCH SEEMINGLY DRAWS TO A CLOSE, ANOTHER SEARCH **CONTINUES**--

--DOWN DARK AND DESERTED ALLEYWAYS--

YIP! YIP! YIP!

--UNTIL, FINALLY--

...WHAT IN--?

DELIVERIES AT THIS DOOR

NATHAN ELLERY'S PENT-HOUSE APARTMENT OCCU-PIES THE WHOLE **TOP FLOOR** OF THIS BUILDING!

BUT IF THAT DOG'S **SCRATCHING** MEANS WHAT I **THINK** IT DOES, THIS PLACE IS ALSO SERVING AS THE **SWAMP THING'S** HIDE--

HUH? SOMEONE COMING UP **BEHIND** ME!

CRUNCH!

BETTER GET OUT OF SIGHT TILL I **SEE** WHO IT IS!

WELL, I'LL BE A--!

THAT ILL-FITTING TRENCH-COAT CAN'T POSSIBLY CON-CEAL ANYTHING BUT--THE **SWAMP THING!**

APPEARS HIS CANINE COM-PANION BEAT HIM **BACK** TO THEIR **HIDE-OUT**--

DIDN'T TAKE ME LONG...TO **FORCE** THIS ADDRESS... OUT OF...

--NOW I'M GOING TO **BEAT** HIM--RIGHT INTO THE **GROUND!**

DELIVERIES AT THIS DOOR

OKAY, GRUESOME-- SURRENDER PEACEABLY-- AND YOU WON'T GET **HURT!**

HUH...? THE...B-BATMAN...! GOT TO TRY...TO **REASON** WITH HIM...!

163

THWUCK

SORRY, UGLY--BUT YOU'RE NOT GETTING THOSE HAM-HOCK HANDS ON ME!

NO...*PLEASE*...YOU DON'T *UNDERSTAND*...! I DON'T WANT...TO *FIGHT* YOU...!

YOU DON'T *UNDERSTAND* ME, DO YOU, MONSTER?

I SAID I'M TAKING YOU *IN*--

THUD!

--IN *HAND-CUFFS*--OR A *BOX*!

THE CHOICE IS *YOURS*!

AMAZING--! THAT WOODEN CRATE--MY *FIST*!

--IT'S ALMOST AS IF HE DOESN'T EVEN *FEEL* THEM!

THWAK

PLEASE... HOW CAN I...MAKE YOU *UNDER-STAND*...?

THAT'S *PECULIAR*! NOW THE THING IS HIDING BEHIND A *TRASH-CAN*--

--PROBABLY PREPARING SOME *SURPRISE* ATTACK!

THIS IS WORKING OUT... ALL *WRONG*...!

I CAN'T... FIGHT *HIM*... I CAN'T...!

WELL, I'M CAPABLE OF A *SURPRISE* OR TWO *MYSELF*!

CHROOM!

COME **ON**, YOU UGLY MONSTER-- FALL--**FALL**!

HE KEEPS COMING...

CLUD

...HE WON'T **QUIT**...!

WHAT CAN I DO...TO **COMMUNICATE**...WITH HIM...?

TWACK

HOW CAN I...MAKE HIM **SEE**...?

NO...IT'S BECOMING **OBVIOUS**...I **CAN'T** MAKE HIM SEE...!

THIS MAN...WILL JUST **KEEP** COMING...UNTIL **ONE** OF US...IS **DEAD**...!

IT'S A **SHAME**...REALLY...!

I WAS HOPING...TO **AVOID** THIS...

SMACK

HUH? MY **FIST**--

--HE'S STOPPED IT **COLD**!

...BUT YOU BROUGHT IT ON **YOUR-SELF**...!

SORRY, HERO...BUT YOUR BLIND...DEDI-CATION TO **DUTY**...CAN SOMETIMES MAKE YOU...MOST **ANNOYING**...!

THUD!

...HE SHOULD BE **OUT**...FOR QUITE A **WHILE**...

...WHICH WILL BE...**PLENTY** OF TIME...FOR ME TO **DO**...WHAT I'VE **COME** TO DO...THEN **LEAVE** THIS...?

HEY...WHAT IS THE **MATTER** WITH YOU, MUTT...?

WHY DO YOU **PERSIST**...IN SQUIRMING LIKE...

WHINE! WHINE!

165

HEY... BLAST YOU... COME *BACK* HERE...!

WE'RE *NOT*... GOING THROUGH *ANOTHER* SCENE... LIKE THE *LAST*...

YIP! YIP! YIP!

WHAT *IS* IT, MUTT...? WHY ARE YOU... *SCRATCHING* AT THE... ...HUH...?

DELIVERIES ALTER DOOR

SCRATCH!

IMPOSSIBLE...! *BATMAN* CAN'T BE... RECOVERING FROM THAT BLOW... *ALREADY*..!?

BETTER GET... OUT OF *SIGHT*... QUICKLY...!

ANOTHER SCUFFLE WITH *HIM*... IS THE *LAST* THING I NEED...!

DAMN! THE *SWAMP THING'S* GONE!

BUT THAT *DOG* OF HIS IS STILL *HERE*--

--SCRATCHING AT THAT *DOOR* LIKE HIS *LIFE* DEPENDED ON IT!

YIP! YIP!

IT'LL TAKE THE POOCH *MONTHS* TO *SCRATCH* HIS WAY INSIDE--

PICK! PICK!

PICK!

--UNLESS I MAKE THINGS A LITTLE *EASIER* FOR HIM!

OKAY, LITTLE FELLA-- IF YOUR MASTER HAS GOTTEN *PAST* ME AND INTO THIS *BUILDING*--

--I WANT YOU TO SHOW ME *WHERE* HE'S GONE!

YIP! YIP!

They **ASCEND**: each in his own fashion...

--UNTIL, AT THE BUILDING'S SUMMIT...

WHAT IN--? THE POOCH IS SCRATCHING AT **NATHAN ELLERY'S** DOOR--

WHINE!
WHINE!

-- BUT THE SWAMP THING CAN'T BE IN **THERE**... CAN HE?

FORGIVE THE SUDDEN **INTRUSION**, FOLKS--BUT THIS IS AN **EMERGENCY!**

OKAY, POOCH-- SHOW ME YOUR **MASTER!**

YIP!
YIP!

NO... **NO!** BATMAN HAS SEARCHED FOR THE CONCLAVE'S **LEADER** FOR MONTHS--

--AND NOW THIS ACCURSED DOG HAS LED HIM RIGHT **TO ME!**

YIP! YIP!

CURSE YOU, BEAST-- YOU'VE **RUINED** EVERYTHING!

GET AWAY FROM ME, I TELL YOU--

--**GET AWAY**-- **GET AWAY!!**

BLAM
BLAM!

OH... MY... **DEAR**... **GOD**... **NO!**

... THE **SWAMP THING** SCALES THE BUILDING'S FACE, HIS POWERFUL FINGERS DIGGING HAND-HOLDS WHERE BEFORE THE WALL WAS SMOOTH--

--THE **BATMAN,** FOLLOWING HIS CANINE CON-SPIRATOR, HIS BREATHING SMOOTH AND REGULAR, HIS MUSCLES TIRELESS STEEL SPRINGS--

THE *SWAMP THING*--WAS HIDING ON THE *BALCONY!* GOT TO--*UUNNFF!*

OUT OF...MY WAY, BATMAN... NOTHING WILL... STOP ME FROM... DOING WHAT I... *MUST*...!

NO... PLEASE!!

THIS *PIG* *MURDERED*... MY *WIFE*...

THWAK!

...*TORTURED*... MY *FRIEND*...

...SHOT DOWN... A *DEFENSELESS* *DOG*...

...AND WHAT HE DID TO *ME*...!

I'LL *KILL*... WITH MY *BARE* *HANDS*...

...*KILL* HIM...

...*KILL*... HIM... Z

NO...I *CAN'T*...I *CAN'T* *BECOME*... *HIS* KIND OF *FILTH*...!

GO ON... GET *AWAY* FROM ME... *FAT* *MAN*...

...BEFORE I *CHANGE*... MY *MIND*...!

HUNFF!

A SINGLE *AWKWARD* STEP...

...A *SQUEAL* OF *ANGUISHED* PAIN...

...AND A *POOR*, *FRIGHTENED* BEAST LASHES OUT TO *DEFEND* ITSELF...

--WHICH, IT SEEMS, IS THE *STRAW*--THAT BREAKS THE *PROVERBIAL* CAMEL'S *BACK*--

NO--LET *GO*-- LET *GO*--

--*LET*--

--AND SUNDRY *OTHER* THINGS AS WELL!

GOOOOOOOO!

TOO LATE--! NOT A *CHANCE* FOR ME TO *SAVE* HIM-- *NOW!*

168

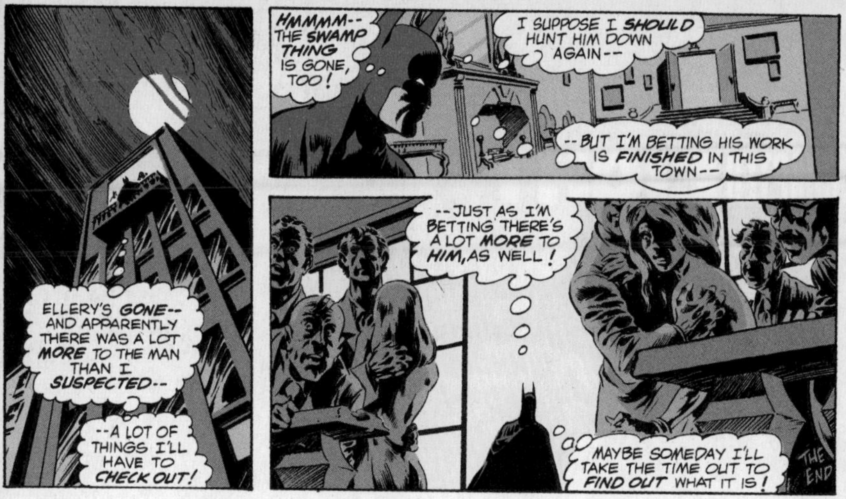
ELLERY'S GONE--
AND APPARENTLY
THERE WAS A LOT
MORE TO THE MAN
THAN I
SUSPECTED--
--A LOT OF
THINGS I'LL
HAVE TO
CHECK OUT!
HMMMM--
THE SWAMP
THING
IS GONE,
TOO!
I SUPPOSE I SHOULD
HUNT HIM DOWN
AGAIN--
--BUT I'M BETTING HIS WORK
IS FINISHED IN THIS
TOWN--
--JUST AS I'M
BETTING THERE'S
A LOT MORE TO
HIM, AS WELL!
MAYBE SOMEDAY I'LL
TAKE THE TIME OUT TO
FIND OUT WHAT IT IS!
THE
END

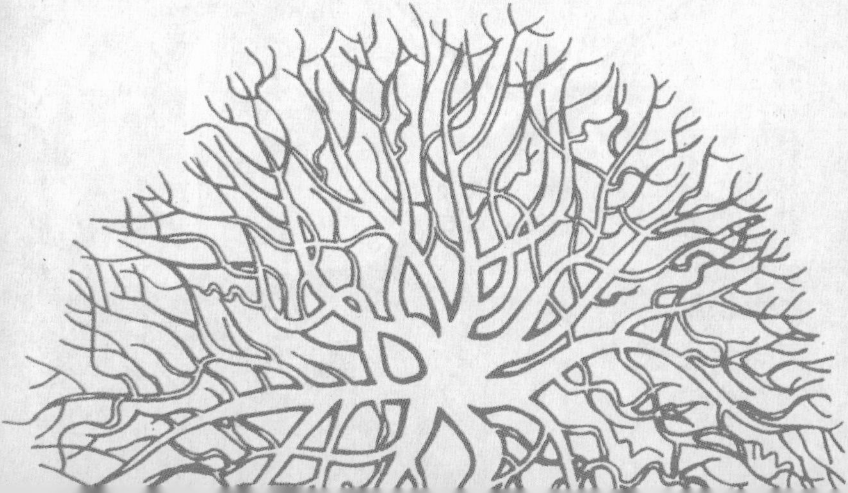

CHAPTER **EIGHT**

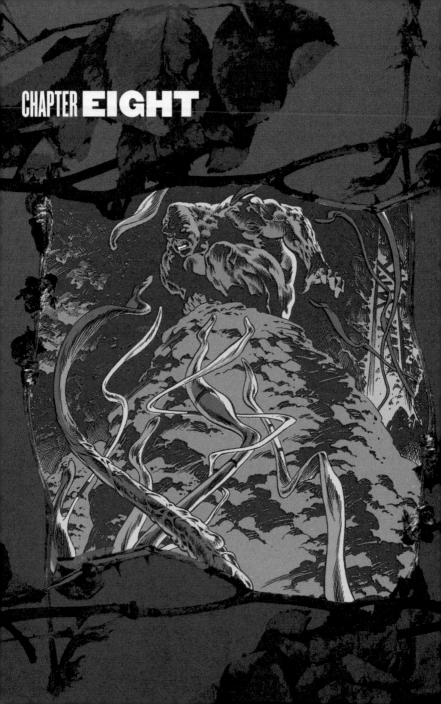

FOR YOUR INFORMATION: THE FREEZING POINT OF WATER IS 32 DEGREES FAHRENHEIT, AND WHEN THE TEMPERATURE FALLS *BELOW* THIS POINT, RAIN BECOMES *SNOW*...

THE FREEZING POINT OF YOUR AVERAGE *PLANT* IS NOT TERRIBLY DIFFERENT FROM THAT OF RAIN-- AND WHEN THIS POINT IS REACHED, SAID PLANT'S METABOLIC RATE DECREASES SHARPLY, SLOWING TO ALMOST A *CRAWL*...

ALL OF WHICH SHOULD HELP TO EXPLAIN THE TERRIBLE *SLUGGISHNESS* FELT BY A CERTAIN MOSSY MAN-BRUTE AS HE SHAMBLES THROUGH A SNOW-SWEPT APPALACHIAN WOOD...

ME AND MY... BRIGHT *IDEAS*...!

GETTING SO *COLD*... I CAN HARDLY *MOVE*....!

IF I DON'T FIND *SHELTER* SOON... I'VE HAD IT...!

"IF ONLY THERE'D BEEN... *ANOTHER* WAY OUT OF... GOTHAM CITY...

"...BUT WITH *THE BATMAN*... HOT ON MY TRAIL... I DIDN'T EXACTLY HAVE *TIME* ...TO *CHOOSE* MY MODE OF TRAVEL...!

"DIDN'T EVEN HAVE *COURAGE* ENOUGH... TO STAY WITH THE TRUCK ONCE WE... WERE *OUT* OF TOWN...

"FIRST STOP THE DRIVER MADE... I GOT OFF...."

...AND NOW I'M... *LOST* IN THE MIDDLE OF...

EEEYAA

WHA...? A SCREAM ...COMING FROM SOMEWHERE *NEAR*...

...COMING FROM THAT *CAVE*...

STORM'S SO *THICK*... I DIDN'T EVEN *SEE* IT...

NEVER *WOULD* HAVE, EITHER... IF THAT SCREAM HADN'T ATTRACTED... MY *ATTENTION*...!

WHOEVER IS *IN* THERE... NEEDS *HELP*... AND I'M GOING TO... FIND OUT *WHY*...!

172

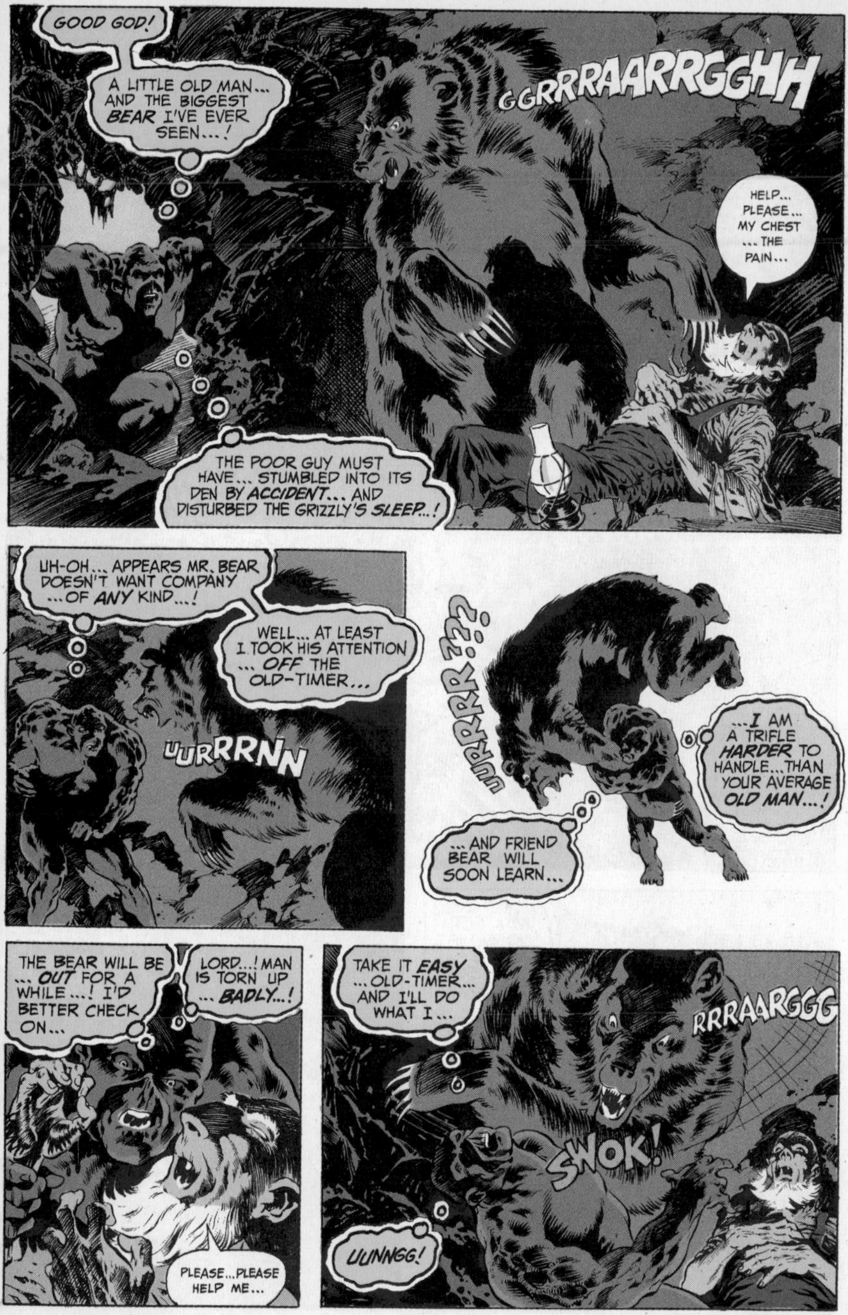
GOOD GOD!
A LITTLE OLD MAN... AND THE BIGGEST BEAR I'VE EVER SEEN...!
GGRRRAARRGGHH
HELP... PLEASE... MY CHEST ... THE PAIN...
THE POOR GUY MUST HAVE... STUMBLED INTO ITS DEN BY ACCIDENT... AND DISTURBED THE GRIZZLY'S SLEEP...!
UH-OH... APPEARS MR. BEAR DOESN'T WANT COMPANY ...OF ANY KIND...!
WELL... AT LEAST I TOOK HIS ATTENTION ... OFF THE OLD-TIMER...
UURRRNN
UURRRR???
...I AM A TRIFLE HARDER TO HANDLE...THAN YOUR AVERAGE OLD MAN...!
... AND FRIEND BEAR WILL SOON LEARN...
THE BEAR WILL BE ... OUT FOR A WHILE...! I'D BETTER CHECK ON...
LORD...! MAN IS TORN UP ... BADLY...!
PLEASE...PLEASE HELP ME...
TAKE IT EASY ...OLD-TIMER... AND I'LL DO WHAT I...
RRRAARGGG
SNOK!
UUNNGG!

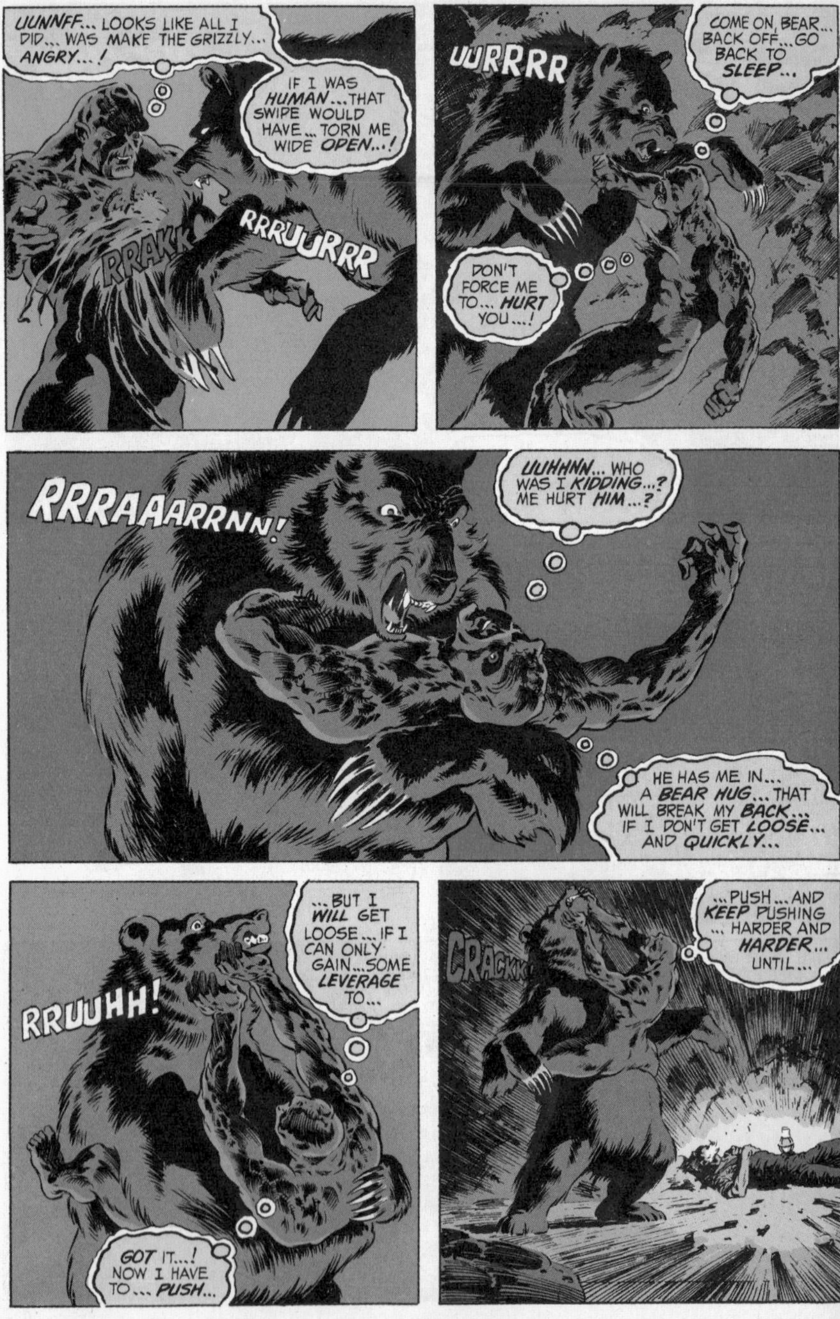
UUNNFF... LOOKS LIKE ALL I DID... WAS MAKE THE GRIZZLY... ANGRY...!
IF I WAS HUMAN... THAT SWIPE WOULD HAVE... TORN ME WIDE OPEN...!
RRAKK
RRRUURRR
UURRRR
COME ON, BEAR... BACK OFF... GO BACK TO SLEEP...
DON'T FORCE ME TO... HURT YOU...!
RRRAAARRNN!
UUHHNN... WHO WAS I KIDDING...? ME HURT HIM...?
HE HAS ME IN... A BEAR HUG... THAT WILL BREAK MY BACK... IF I DON'T GET LOOSE... AND QUICKLY...
RRUUHH!
...BUT I WILL GET LOOSE... IF I CAN ONLY GAIN... SOME LEVERAGE TO...
GOT IT...! NOW I HAVE TO... PUSH...
CRACKK
...PUSH... AND KEEP PUSHING ... HARDER AND HARDER... UNTIL...

FOR THE BRIEFEST INSTANT, THE SHAGGY BEHEMOTH TOTTERS ON ITS FEET, ITS TINY EYES SLOWLY GLAZING OVER-- THEN, LIKE A POLEAXED TREE--

--IT FALLS!

HATED TO SNAP ITS *NECK* LIKE THAT... BUT IT GAVE ME... *NO* CHOICE...!

HAVE TO GET THIS CARCASS *OFF* ME... AND SEE ABOUT THE... *OLD MAN...*!

THWUM

BUT THE OLD MAN'S BLOOD-RIMMED EYES ARE TOO FAR GONE TO SEE IN TURN THE MOSS-ENCRUSTED MONSTROSITY THAT KNEELS AT HIS SIDE MERE MOMENTS LATER...

THANK YOU, STRANGER... FOR WHAT YOU DID FOR ME...

...BUT IT'S TOO LATE...

...TOO LATE TO HELP ME... *NOW*...

...AND ALL I CAN GIVE TO REPAY YOU FOR YOUR KINDNESS... IS A *WARNING*...

...IF YOU'RE A STRANGER IN THESE PARTS... *STAY* A STRANGER...

WHATEVER YOU DO... DON'T GO INTO *PERDITION*... DON'T GO INTO TOWN...

NOT THAT PERDITION WASN'T A *GOOD* TOWN ONCE... IT WAS A *FINE* TOWN ...A *MINING* TOWN ...RICH IN COAL AND PRECIOUS ORES...

175

"...BUT THEN THE COAL *RAN OUT*... AND THE *PEOPLE* STARTED RUNNING OUT AS WELL..."

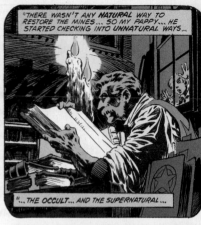

"THERE WASN'T ANY *NATURAL* WAY TO RESTORE THE MINES... SO MY PAPPY... HE STARTED CHECKING INTO *UNNATURAL* WAYS..."

"...THE OCCULT... AND THE SUPERNATURAL..."

"THEN, ONE NIGHT... I GUESS HE THOUGHT HE WAS READY..."

"HE GATHERED UP ALL THE MYSTIC BOOKS AND SUCH HE'D BEEN COLLECTING... AND CARRIED THEM INTO THE MINE..."

SPELLS AND INVOCATIONS

"...AND THAT WAS THE *LAST* ANYONE EVER SAW OF MY PAPPY..."

"OH, THERE WAS THE *SCREAM* THAT NIGHT, OF COURSE..."

"...CAME ROLLING OUT OF THE MINE... SPILLING ACROSS THE STREETS OF TOWN... BUT NEVER ANY SIGN OF THE MAN WHO *MADE* THE HORRID SOUND..."

"...THINGS HAVEN'T BEEN THE SAME IN PERDITION SINCE THEN... THE STRANGE *DISAPPEARANCES* OF ANYBODY GOING TOO CLOSE TO THE MINES..."

"...THE *GNAWING FEAR* THAT EVERYBODY LIVES THERE WITH..."

"...AND THE FACT THAT SINCE MY PAPPY VANISHED ...NOBODY ELSE HAS EVER LEFT TOWN..."

...UNTIL *ME*, THAT IS...

I WAS LEAVING TOWN... I WAS *RUNNING* FROM IT... WHEN I MET UP WITH THAT BEAR...

NOW, I GUESS ...THEY'LL NEVER GET ME *BACK* THERE AGA... UUNNHHH...

OLD MAN...?

HE'S... *GONE*...!

176

THE FALLING SNOW IS COLD --COLDER, PERHAPS, THAN IT WAS A SHORT WHILE BEFORE--

--BUT A SOLEMN SWAMP THING NO LONGER SEEMS TO FEEL THE COLD AS HE CARRIES A FRAIL, LIMP BURDEN SEEMINGLY ENDLESSLY THROUGH THE IVORY-FROSTED WOODS...

COULDN'T JUST LEAVE THE OLD MAN... IN THE CAVE...!

HE SHOULD HAVE A...PROPER BURIAL...! HIS FAMILY SHOULD BE NOTIFIED...

...IF HE HAS ONE...

STILL... I CAN'T CARRY HIM FOREVER...!

HAVE TO FIND SOMEWHERE... TO TAKE HIM...DECIDE SOME DESTINATION ...BEFORE I CAN...

GOOD LORD...!

IT SEEMS MY DECISION ...HAS BEEN MADE... FOR ME...!

UNLESS I MISS MY GUESS... BY A LONG SHOT... THIS IS THE TOWN ...OF PERDITION...!

I'VE CARRIED THE OLD MAN ... HOME...!

177

BUT AS THE MOSS-ENCRUSTED MAN-BRUTE SHAMBLES ALONG THE DECREPIT TOWN'S MAIN STREET...

OH, MILORD, HECTOR-- LOOK!

IT--IT'S SOME SORT'A MONSTER-- AN' HE'S KILLED OLD EZEKIEL!

MONSTER, HUH?

WELL, WE'LL SHOW IT NO BLAMED MONSTER KIN KILL ONE'A OUR PEOPLE AN' GIT AWAY WITH IT!

OH, NO... NOT ANOTHER MINDLESS MOB...!?!

WHEREVER I GO...

SWACT!

...I'M ATTACKED BY WEAPON-WIELDING CRETINS...

...AND TO TELL THE HONEST TRUTH...

LORDY-- IT AIN'T POSSIBLE--!

CHUK!

...I'M SICK AND TIRED OF IT...!

WHUMP!

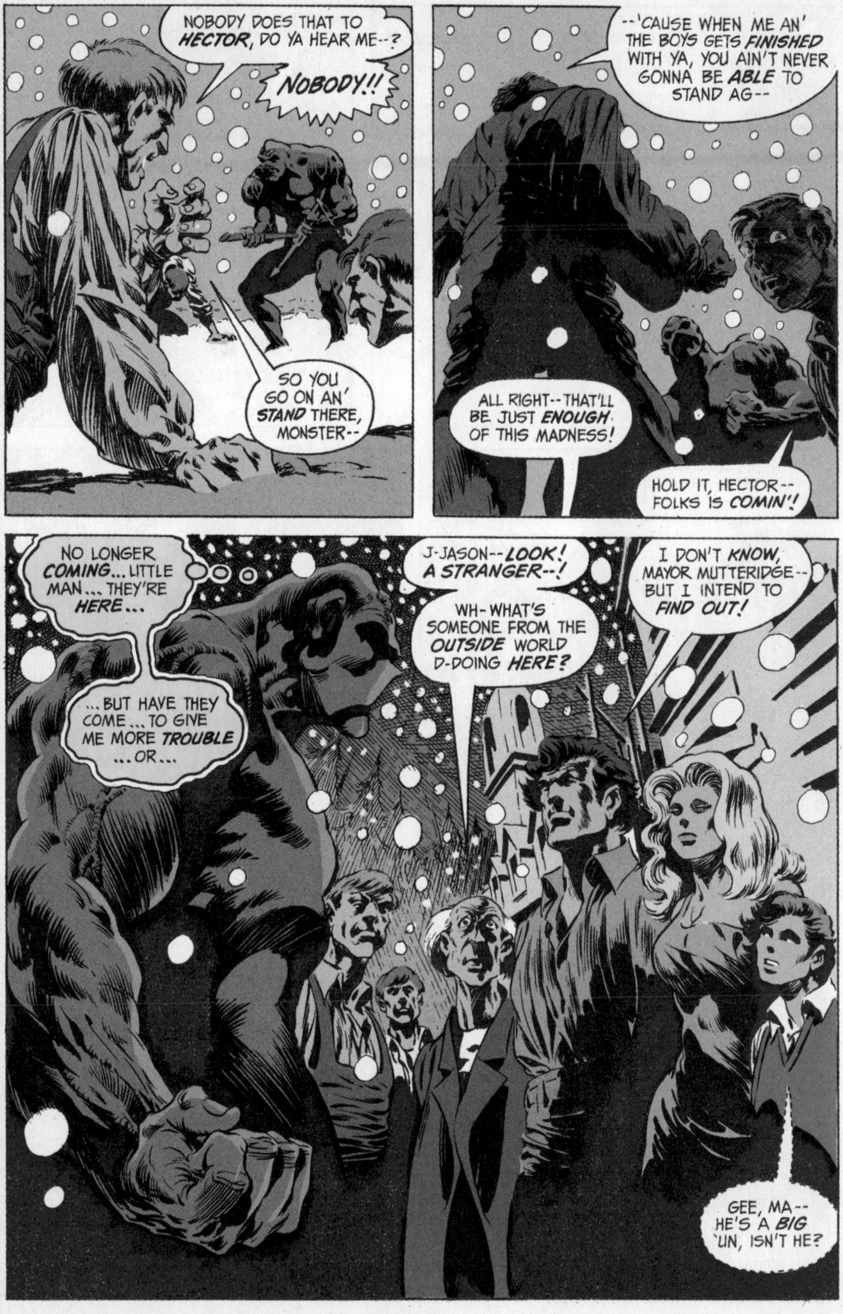

NOBODY DOES THAT TO HECTOR, DO YA HEAR ME--?
NOBODY!!
SO YOU GO ON AN' STAND THERE, MONSTER--
--'CAUSE WHEN ME AN' THE BOYS GETS FINISHED WITH YA, YOU AIN'T NEVER GONNA BE ABLE TO STAND AG--
ALL RIGHT--THAT'LL BE JUST ENOUGH OF THIS MADNESS!
HOLD IT, HECTOR--FOLKS IS COMIN'!
NO LONGER COMING... LITTLE MAN... THEY'RE HERE...
...BUT HAVE THEY COME... TO GIVE ME MORE TROUBLE ...OR...
J-JASON--LOOK! A STRANGER--!
WH-WHAT'S SOMEONE FROM THE OUTSIDE WORLD D-DOING HERE?
I DON'T KNOW, MAYOR MUTTERIDGE--BUT I INTEND TO FIND OUT!
GEE, MA--HE'S A BIG 'UN, ISN'T HE?

DOIN' HERE? I'LL TELL YA WHAT HE'S DOIN' HERE, JASON -- HE'S COMMITTIN' *MURDER!*

G'WAN -- LOOK FER *YOURSELF!* THAT MONSTER KILLED YER *PAPPY!*

MY *FATHER?* NO -- HE *COULDN'T* HAVE --!

MURDER, YOU SAY? THEN CHECK THE *BODY!*

MY FATHER WASN'T KILLED BY THE *STRANGER* --

-- HE WAS *CLAWED* TO DEATH -- BY A *BEAR!*

W-WHY -- YES, HE *WAS* -- HE WAS *INDEED*, BY GEORGE!

YOU *SEE?* THE STRANGER'S *INNOCENT!* YOU ATTACKED HIM FOR *NO REASON!*

C'MON NOW, HECTOR -- *ADMIT* YOUR MISTAKE!

TELL THE STRANGER YOU DIDN'T *MEAN* TO CALL HIM A *MONSTER!*

SHUCKS, STRANGER -- I'M DOWNRIGHT *SORRY* IF I *OFFENDED* YA!

WHAT KIND OF TOWN ... *IS* THIS ...? THEY'RE ALL ... *CRAZIER* THAN ...

OH, MA -- *LOOK!* THE BEAR CLAWED THE *STRANGER*, TOO! HE'S *HURT!*

SO HE *IS!* HOW *TERRIBLE!*

YOU'D BETTER COME HOME WITH *US*, STRANGER -- AND LET LYDIA *TEND* TO THOSE CUTS!

WITH *PLEASURE* ...! CRAZY OR NOT ... THAT'S THE FIRST *INVITATION* ... I'VE RECEIVED IN ... A *LONG* TIME ...!

He awakens...

THERE YA GO, PAL! LYDIA'S NOT *HURTIN'* YA NONE NOW, *IS* SHE?

GOOD! NOW YOU JUST REST *EASY*--AN' EVERYTHIN'S GONNA BE *FINE!*

YES--ER--*YES! MIGHTY* FINE, INDEED--*INDEED!* YOU'LL BE GOOD AS *NEW*-- FIRST-CLASS SHAPE!

AFTER ALL, WE--ER-- WOULDN'T WANT TO *LOSE* THE FIRST *VISITOR* THIS TOWN'S HAD IN *YEARS* NOW--ER-- *WOULD* WE?

THE MAYOR'S *RIGHT*, FRIEND-- YOU JUST RELAX AND *RECU-PERATE!* WE ALL WANT YOU BACK IN *PERFECT CONDITION*-- ABSOLUTELY *PERFECT* CONDITION-- *HA HA HA HA!*

...and awakening, He becomes aware...

EVERYONE LAUGHS HEARTILY AT JASON'S LITTLE JEST--EVERYONE SAVE THE *SWAMP THING*, THAT IS--

--FOR HE SEES NO *HUMOR* IN JASON'S SIMPLE COMMENT--AND THE FACT THAT THEY ALL *DO* SENDS SHIVERS UP HIS MIS-SHAPEN SPINE ...

THE LAUGHTER FADES QUICKLY-- BUT THE AIR OF MERRIMENT DOES *NOT*--

THE CONVIVIAL *CHATTER* DRONES ON --

--THE BANAL *BANTER* THAT IS THE LIFE-BLOOD OF *ANY* PARTY FILLS THE ROOM--

--AND, AS IS *ALSO* TRUE OF THE AVERAGE PARTY, NOBODY NOTICES THE SILENT, STIFF-LIMBED *DEPARTURE* OF ONE OF ITS SMALLER GUESTS--

--NOBODY NOTICES *ANYTHING*, IN FACT--

--FOR, THOUGH THE MUNDANE CONVERSATION HAS NOT FLAGGED, EVERYONE SEEMS SOMEHOW *DISTRACTED* NOW--

--AS IF SOME MUTUALLY *UNPLEASANT* THOUGHT HAS TAKEN NEST IN THE BACK OF THEIR MINDS--

--AND ALTHOUGH THE BEWILDERED MAN-MONSTER *SENSES* THE UNEASINESS THAT GNAWS AT THE GATHERED THRONG, THEY DO THEIR BEST TO *CONCEAL* IT--

--UNTIL IT CAN BE *HIDDEN* NO LONGER...

EEEIIIEEEEE

LYDIA? GOOD LORD, WOMAN-- WHAT *IS* IT?

JASON-- IT'S *JODY!*

OUR SON IS-- *GONE!*

GONE? WHAT DO YOU MEAN--GONE? HE HAS TO BE HERE SOMEPLACE!

BUT HE'S NOT, JASON--I CHECKED THE ENTIRE H-HOUSE!

OH, GOD, JASON-- OUR CHILD IS WANDERING LOST--OUTSIDE!

IF HE IS, LYDIA, WE'LL--ER--FIND HIM! WE'LL ORGANIZE--ER--A SEARCH PARTY -- THAT'S WHAT WE'LL DO-- A SEARCH PARTY!

YOU BET WE WILL!

C'MON--LET'S GET MOVIN'!

...and coming aware, He has called...

THE SNOW HAS STOPPED FALLING NOW--AND IT LIES UPON THE LANDSCAPE LIKE A SHROUD OF SCATTERED DREAMS--

--DREAMS NOW BROKEN-- EVEN AS THE SNOWY CRUST IS BROKEN--

--BY THE TRACK OF TWO SMALL SNEAKERED FEET...

THEY'RE JODY'S TRACKS, AL'RIGHT --I'D RECOGNIZE THEM ANYWHERE!

THIS SNOW IS A GODSEND! WHEREVER THOSE TRACKS LEAD, WE CAN FOLLOW!

AND SO IT GOES--

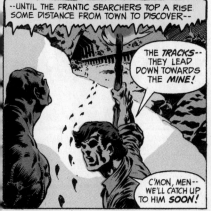

--UNTIL THE FRANTIC SEARCHERS TOP A RISE SOME DISTANCE FROM TOWN TO DISCOVER--

THE TRACKS-- THEY LEAD DOWN TOWARDS THE MINE!

C'MON, MEN-- WE'LL CATCH UP TO HIM SOON!

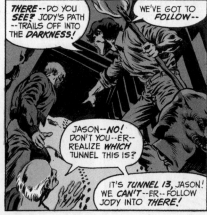

THERE--DO YOU SEE? JODY'S PATH --TRAILS OFF INTO THE DARKNESS!

WE'VE GOT TO FOLLOW--

JASON--NO! DON'T YOU--ER-- REALIZE WHICH TUNNEL THIS IS?

IT'S TUNNEL 13, JASON! WE CAN'T--ER-- FOLLOW JODY INTO THERE!

183

MAYBE **YOU** CAN'T, MUTTERIDGE--BUT HE'S **MY** SON!

I'M GOING IN THERE **ALONE** IF I HAVE...

EH?

NO, JASON... YOU'RE **NOT** ...GOING IN THERE...!

I AM GOING IN THERE... IN YOUR **PLACE**...! I **OWE** YOU... THAT MUCH AT LEAST...!

YOU JUST **STAY** HERE ...AND **WAIT**...! I'LL BE BACK...WITH YOUR **SON**...

...OR I **WON'T** BE BACK...AT ALL...!

DETERMINEDLY, THE HULKING MAN-BRUTE SHAMBLES INTO THE TUNNEL'S DEPTHS, HIS MOSS-HOODED EYE PEERING INTENTLY AHEAD--AND THAT IS **UNFORTUNATE**--

--FOR WERE HE TO GLANCE BACK AT THE CROWD GATHERED BEHIND HIM, HE MIGHT NOTICE A MOST BIZARRE **EXPRESSION** UPON THEIR SHADOWED FACES--

--A GLEAMING GRIN OF **TRIUMPH!**

BUT THE SWAMP THING DOES **NOT** GLANCE BACK-- AND SO HE LUMBERS ON--

--FOLLOWING THE TRACKS OF A RUSTY ORE CAR DEEP INTO THE CLUTCHING DARKNESS--

--UNTIL THE TRACKS ABRUPTLY **END**-- AND THERE IS **NOTHING** FOR HIM TO FOLLOW--

--SAVE AN INNER **VOICE** THAT DRAWS HIM ONWARD--

--ONWARD INTO THE TUNNEL'S DARKEST RECESSES --AND THE RIM OF AN **UNNATURAL PIT**--

...for He has called and, at last, He has been answered...

...and having been answered, **He** is satisfied...most satisfied...

...for He is M'Nagalah... and he lives...

...Dear, dear God in Heaven... He **LIVES!!!**

...AND TO THE NAUSEATED SWAMP THING'S MIND, *HE SPEAKS*--IN A VOICE THAT IS LIKE A GUTTURAL *WHISPER* FROM BEYOND THE GRAVE, LIKE A FLESH-CURDLING *HISSING* OUT OF HELL...

WELCOME, YOU WHO WERE ONCE DOCTOR ALEC HOLLAND...

...M'NAGALAH HAS BEEN... *EXPECTING* YOU!

COME TO ME, DOCTOR ALEC HOLLAND ...M'NAGALAH HAS NEED OF YOU!

WHA...? THAT UNHOLY OBSCENITY... HAS GRABBED HOLD... OF MY ANKLES...

...BUT IF IT THINKS... IT WILL PULL ME... DOWN THERE...

...IT WILL HAVE TO... THINK AGAIN...!

AND AS THE SWAMP THING WRENCHES FREE THE TUNNEL WALLS SHUDDER...SLIGHTLY...

COME, DOCTOR HOLLAND... DO NOT BE FOOLISH! YOU CANNOT HOPE TO DENY M'NAGALAH...

...FOR M'NAGALAH IS ETERNAL... THE GIVER OF ALL THINGS...

...IT WAS M'NAGALAH WHO DECREED THE BIRTH OF LIFE ON YOUR WORLD...

...M'NAGALAH WHO SAW TO THE COMING OF MAN... AND BESTOWED HIM WITH THE CAPACITY FOR MINDLESS VIOLENCE...

...BUT M'NAGALAH HAS BEEN GENEROUS AS WELL... FOR HE HAS TOUCHED THE MINDS OF YOUR GREATEST SCRIBES... LOVECRAFT... BIERCE... POE...

...BUT M'NAGALAH HAD DONE ALL THIS FROM A VERY **FAR** PLACE... A PLACE **NOT** OF YOUR WORLD... AND THERE, **ALONE,** M'NAGALAH WOULD HAVE **STAYED...**

...HAD NOT **ABRAHAM**... FATHER OF EZEKIEL... GRAND-FATHER OF JASON ...SPOKEN THE SPELL THAT FREED M'NAGALA FROM HIS DISTANT PRISON...

M'NAGALAH CAME **INTO** YOUR WORLD MOST SLOWLY... AS A **GROWTH** ON THE LIMB OF HE WHO HAD **RELEASED** M'NAGALAH...

...UNTIL, AT LAST, M'NAGALAH **CONSUMED** HIM... AND TOOK ABRAHAM'S PHYSICAL **MASS** AS HIS OWN...

...BUT M'NAGALAH GREW **HUNGRY** THEN... HUNGRY FOR **MORE** MASS TO CLAIM AS HIS OWN... HUNGRY TO DRINK THE **MINDS** OF THOSE WHOSE MASS HE CLAIMED...

...AND SO M'NAGALAH WENT SEARCHING... AND **FOUND** MORE MASS TO THRIVE ON... MORE MINDS TO ENJOY...

...**LARGE** MASS, **SMALL** MASS... ALL THE **SAME** TO M'NAGALAH... FOR M'NAGALAH MUST HAVE MUCH MASS TO GROW...

...TO GROW TO HIS **FULL** SIZE ...BEFORE ALL THE UNIVERSE REACHES **PRIME**...

...FOR SOON...SOON...THE GREAT GEOMETRIC PROGRESSION THAT WAS BEGUN AT THE BIRTH OF THE COSMOS WILL BE *FINISHED* AT LAST... SOON EACH INTERGALACTIC BODY WILL BE IN POSITION TO *COMPLETE* THE VAST CELESTIAL CIRCUITRY THAT WILL MAKE M'NAGALAH THE *MASTER* OF ALL THAT IS... BUT *ONLY* IF M'NAGALAH HAS ATTAINED HIS *FULL MASS*...

...AND *YOU*, DOCTOR ALEC HOLLAND...WILL FINALLY *PROVIDE* M'NAGALAH WITH *SUBSTANCE* ENOUGH TO BE FULFILLED...

SO *COME*... COME AND MAKE M'NAGALAH *WHOLE*...

COME...AND LET MYSELF BE *DEVOURED*... BY A PULSATING *CANCER*... LIKE *YOU*...?

RRUNCH!

IN A *WORD*... M'NAGALAH...

NO!!

WHUNCH!

FOOL... YOU DARE TO DISRUPT M'NAGALAH'S MASS?

M'NAGALAH IS ENRAGED...

HUH...? M'NAGALAH IS PULSATING SO FURIOUSLY... HE'S MAKING THE ENTIRE CAVERN TREMBLE...

...AND WITHOUT THE POST I THREW... TO HELP SUPPORT ITS CEILING...

... THE TUNNEL IS... CAVING IN...!

ONCE AGAIN, THE TUNNEL WALLS SHUDDER -- BUT THIS TIME, THEY DO NOT SHUDDER SLIGHTLY...

THIS TIME, THOSE SHUDDERS ARE DEATH THROES...

AND IS IT THE CHALKY *DUST* BILLOWING FROM THE COLLAPSED TUNNEL'S ENTRANCE -- OR AN OVERWHELMING SHIVER OF *RELIEF* -- THAT CHOKES JASON'S WORDS TO A *WHISPER*...

N-NOTHING COULD HAVE SURVIVED *THAT!* BOTH MONSTERS ARE *DEAD* -- THEY HAVE TO BE!

AT LONG LAST -- IT'S *OVER!*

IS IT *REALLY*, JASON?

GOD -- *NO!* IT'S *IMPOSSIBLE!* ONE OF THEM IS S-STILL -- *ALIVE!*

NO THANKS TO *YOU*... "FRIEND"...!

I WENT INTO... THAT GHASTLY BLACK HOLE... ON *YOUR* BEHALF... ON AN ERRAND OF *MERCY*... I THOUGHT...

...BUT *YOU*... YOU FILTHY SCUM... YOU SENT ME IN THERE ... AS A *SACRIFICE!* ... I OUGHT TO...

NO -- PLEASE -- DON'T *HURT* ME --!

W-WE DIDN'T *WANT* TO DO THIS TO YOU -- BUT TH-THAT *THING* INSIDE THE MINE -- IT *FORCED* US TO -- *CONTROLLED* US -- MADE US FAKE JODY'S DISAPPEARANCE --!

P-PLEASE -- WE'RE *SORRY* --! DON'T *HURT* ME --!

HURT YOU, JASON...?

NO... I WON'T *HURT* YOU...!

AS YOU SAID... IT'S *OVER*...!

THE SWAMP THING TURNS SILENTLY, THEN SHAMBLES OFF INTO THE WOODS...

-- AND, IN HIS SOLEMN MIND, THE WORDS *ECHO:* "IT'S *OVER!*"

BUT, AS USUAL, THE WORDS ARE *WRONG!*

IT'S *NEVER* OVER!

THE END?

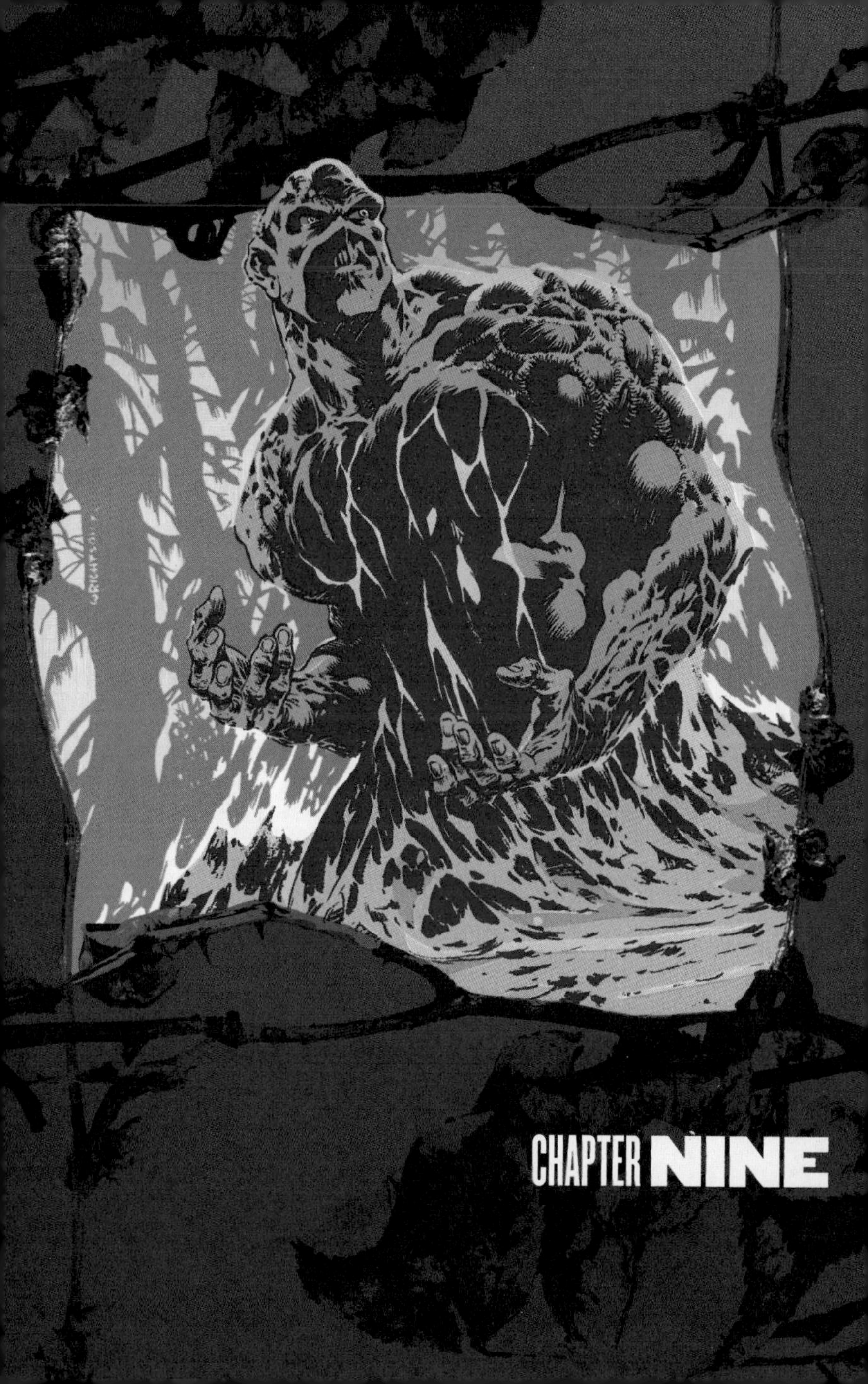

CHAPTER NINE

NIGHT FREIGHT: CLATTERING DOWN OUT OF *PITTSBURGH*, CHEWING UP TRACK TOWARD *BATON ROUGE*...

TO THE *DREAMERS* IT PASSES, THE OLD TRAIN'S MOURNFUL WAIL BRINGS *VISIONS*-- OF THOSE DISTANT EXOTIC PLACES THEY KNOW THEY'LL NEVER SEE--

--BUT PERHAPS THEY ARE *FORTUNATE* FOR THIS -- FOR WE SHALL FOLLOW THIS LUMBERING LOCOMOTIVE INTO A DREAM THAT CAN ONLY BE CALLED... *NIGHTMARE!*

YO' SURE THIS'S *SAFE*, RUFE?

'COURSE I AM, ELMO! THIS 'BO AIN'T SO MUCH AS *TWITCHED* SINCE WE GOT ON THIS FREIGHT!

SORRY TA *DISTURB* YA, 'BO --

--BUT JEST SOON'S ELMO AN' ME *ROB* YA, YA KIN GO BACK TO--

-- SLEEP?

APPARENTLY, THE SILENT SLEEPER DOES *NOT* LIKE BEING DISTURBED...

914 246962

KWARAM

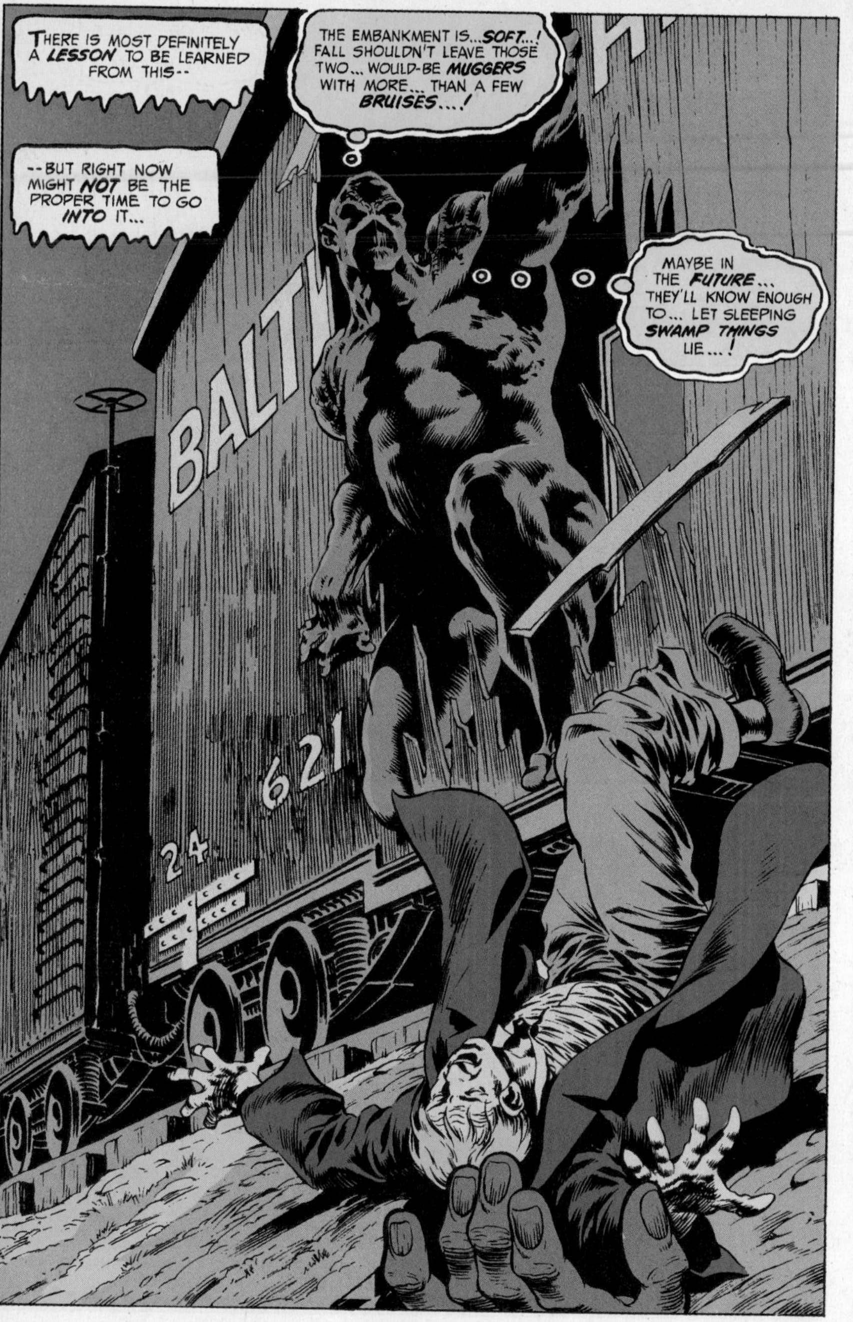
THERE IS MOST DEFINITELY A LESSON TO BE LEARNED FROM THIS--
THE EMBANKMENT IS... SOFT...! FALL SHOULDN'T LEAVE THOSE TWO... WOULD-BE MUGGERS WITH MORE... THAN A FEW BRUISES...!
--BUT RIGHT NOW MIGHT NOT BE THE PROPER TIME TO GO INTO IT...
MAYBE IN THE FUTURE... THEY'LL KNOW ENOUGH TO... LET SLEEPING SWAMP THINGS LIE...!
BALT
24 621

BUT AS THE LUMBERING MAN-BRUTE STARTS TO TURN AWAY FROM THE NEWLY-FORMED PORTAL...

HUH...? OFF-BALANCE ...SUDDEN LURCH... PITCHING ME OUT...!

GOT TO... GRAB HOLD OF SOMETHING...OR...

OH...NO... HERE I GO AGAIN...!

UUNNFF... EMBANKMENT REALLY IS SOFT...

...TOO SOFT FOR ME... TO REGAIN MY FOOTING...

...BUT I HAVE TO GET... BACK UP TO THAT TRAIN AGAIN ...BEFORE...

TOO LATE...!

NOT A CHANCE OF... CATCHING THAT OLD FREIGHT NOW...!

GUESS I'LL HAVE TO START ...WALKING...!

AND WALK THE SWAMP THING DOES--MILE AFTER COUNTLESS MILE-- LEAVING AN OOZING, SLIME-CAKED TRAIL BEHIND HIM, HE WALKS--

--UNTIL, AT LAST, THE AIR GROWS THICKER, PUNGENT WITH THE SMELL OF OLD MOSS AND DECAY--A FAMILIAR SMELL--HIS SMELL--

--AND HE WHO WAS ONCE DOCTOR ALEC HOLLAND KNOWS HE HAS COME HOME--

-- TO THE STAGNANT SWAMP THAT SPAWNED HIM!

MAKE IT THE PREVIOUS *AFTERNOON* ON A SECLUDED FLORIDA *BEACH*. THE *SKY* IS A DISMAL GRAY, AWASH WITH THE PROMISE OF STORM; THE *WATERS*, CHOPPY AND CHILL--

--AND THE HEART OF ONE *MATTHEW CABLE* THIS DAY IS GRAYER AND BLEAKER THAN ALL OF NATURE'S WONDER COULD EVER *HOPE* TO BE--

DONE SWIMMING SO *SOON*, ABIGAIL?

SWIMMING? FREEZING IS MORE LIKE IT!

SOMEBODY MUST HAVE TOLD THE OCEAN IT'S ONLY A FEW WEEKS TILL *CHRISTMAS!*

YOU *ALL RIGHT*, MATTHEW?

DEPENDS ON HOW YOU *DEFINE* THE TERM, ABBY--

IF YOU MEAN ALL RIGHT IN *BODY*--YES! I'VE HEALED UP JUST *FINE* SINCE THAT *CONCLAVE* AFFAIR--

--BUT IF YOU MEAN ALL RIGHT IN *SPIRIT* ...I DON'T *KNOW!*

I'VE BEEN *SITTING* HERE, ABBY--*THINKING* ABOUT MYSELF--ABOUT THE *SWAMP THING*--

--WONDERING IF I'VE SOMEHOW LET MY UNYIELDING HATRED *BLIND* ME TO THE *TRUTH* ABOUT HIM--!

TRUTH IS SUCH A --*NEBULOUS* THING, MATT!

YOU'VE DONE WHAT YOU THOUGHT *RIGHT* THROUGH ALL THIS AND PERHAPS--

HEY--! HEY YOU ON THE BEACH--!

MATTHEW, SOMEONE'S *COMING*--

--AND FROM HIS *ATTIRE*, I'D SAY HE'S *NOT* INTERESTED IN SUN-BATHING!

OH NO--I RECOGNIZE THE *EX-PRESSION* ON THAT *FACE*--!

I'LL LAY ODDS THE HOME OFFICE SENT HIM TO FETCH US BACK TO *WASHINGTON!*

MR. CABLE? MS. ARCANE? I'M *SMITHERS!* THE *HOME OFFICE* SENT ME!

I *KNEW* IT! I *KNEW* IT! SOMEBODY UPSTAIRS *HATES* ME!

HATE TO *DO* THIS ON YOUR *VACATION*-- BUT YOU'RE *NEEDED* BACK IN D.C.--!

THE ROOM YOU HAVE JUST ENTERED DOES NOT *EXIST* ON ANY ARCHITECT'S BLUEPRINT--NOR IS IT ON FILE WITH THE DISTRICT OF COLUMBIA ZONING BOARD OF RECORD--

--FOR IT IS THE COMMAND BASE OF A MOST *UNIQUE* GOVERNMENT AGENCY--

--AND IT IS *HERE* WE NEXT FIND LIEUTENANT MATT CABLE...

MATT, I'D LIKE YOU TO MEET *CAPTAIN BRAD SAMSON!*

HE'LL BE HANDLING THE *MILITARY* END OF THIS OPERATION!

SO *YOU'RE* CABLE, HUH? BEEN HEARIN' SOME PRETTY *GOOD* THINGS ABOUT YOU!

GLAD YOU'LL BE ALONG FOR THE RIDE--

--'CAUSE WE'RE RIDING A GRADE-A, FIRST-CLASS *WHIRLWIND,* PAL!

THE *BIG BOYS* AT THE PENTAGON'VE ALREADY GOT A *NAME* FOR IT--

--"OPERATION SPACE-FACE"!

"SPACE-FACE"? HEY, THAT DOESN'T MEAN WHAT I *THINK* IT DOES--?

OH, BUT IT DOES, PAL-- IT *DOES!*

SEEMS LIKE *A.I.D.--* THE *AGENCY OF INTERSTELLAR DISCOVERY--* HAS FINALLY *EARNED* ITS KEEP!

WE *SPOTTED* ONE, BOY-- AN HONEST-TO-GOD UFO*--TRACKED IT, TILL IT *LANDED--*

--*HERE*--DEEP IN THE LOUISIANA SWAMPLANDS!

*UNIDENTIFIED FLYING OBJECT.

I WANTED TO TAKE IN SOME OF MY BOYS RIGHT AWAY--

--BUT THE BRASS FIGURED SINCE *YOU* WERE IN CHARGE OF THE HOLLAND OPERATION DOWN THERE--

--YOU OUGHTTA *TAG ALONG*--TO MAKE SURE WE DON'T STEP ON ANY *OTHER* BRANCH'S TOES!

I'M NOT ENTIRELY SURE I *LIKE* THE IDEA OF PLAYING *NURSEMAID*--

--BUT IF THAT'S WHAT UNCLE SAM *WANTS*--I'LL DO WHAT I CAN TO *HELP!*

GOOD! YOU *DO* THAT, PAL!

JUST TRY TO KEEP *OUT* OF THE WAY-- AND WE'LL GET ALONG JUST *FINE!*

I DON'T THINK I'M GOING TO *LIKE* THIS MAN!

AND HOURS LATER, IN THOSE LOUISIANA SWAMP-LANDS, A CERTAIN MOSSY MAN-BRUTE SHAMBLES HESITANTLY TOWARDS THE SINGLE WOODEN STRUCTURE THAT RISES FROM THE BOG...

THERE IT IS...!

THE STORY OF THE *SWAMP THING*... *BEGAN* IN THAT OLD CONVERTED *BARN*...!

ALL BOARDED UP NOW... MUST HAVE *TAKEN* ALMOST EVERYTHING... *WITH* THEM WHEN THEY CLOSED DOWN...

BUT IF THEY LEFT ANYTHING *BEHIND*...

...*ANYTHING* AT ALL...

...I'LL HAVE A *STARTING PLACE*... TO BEGIN THE WORK OF... *CURING* MY...

...*LORD*...!

A SPACECRAFT... SURELY NEVER DESIGNED BY... ANY ASTROPHYSICIST OF *THIS* EARTH...!

IT'S BANGED UP PRETTY *BADLY*... ITS PILOT MUST HAVE BROUGHT IT... INTO THE *HAVEN* OF THIS OLD BARN... FOR *REPAIRS*...!

WELL... I SUPPOSE THAT'S *HIS* BUSINESS...!

AS LONG AS HE DOESN'T *INTERFERE* WITH *MY* WORK, HE CAN...

OH, GOD ... *NO*...!

SOME EQUIPMENT *WAS* LEFT BEHIND... BUT IT'S BEEN *DISMANTLED*...

...ITS COMPONENTS USED... TO *REPAIR* THAT BLASTED *SHIP*...!

I'M *FINISHED*... MY *LAST* HOPE TO DISCOVER A CURE ...*RUINED*...!

IF I COULD GET MY *HANDS*... ON THE ONE *RESPONSIBLE* FOR THIS, I'D...

HUH?

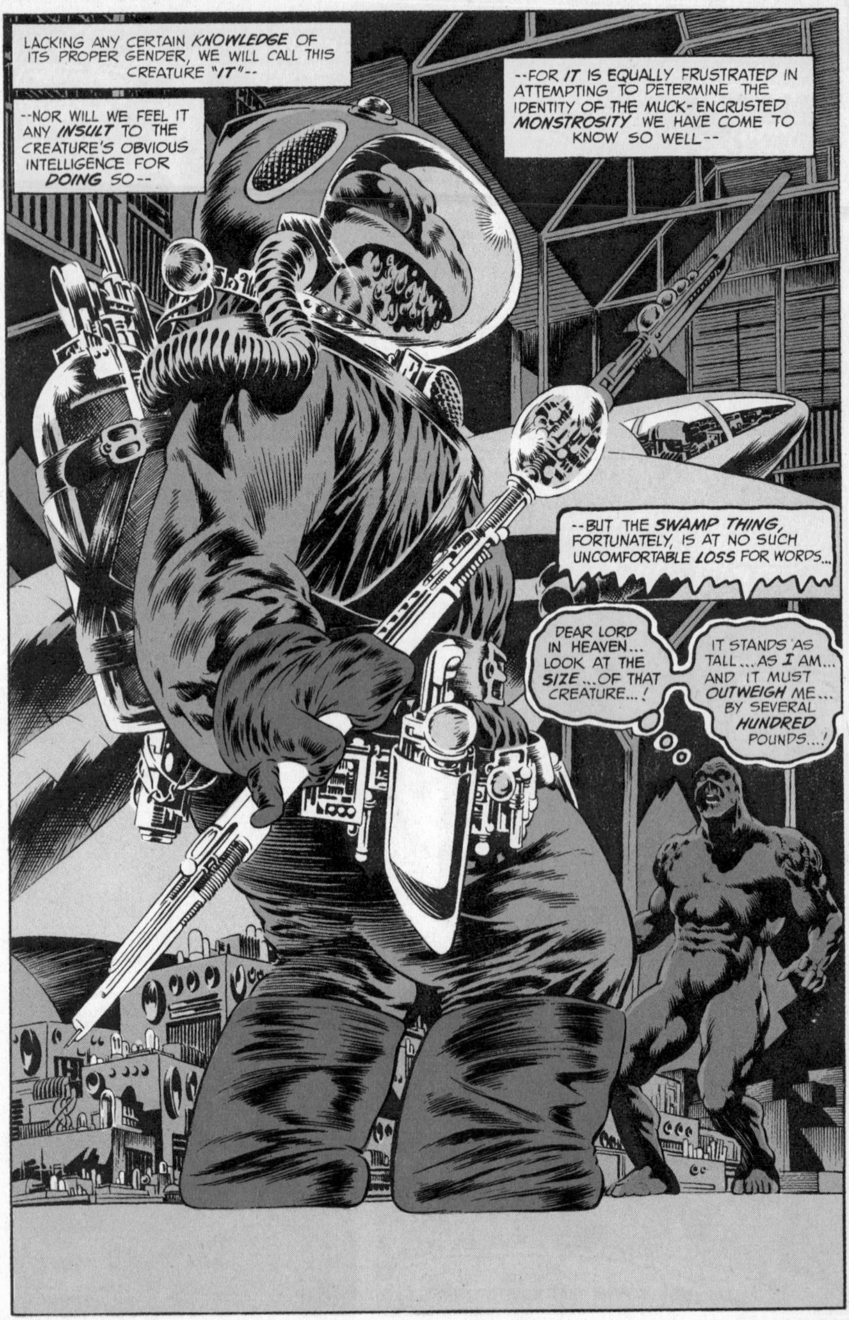
LACKING ANY CERTAIN KNOWLEDGE OF ITS PROPER GENDER, WE WILL CALL THIS CREATURE "IT"--
--NOR WILL WE FEEL IT ANY INSULT TO THE CREATURE'S OBVIOUS INTELLIGENCE FOR DOING SO--
--FOR IT IS EQUALLY FRUSTRATED IN ATTEMPTING TO DETERMINE THE IDENTITY OF THE MUCK-ENCRUSTED MONSTROSITY WE HAVE COME TO KNOW SO WELL--
--BUT THE SWAMP THING, FORTUNATELY, IS AT NO SUCH UNCOMFORTABLE LOSS FOR WORDS...
DEAR LORD IN HEAVEN... LOOK AT THE SIZE ...OF THAT CREATURE...!
IT STANDS AS TALL ...AS I AM... AND IT MUST OUTWEIGH ME... BY SEVERAL HUNDRED POUNDS...!

FOR A MOMENT, THESE TWO AWESOME **BEHEMOTHS** **STAND**, EACH STUDYING THE OTHER, AS IF TRYING TO DECIDE HOW TO **DEAL** WITH THIS UNEXPECTED SITUATION...

THE ALIEN FROM SPACE PEERS AT THE SWAMP THING -- AND WONDERS IF **ALL** WHO INHABIT THIS PRIMITIVE LITTLE WORLD ARE AS **FRIGHTENING** IN THEIR VISAGE --

-- WHILE THE ALIEN FROM **EARTH** WONDERS, IN TURN, WHAT SORT OF HELL-SPAWNED **MONSTER** WOULD STEAL AWAY A MAN'S FINAL CHANCE TO REGAIN HIS **HUMANITY** --

-- THEN, UNABLE TO **CONTAIN** HIS SEETHING RAGE ANY LONGER, THE SWAMP-BRUTE **ACTS** --

-- AND HIS STAR-BORN OPPONENT **REACTS** WITH STAGGERING SPEED...

ZZKAKK

HUH...? THAT **RAY** OF HIS... **DISINTEGRATED** MY HAND...

...BUT IF HE THINKS... THAT WILL **KEEP** ME... FROM MAKING HIM **PAY**...

...FOR WHAT HE'S DONE... TO MY **HOPES**... MY **DREAMS**...

...HE'S **WRONG**...

...**DEAD** WRONG...!

SKRUNCH!

WHAT I DID TO YOUR *WEAPON*, UGLY... IS ONLY A *SAMPLE*... OF WHAT I'M GOING TO DO... TO *YOU*...!

LITERALLY *MAD* WITH GRIEF, THE THING THAT WAS ONCE *ALEC HOLLAND* LUNGES FOR WHAT HE ASSUMES IS HIS OPPONENT'S *THROAT*--

--AND, HAVING NO OTHER RECOURSE, THE ALIEN LASHES OUT WITH AN ELEPHANTINE LIMB TO *DEFEND* ITSELF...

WHUD!

SKRACK

NO...! I'VE *SHATTERED* THE STARSHIP'S... *SUPPORT* POST...!

THEN, BEFORE THE MOSSY BRUTE CAN EVEN *HOPE* TO MOVE OUT OF THE WAY--

--THE STARSHIP--*FALLS!*

THWOOM!

THE REVERBERATIONS FADE AND THE OLD BARN FLOODS UP WITH *SILENCE*--

--WITH *MUTE ACCUSATIONS* THAT SWIRL ABOUT THE SWAMP THING'S SPRAWLED, UNMOVING BODY --

--AND IF ONE COULD DISCERN *EMOTION* IN THE ALIEN'S IMMOBILE FACE, ONE MIGHT DISCOVER IT SUFFUSED WITH --*REGRET!*

SILENCE SEEMS TO *FOLLOW* THE ALIEN CREATURE AS IT CARRIES A MUCK-ENCRUSTED BODY OUT INTO THE *SWAMP-LAND* THAT SURROUNDS THE OLD BARN--

THE LEAVES *CEASE* THEIR RUSTLING AS THE SPACE TRAVELER PASSES -- THE BIRDS *HESITATE* IN THEIR SONG--

--BUT STILL THE ALIEN MOVES ONWARD--AS IF SOMEHOW *SENSING* THE BIZARRE *BOND* THAT EXISTS BETWEEN ITS VICTIM AND THIS MARSH--

--THEN, SOFTLY, IT LAYS ITS MOSSY BURDEN DOWN AT THE STAGNANT WATERS' *EDGE*--

--AND, IF IT BELIEVES IN SOME SUPREME DEITY, PERHAPS THE ALIEN OFFERS UP A *PRAYER* FOR THE SWAMP THING'S *SOUL*--

--BEFORE IT GENTLY ROLLS THE MOSS-WET BODY BACK INTO THE CLAMMY EMBRACE OF THE *BOG*--

--THEN SOLEMNLY, REMORSEFULLY, THE ALIEN TURNS AND SHAMBLES BACK TOWARDS ITS *WORK*--

--LEAVING BEHIND ONLY A HANDFUL OF BILIOUS *BUBBLES* TO MARK THE FINAL RESTING PLACE OF WHAT ONCE HAD BEEN -- A *MAN!*

201

A SHORT WHILE LATER... A SHORT *DISTANCE* AWAY...

NOT MUCH FARTHER *NOW*, GENTS.

HOW MUCH IS "NOT MUCH," CABLE? I'M STARTIN' TO GET *ITCHY*.

KNOW WHAT YOU *MEAN*, CAPTAIN, SIR.

THESE SPECIAL *SUITS* THE LAB BOYS DESIGNED FOR US MIGHT BE GREAT FOR KEEPIN' OUT *HEAT*, BUT *MOSQUITOES* -- FORGET IT!

THERE! YOU CAN *SCRATCH* YOUR ITCH IN JUST A MINUTE, SAMSON.

THAT'S THE OLD *BARN* I TOLD YOU ABOUT. WE CAN SET UP OPERATIONS *THERE*.

THEN LET'S GET *WITH* IT, CABLE. SOONER WE HUNT UP THE *UFO*, THE *BETTER!*

IS *NOW* SOON ENOUGH FOR YOU, CAPTAIN SAMSON?

THE *UFO* -- STASHED RIGHT IN THE *BARN!*

I DON'T *BELIEVE* IT -- !

LORD, SHIP AIN'T LIKE NOTHIN' I EVER SAW ON *THIS* EARTH!

YEAH -- AN' NEITHER IS THE THING THAT *OWNS* IT! *LOOK!*

WE'VE GOT TO FIGURE OUT HOW TO *COMMUNICATE* WITH IT -- DISCOVER WHERE IT *COMES* FROM AND --

HEY -- THAT MONSTER'S PULLING A *WEAPON* ON US --

-- BUT HE AIN'T GONNA WASTE *ME!*

HOLD YOUR *FIRE*, PVT. OPTIK -- *NOW!*

CHASH!

THAT DEVICE LOOKED MORE LIKE A *WELDING TORCH* THAN A *WEAPON*.

BESIDES, OUR ORDERS ARE TO BRING BACK ANY-THING WE FIND OUT HERE -- *ALIVE!*

BLAN!

ALIVE, HUH? THAT'S EASY FOR THE BRASS BACK *HOME* TO SAY --*THEY* AIN'T STANDIN' HERE *FACIN'* THAT BRUTE!

BUT IF THAT'S THE WAY THEY *WANT* IT--

--THAT'S THE WAY THEY'LL *GET* IT! *RIGHT*, CAPTAIN, SIR?

O'REILLY, YOU *FOOL* -- COME *BACK* HERE! I DIDN'T GIVE THE *ORDER*!

AT FIRST, THE ALIEN WAS *STARTLED* --THESE NEW INTRUDERS SEEMED SO *UNLIKE* THE ONE IT HAD ACCIDENTALLY *SLAIN*--

KRAK!

--BUT ONLY IN *APPEARANCE* --FOR THEY TOO ATTACK *UNPROVOKED*--FORCING IT AGAIN TO *DEFEND* ITSELF!

--AND IN SO DOING, TO LEARN A *NEW* THING --

--WHEN THESE SMALL CREATURES ARE *STRUCK* --THEY *BREAK*!

O'REILLY? SO HELP ME, IF THAT MONSTER *HURT* THE KID, I'LL...

THIS IS THE *SECOND* LIFE THE ALIEN HAS ALMOST *TAKEN* ON THIS STRANGE WORLD--

--AND THAT THOUGHT IS NEARLY *MORE* THAN IT CAN BEAR...

O'REILLY'S JUST *DAZED* -- BUT LOOK AT THE *ALIEN*--!

IT'S NOT *MOVING*--ALMOST AS IF IT *REGRETS* WHAT IT'S DONE!

YEAH? WELL, I DON'T REGRET WHAT I'M ABOUT TO DO --

DON'T REGRET IT ONE *BIT!*

CLAKT!

IT IS NEARLY *DUSK* WHEN MATT CABLE AND HIS COMPANIONS AT LAST MAKE *CAMP* A SHORT DISTANCE FROM THE MOLDERING *BARN...*

WE'RE BETTER OFF OUT *HERE* -- LESS CHANCE OF US ACCIDENTALLY *DESTROYING* ANY OF THE ALIEN'S *EQUIPMENT.*

LORD ONLY KNOWS WHAT *SCIENTIFIC KNOWLEDGE* MIGHT BE *LOST* THAT WAY.

AND *SPEAKING* OF THAT -- DON'T YOU THINK WE OUGHT TO LET *HOME BASE* KNOW HOW THINGS WENT, SAMSON?

HUH? OH -- ER -- *SURE.*

TRUMBO, GET ON THE *"HORN"* AND CONTACT THE *BASE.*

TELL 'EM TO SEND IN A *CHOPPER* IN THE MORNIN' FOR US AND OUR SPECIAL -- ER -- *PACKAGE.*

YES SIR, CAPTAIN -- RIGHT AWAY.

BUT BRIEF MOMENTS LATER...

CAN'T *UNDERSTAND* IT, CAPTAIN.

THE RADIO DON'T SEEM TO BE *WORKIN'!*

NOT *WORKIN'?* ANY IDEA WHAT'S *WRONG?*

DON'T *KNOW*, SIR, SHE CHECKED OUT *A-OK* BACK AT THE *BASE* BUT --

WHAT IN --? THE MASTER TRANSMITTER TUBE -- IT'S *GONE* --

-- AN' *WITHOUT* IT, WE AIN'T *CALLIN'* NOBODY FOR *NOTHIN'!*

SWELL! THEN WE MAY *NEVER* GET THE ALIEN OUT OF THIS SWAMP!

LOOKS LIKE WE GOT OURSELVES A *PROBLEM*, THEN, DON'T IT?

WONDER WHERE THAT FLAMIN' RADIO TUBE *WENT* TO, ANYHOW?

204

WHILE A DOZEN YARDS AWAY, AS IF *RECOILING* FROM CAPTAIN SAMSON'S *COLD-BLOODED SARCASM*, THE STAGNANT SWAMP WATERS BEGIN TO RIPPLE AND STIR--

--BRACKISH *BUBBLES* ARE BELCHED UP ANEW TO BREAK THE MIRE'S *SURFACE*...

...FOLLOWED BY WHAT HAS NOW BECOME A MOST *FAMILIAR* HAND.

HIS VERY *ESSENCES* RESTORED BY THE CHEMICAL-TAINTED OOZE THAT CONCEIVED HIM, THE *SWAMP THING* LIVES AGAIN--

--IF ONE COULD TRULY CALL THIS *LIVING!*

THOUGHT THAT FALLING ROCKET... HAD *KILLED* ME... BUT THIS CURSED BOG... *REVIVED* ME SOMEHOW...!

DON'T KNOW HOW LONG... I'VE BEEN *OUT*... SO I'D BEST... GET *BACK* TO THE BARN... AS *QUICKLY* AS POSSIBLE...!

I STILL HAVE A *SCORE* ...TO SETTLE WITH... A CERTAIN ALIEN *SQUATTER* WHO...

HUH...?

THIS IS NOT... QUITE AT ALL... WHAT I'D *EXPECTED*...!

THE *ALIEN*... A *PRISONER* OF MATT CABLE... AND FIVE *OTHERS*...!

BETTER KEEP OUT OF *SIGHT*... UNTIL I KNOW EXACTLY... WHAT'S *GOING ON*...!

LOOK AT THAT UGLY BRUTE--STANDIN' THERE QUIET AS A *TOMB.*

YOU KNOW, IF I WAS A *RELIGIOUS* MAN, I'D SWEAR IT WAS AN AGENT OF THE *DEVIL* HIMSELF.

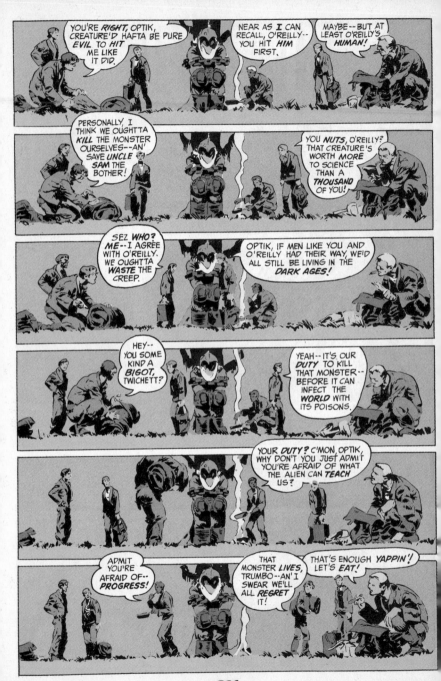

YOU'RE *RIGHT*, OPTIK, CREATURE'D HAFTA BE PURE *EVIL* TO *HIT* ME LIKE IT DID.

NEAR AS *I* CAN RECALL, O'REILLY-- YOU HIT *HIM* FIRST.

MAYBE-- BUT AT LEAST O'REILLY'S *HUMAN!*

PERSONALLY, I THINK WE OUGHTTA *KILL* THE MONSTER OURSELVES--AN' SAVE *UNCLE SAM* THE BOTHER!

YOU *NUTS*, O'REILLY? THAT CREATURE'S WORTH *MORE* TO SCIENCE THAN A *THOUSAND* OF YOU!

SEZ *WHO? ME*--I AGREE WITH O'REILLY. WE OUGHTTA *WASTE* THE CREEP.

OPTIK, IF MEN LIKE YOU AND O'REILLY HAD THEIR WAY, WE'D ALL STILL BE LIVING IN THE *DARK AGES!*

HEY-- YOU SOME KIND A *BIGOT*, TWICHETT?

YEAH-- IT'S OUR *DUTY* TO KILL THAT MONSTER-- BEFORE IT CAN INFECT THE *WORLD* WITH ITS POISONS.

YOUR *DUTY?* C'MON, OPTIK, WHY DON'T YOU JUST ADMIT YOU'RE AFRAID OF WHAT THE ALIEN CAN *TEACH* US?

ADMIT YOU'RE AFRAID OF-- *PROGRESS!*

THAT MONSTER *LIVES*, TRUMBO--AN' I SWEAR WE'LL ALL *REGRET* IT!

THAT'S ENOUGH *YAPPIN'!* LET'S *EAT!*

"*SAVE* THE CREATURE OR *SLAY IT?*" THE QUESTION SEEMS PURELY *RHETORICAL*--A WAY TO BLOW OFF *STEAM*--SO THE SIX MEN EAGERLY *CONTINUE* THEIR ARGUMENT LONG INTO THE EVENING--

--BUT IN THE MORNING WILL COME THE DIFFICULT TASK OF BRINGING THE ALIEN OUT OF THE SWAMP *ON FOOT* AND THESE MEN WILL NEED THEIR *REST*--SO, AT LAST, THE HEATED CONVERSATION COOLS TO A *WHISPER*--AND SOON ALL ARE *ASLEEP*--

--ALL SAVE *ONE!*

CL-K

YOU BEEN *LISTENIN'*, HAVEN'T YA, MONSTER? YOU HEARD EVERYTHING WE *SAID* TONIGHT, DIDN'T YA?

WELL, THEY'RE *RIGHT*, YA KNOW -- OPTIK AN' O'REILLY--YOU *ARE* A MENACE--A *DISEASE!*

BRING YOU BACK TO *CIVILIZATION* --AN' EVERY BLEEDIN'-HEART KID IN THE COUNTRY'LL HAVE A *NEW* CAUSE TO RALLY AROUND.

SURE, I CAN SEE THE HEADLINES NOW, "*MENACE ...OR MESSIAH?*"

HELL, WITHOUT HALF *TRYIN'*, YOU COULD BECOME THE MOST *POWERFUL* THING ON EARTH--AN' I CAN'T *ALLOW* THAT.

YOU'RE *FOREIGN* -- A DAMNED *ALIEN*--YOU DON'T *BELONG* HERE--

--AND I'M NOT GONNA LET YOU *STAY* AN' DESTROY WHAT LITTLE *CHANCE* THIS PLANET HAS LEFT.

YOU UNDERSTAND THIS IS NOTHIN' *PERSONAL*, DON'T YA?

JUST THOUGHT YOU SHOULD KNOW THE REASONS *WHY*--

BLAM!

--HUH?

AND THE *REACTION* TO THAT SINGLE THUNDERCLAP IS INSTANTANEOUS...

WH- WHAT'S *GOING ON?* WHO--?

SAMSON!?! WHAT IN GOD'S NAME ARE YOU DOING WITH THAT *GUN?*

IT WAS A--ER--A *BEAR!*

CAUGHT ONE SNEAKIN' INTO CAMP--AN' TOOK A *SHOT* AT IT.

I'VE GOT *NEWS* FOR YOU, SAMSON -- THERE ARE *NO* BEARS IN THE BAYOU.

YOU WERE TRYING TO SHOOT THE *ALIEN*, WEREN'T YOU, MANIAC?

WEREN'T YOU??

AND WHAT IF I *WAS*, BRIGHT BOY?

I WAS DOIN' IT TO SAVE *YOUR* SKIN, TOO.

I'M DOIN' IT TO SAVE *EVERYONE* -- BEFORE THAT MONSTER *DESTROYS* US ALL FROM *WITHIN*--

--AND I'LL *KILL* ANYONE WHO TRIES TO *STOP* ME!

WHOK!

SURE HOPE YOU DON'T MIND MY *SAYING* SO, CAPTAIN, SIR--

--BUT YOU HAVE GONE *OUT* OF YOUR *EVER-LOVIN'* MIND!

UUNNFF!

"*SAVE* THE CREATURE OR *SLAY* IT?" THE MATTER HAD INDEED SEEMED QUITE *RHETORICAL* BEFORE--

--BUT SAMSON'S VIOLENT *ACTION*--AND TRUMBO'S VIOLENT *RESPONSE*--HAVE MADE THAT QUESTION THE *CRUX* OF A DESPERATE CONFLICT--

--AS MEN WHO HAD BEEN *FRIENDS* OF A SORT MERE *HOURS* AGO STRUGGLE TO *RESOLVE* THE QUESTION IN MANKIND'S *USUAL* FASHION ...

THE ALIEN OBSERVES THIS ALL IN *SILENCE*, ITS *LIDLESS* EYES NEVER *WAVERING* FROM THE SCENE OF COMBAT...

PERHAPS IT WONDERS AT WHAT *FOOLS* THESE CREATURES BE... *PERHAPS.*

NO ONE CAN SAY FOR CERTAIN HOW *LONG* THE BATTLE RAGES--GROWING MORE AND MORE *HEATED* --UNTIL, ONCE MORE, THE STACCATO SOUND OF *GUN-FIRE* ECHOES THROUGH THE CLEARING--

BLAM
BLAM

--AND MATT CABLE SUDDENLY *REALIZES...*

STOP! FOR GOD'S SAKE, STOP *SHOOTING!*

ONE OF THOSE WILD SHOTS IS LIABLE TO *HIT* THE...

...ALIEN...?

IN *FACT*, MATT CABLE, ONE OF THOSE WILD SHOTS HAS ALREADY DONE JUST *THAT*-- INSTANTS BEFORE A MOSS-ENCRUSTED MONSTROSITY TORE THE ALIEN'S SHACKLES *ASUNDER*--

--THEN MOVED TO HELP THE FAST-WEAKENING WAY-FARER *BACK* TO THE MUSTY OLD BARN--AND THE GREAT GLEAMING *SHIP* WITHIN--

209

NO *WORDS* NEED BE SPOKEN HERE. THE ALIEN PLACES ITS EXTREMITY UPON THE MOSSY MAN-BRUTE'S SHOULDER IN A *UNIVERSAL* GESTURE--

--A GESTURE THAT HAS A RATHER *SINGULAR* EFFECT.

THE SWAMP THING *VANISHES*--

--AND AS THE SPACE TRAVELER TURNS TO ENTER ITS SHIP...

DON'T *MOVE!* *STOP* WHERE YOU ARE OR...

NO--THIS--TIME--IT--IS--YOU--WHO--WILL--STOP--!

HUH? H-H-E'S THROWN UP SOME SORT OF *FORCE FIELD* AROUND US--?

AND HE--HE'S *TALKING!*

YES--I--HAVE--HEARD--ENOUGH--OF--YOUR--LANGUAGE--AT--LAST--TO--COMMUNICATE--WITH--YOU--

--BUT--WHAT--I--HAVE--HEARD--SICKENS--ME--!

I--CAME--TO--YOU--IN--PEACE--BUT--I--HAVE--FOUND--ONLY--VIOLENCE--HERE--!

I--LANDED--HERE--BY--ACCIDENT--A--VICTIM--OF--A--COSMIC--STORM--!

I--NEEDED--ONLY--YOUR--HELP--IN--REPAIRING--MY--SHIP--AND--WOULD--HAVE--GIVEN--YOU--MUCH--IN--RETURN--

BUT--NOW--ALL--I--HAVE--FOR--YOU--IS--*PITY*--!

HEY--THE *BUBBLE'S* DISSOLVING!

THEN LET'S GET *OUT* OF HERE --*FAST!*

THAT SHIP IS TAKING OFF!

IT MAKES SURPRISINGLY LITTLE *SOUND* FOR SOMETHING SO AWESOME, THIS GREAT, GLEAMING *VESSEL* OF THE STARS...

THERE IS THE INITIAL *ROAR* AS TONGUES OF FLAME ARE PUSHED AGAINST THE DAMP EARTH -- THE SPLINTERING *CRASH* AS THE SHINING STELLAR ARROW ERUPTS UP THROUGH THE OLD BARN ROOF --

--THEN ONLY A LOW *WHISTLE*, LIKE THE TRILLING OF MELANCHOLY *BIRDS* --

--AND LIKE A BIRD, IT *SOARS*, ARCHING SKYWARD, SINGING THE PRAISES OF THE *STARS* --

--ONLY TO *FALTER* AT HEAVEN'S VERY GATE, THERE TO *PLEAD* SILENTLY FOR LESS THAN A MOMENT --

--THEN, LIKE *ICARUS* COMING TOO NEAR THE SUN --

--TO *FALL!*

EPILOGUE...

"WELL, SAMSON -- ARE YOU HAPPY *NOW?* YOU WON'T HAVE TO WORRY ABOUT THE *ALIEN* ANYMORE."

"OF COURSE I'M HAPPY, CABLE. THAT MONSTER WAS *EVIL* --A *MENACE* --"

"YOU STILL *BELIEVE* THAT-- EVEN AFTER WHAT THE ALIEN *SAID?* WHY, SAMSON -- BECAUSE HE WAS *DIFFERENT* -- BECAUSE HE WASN'T *HUMAN?*"

"DON'T PLAY SO HIGH-AN'-MIGHTY WITH ME, CABLE. I'LL BET THERE'S SOMETHING IN YOUR LIFE YOU'VE FELT EXACTLY THE SAME WAY ABOUT."

"DON'T BE *RIDICULOUS*, SAMSON. I NEVER...I...I... OH, MY GOD, SAMSON. THERE IS...THERE *IS!*"

THE END

CHAPTER TEN

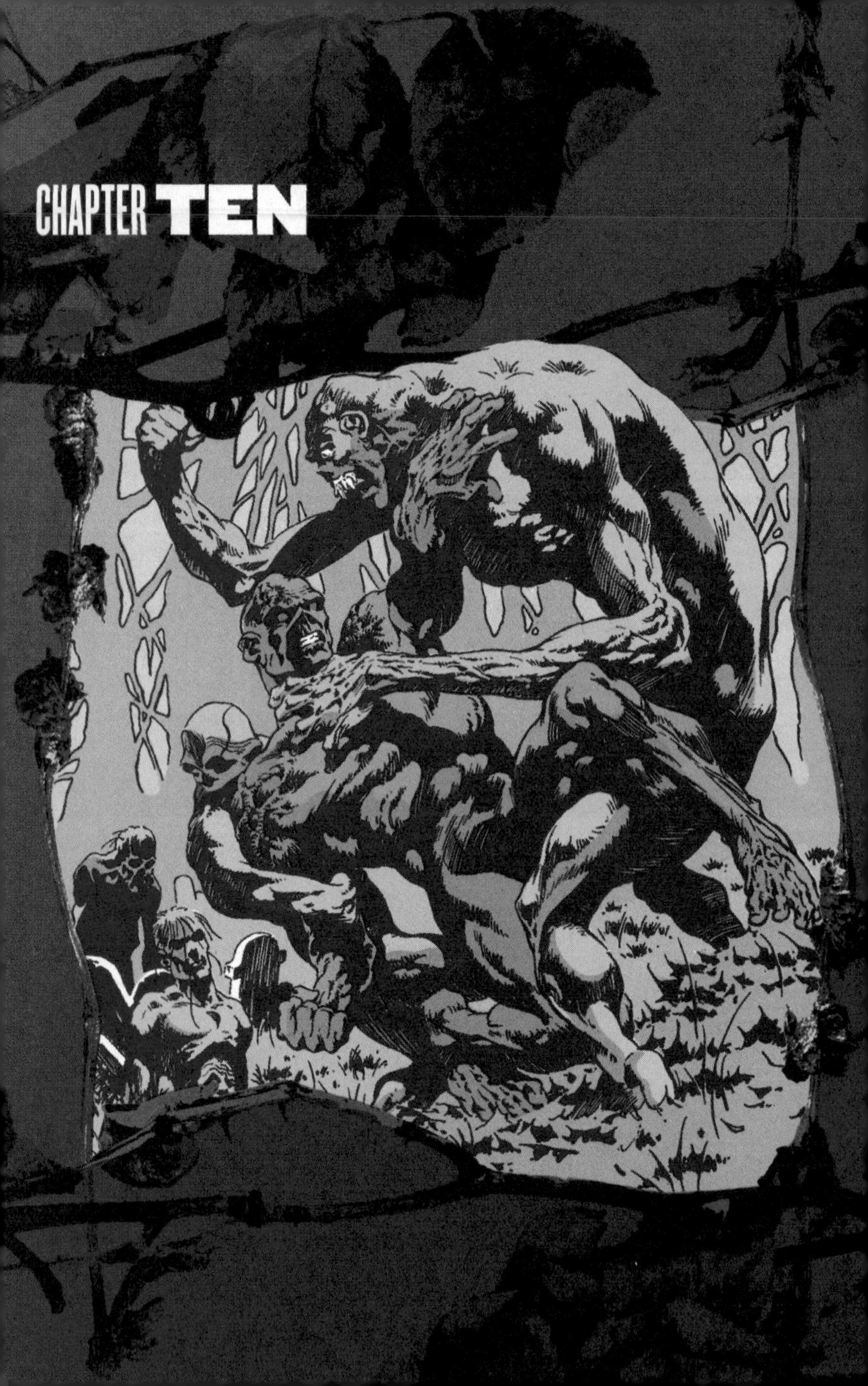

HE HAS BEEN *RUNNING* FOR MANY HOURS NOW, IGNORING THE SEARING *PAINS* THAT LANCE THROUGH HIS CHEST--AND, AT LAST, HE HAS LEFT THE MOURNFUL BAYING OF THE *BLOODHOUNDS* FAR BEHIND...

HIS NAME IS *"HUNK" DORRY*, NUMBER 2431975. HE IS A *FUGITIVE* FROM A CHAIN GANG. IN HIS TIME, HE HAS BEEN CONVICTED OF MURDERING *MANY MEN* --

--AND HE FIGURES THAT, AT THIS LATE DATE, *ANOTHER* VICTIM MORE OR LESS WILL NOT MAKE A BIT OF *DIFFERENCE*...

...BUT TO THE HUGE, SHAMBLING, MOSS-ENCRUSTED MONSTROSITY STANDING IN THE SHADOWS AT THE CLEARING'S EDGE, IT MAKES *ALL* THE DIFFERENCE IN THE WORLD!

DON'T KNOW *WHUT* YOU COOKIN' IN THET *POT O'* YOURS, OLD WOMAN--

--BUT I BEEN *RUNNIN'* SO LONG-- *HURTIN'* SO BAD-- *FEELIN'* SO MEAN-- THET I AIN'T ABOUT TO *ASK* FER NO HANDOUT *NOW!*

I'M JEST GONNA *KNOCK YOU OFF--* AN' *TAKE* WHUT I--!

NO!!

HUH? AIN'T *NOBODY* TELLS "HUNK" DORRY WHUT TO DO--!

BUT THE *SWAMP THING* LUMBERS OUT OF THE DARKNESS THEN, DRIPPING A MOSSY WET TRAIL BEHIND HIM--AND THE *BLOOD* OF THE MAN NAMED "HUNK" DORRY SUDDENLY RUNS *COLDER* THAN EVER IT HAS BEFORE...

LORD A'MIGHTY!

WH-WHUT INNA NAME O' MARY IS-- *THAT?*

DON'T KNOW WHUT KIND O' *MONSTER* YOU KEEP AS A *PET*, OLD WITCH--

--BUT "HUNK" DORRY AIN'T NEVER RUN FROM NO FIGHT WITH *NOTHIN'*--

--AN' I AIN'T--

--ABOUT TO--

--START--

--NOWWWW--

NO USE FUSSIN' OVER *HIM*, CHILE-- HE'S STONE *DEAD!*

AIN'T *NOBODY* THAT KIN LIVE TOO LONG WITH THAT MANY *BULLETS* IN HIM--

--'CEPTIN' MAYBE *YOU*, I WAGER!

S'POSE YOU WONDERIN' WHY YOUR OLD *AUNTIE BELLUM* IS JEST SETTIN' HERE *TALKIN'*--

--'STEAD O' *SCOOTIN'* AWAY FROM YOU LIKE THAT OLE *DEVIL* WAS ON MAH TAIL?

JEST TOO *OLD*, I RECKON!

SEEN TOO MANY DOWNRIGHT *AWFUL* THINGS TO *CARE* MUCH ANYMORE!

YES'M, CHILE-- THIS OLE LAND'S GOT A POWERFUL *MEAN* WAY OF TREATIN' THE FOLKS WHUT *LIVES* HERE!

NOT THAT IT WAS *ALWAYS* THIS WAY, MIND YOU!

TIME WAS THIS LAND WAS *RICH* AN' *GREEN*-- AN' SO AL'MIGHTY *BEAUTIFUL* THE GOOD LORD HIMSELF MUST'A *ENVIED* IT!

"THERE WAS A COTTON *PLANTATION* HERE THEN, A GREAT WARM WHITE-BRICK *BUILDIN'* FRONTED WITH TALL MARBLE COLUMNS, BORDERED WITH *ROSES* AS SWEET AS A SUMMER'S *DAWN*--

"--AN' FOR A *SLAVE*, PLANTATION LIFE MIGHT O' BEEN ALMOST *PLEASANT*--

"--IF'N IT WASN'T FOR THE *MONSTER* THAT OWNED IT!

"*SAMSON PARMINTER*, HIS NAME WAS-- BUT THEY MIGHT JUST AS WELL CALLED HIM *LUCIFER*... *BEELZEBUB*... OR *SATAN*!

"A *CUSSED MEAN* ONE, HE WAS-- BORN WITH SOMETHIN' *MISSIN'* IN HIS SOUL-- BORN WITH A POWERFUL NEED TO *HURT*--TO *PAIN* THOSE WHAT SERVED HIM!

"THE SLAVES, THEY ALL *HATED* PARMINTER-- BUT THERE WAS NOTHIN' THEY COULD *DO*--

"--TILL THE DAY PARMINTER TOOK A SHINE TO A PURTY YOUNG THING NAMED *ELSBETH*!

"NOW *ELSBETH*, SHE WOULDN' HAVE NO *PART* O' PARMINTER--TOLD HIM SHE WAS ALREADY PROMISED TO *AN-OTHER*--

"--AND *PARMINTER*-- WELL, HE DECIDED HE'D JEST AS SOON HAVE HER *TORN LIMB-FROM-LIMB* AS *SPIT* ON HER!

"THAT WAS PARMINTER'S BIGGEST *MISTAKE*-- 'CAUSE THAT'S WHEN *BLACK JUBAL* STEPPED OUT FROM THE SLAVES! SEEMS *HE* WAS THE ONE ELSBETH WAS PROMISED TO!

"NOW BLACK JUBAL, HE JEST STOOD RIGHT *UP* TO OLE PARMINTER-- TOLD HIM OFF STRAIGHT TO HIS FACE--

"--AN' PARMINTER, HE DIDN'T *LIKE* THAT!

"NO, HE DIDN'T *LIKE* THAT A'TALL!

216

"NOW PARMINTER *COULDN'T* TEAR JUBAL'S LIMBS OFF-- HE'D ALREADY TAKEN *ONE* ARM WHEN JUBAL WAS JEST A *CHILE*--

"--SO THAT MONSTER DECIDED TO *BURN* JUBAL INSTEAD-- SAID IT WAS THE WAY *ALL* GOOD MARTYRS DIED!

"WELL, AS THEM *FLAMES* LICKED UP AROUND JUBAL'S BODY, THE BIG MAN SWORE AN *OATH*--

"--SAID EVEN *DEATH* WOULDN' STOP HIM FROM *DEALING* WITH PARMINTER FOR GOOD -- SAID PARMINTER'S BREED WOULD *PAY IN KIND* FOR THE AL'MIGHTY *SINS* THEY COMMITTED 'GAINST THEIR FELLOW MAN--

"-- BUT *PARMINTER,* HE JEST *LAUGHED* --AND ONCE BLACK JUBAL WAS BURIED AN' GONE, HE WENT RIGHT ON BACK TO HAVIN' HIS *FUN*!--

"--AN' IF THE SINS HE'D COMMITTED *BEFORE* WERE BAD-- THEM THAT FOLLOWED WAS *WORSE*--

"--ALMOST AS IF HE WAS *DARIN'* OLE BLACK JUBAL TO RISE ON UP OUT O' THE GROUND AN' *MAKE* HIM STOP LIKE HE *SWORE* HE WOULD!

"NOW THE *SLAVES,* ALL THEY COULD DO WAS SUFFER AN' *PRAY* SOMEBODY *ELSE* WOULD COME ALONG TO STOP PARMINTER-- AN' ONE NIGHT, SOMEBODY-- OR SOME *THING*-- *DID*!

"THEY HEARD *NOISES* FROM THE OLE PLANTATION-- SOUNDS LIKE THE AGONIZED SCREAMIN' O' SOMETHIN' *UNHUMAN*--

"--AN' WHEN THEY RUSHED INSIDE, THEY *FOUND* MISTER PARMINTER-- IN THE *FOYER*-- THE *LIVIN' ROOM*-- THE *PANTRY*-- THE *DEN*--!

"SOMETHING HAD TORN SAMSON PARMINTER *LIMB-FROM-LIMB!*

THINGS KIND O' *FELL APART* AFTER THAT, CHILE!

MOST O' THE *SLAVES*, THEY RUN AWAY -- LET THE OLE PLANTATION TUMBLE INTO *RUIN* --

--BUT OLE *AUNTIE BELLUM* -- WELL, I JEST DID'N' HAVE NOWHERES *ELSE* TO GO!

NOT THAT I *MINDS* MAH LOT, CHILE -- I KNOW IT'S FOR THE *BEST!*

WHEN YOU GETS AS OLD AS OLE *AUNTIE* -- YOU KNOWS ALL *KINDS* O' STUFF!

--LIKE I KNOWS THAT THE EYES OF *UNHOLY THINGS* ARE STARIN' AT US RIGHT THIS VERY SECON'!

THE EYES OF ... *WHAT* ...??

THE OLD WOMAN IS *RIGHT* ...! I CAN *SEE* THE EYES ... GLEAMING OUT OF THE *DARKNESS* ...

... AND I THINK I'D BETTER ... FIND OUT *WHO* THEY BELONG TO ...!

MOVING HIS GREAT SHAMBLING BULK FAR *FASTER* THAN ONE COULD BELIEVE POSSIBLE, THE CREATURE WHO WAS ONCE *DOCTOR ALEC HOLLAND* PURSUES HIS GROTESQUE QUARRY THROUGH THE SHADOWY *SWAMP*--

--AND SOME SMALL MOTE OF *MEMORY* TUGS AT HIS *SLUGGISH* MIND: HE'S *SEEN* THIS PECULIAR, AWKWARD GAIT *BEFORE*--

--IF *ONLY*-- IF ONLY HE COULD REMEMBER *WHEN*...

CAN'T GET A REALLY GOOD LOOK AT THEM...!

THEY MOVE TOO QUICKLY... STAY TOO CLOSE TO THE *SHADOWS*...

...BUT THEY SEEM TO BE... HEADING FOR THAT *CLEARING* UP AHEAD...

...AND MAYBE *THERE* I CAN...

CAUTIOUSLY, THE ROOT-ENTANGLED MONSTROSITY SHUFFLES TO THE SECLUDED CLEARING'S EDGE--

--AND HIS RHEUMY RED-RIMMED EYES SUDDENLY GO *WIDE* WITH THE SHOCK OF *RECOGNITION*--

--AND THE DEPRESSING REALIZATION THAT THE TIRED OLD ADAGE IS *TRUE*--

219

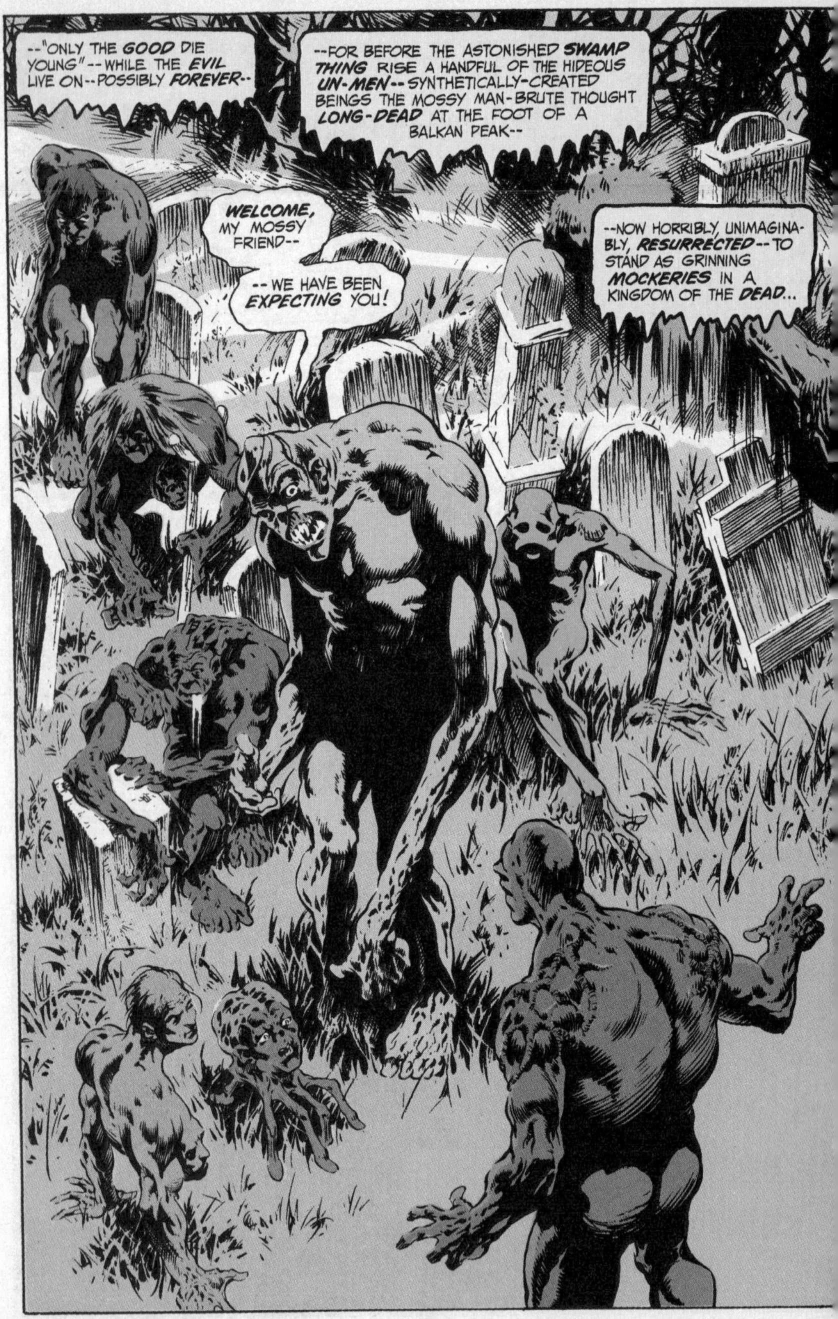
--"ONLY THE GOOD DIE YOUNG"--WHILE THE EVIL LIVE ON--POSSIBLY FOREVER--
--FOR BEFORE THE ASTONISHED SWAMP THING RISE A HANDFUL OF THE HIDEOUS UN-MEN--SYNTHETICALLY-CREATED BEINGS THE MOSSY MAN-BRUTE THOUGHT LONG-DEAD AT THE FOOT OF A BALKAN PEAK--
WELCOME, MY MOSSY FRIEND--
--WE HAVE BEEN EXPECTING YOU!
--NOW HORRIBLY, UNIMAGINABLY, RESURRECTED--TO STAND AS GRINNING MOCKERIES IN A KINGDOM OF THE DEAD...

AH, I SEE *CONFUSION* IN YOUR EYES! YOU RECOGNIZE MY *UN-MEN* --BUT NOT *ME!*

THEN PERMIT ME TO *REINTRODUCE* MYSELF--

--I AM-- *ARCANE--*

--AND I HAVE COME TO CLAIM WHAT IS *MINE!*

SEIZE HIM, MY PETS!

LIKE CHILDREN IN A SCHOOLYARD, THE *UN-MEN* SCAMPER FORWARD --AND BEFORE THE STARTLED *SWAMP THING* HAS TIME TO REACT--

--HE HAS ALREADY *LOST* THE GAME!

DO NOT ATTEMPT TO *RISE*, MY FRIEND--

--OR WE WILL ONLY BE FORCED TO *REPEAT* THIS PERFORMANCE--

--MORE *VIOLENTLY* THAN BEFORE!

UNDOUBTEDLY, YOU ARE WONDERING HOW I *SURVIVED* THE FALL FROM MY TOWER--AND HOW MY MAGNIFICENT *MIND* CAME TO BE IN THIS GROSS, MISSHAPEN FORM--

--AND SINCE *YOU*, ABOVE ANYONE ELSE IN THIS WORLD, WOULD APPRECIATE THE *IRONY* OF IT ALL--

--I SHALL *TELL* YOU!

"IN TRUTH, I DID *NOT* SURVIVE THE FALL! THOUGH THE SPARK OF *LIFE* REMAINED WITHIN ME--

"I HAD *SHATTERED* EVERY SINGLE BONE IN MY BODY!

"THOSE *FEW* REMAINING OF MY *UN-MEN*, UNDER THE DIRECTION OF THE LIVING BRAIN, *CRANIUS*, CARRIED MY BROKEN BODY TO A SECRET *LABORATORY*--

"--WHERE UNDER MY SEMI-TELEPATHIC CONTROL, CRANIUS SUPERVISED THE PRODUCTION OF A *MIRACLE!*

"FROM A VAST SUPPLY OF COMPONENT PARTS I HAD STORED THERE FOR JUST SUCH AN EMERGENCY, THEY CONSTRUCTED A *SYNTHETIC BODY* TO HOUSE MY UNDAMAGED *MIND*--

"--BUT, WITHOUT MY MASTERFUL HAND TO *GUIDE* THEM, THE RESULTS OF THE OPERATION WERE--

"--ER-- SOMEWHAT LESS THAN *PERFECT!*

"REALIZING I COULD NOT SPEND *ETERNITY* IN THIS CUMBERSOME, MORTAL FORM, I RESOLVED ONCE MORE TO POSSESS *YOUR* BODY--FOR, AS YOU KNOW, MY EARLIER TESTS OF IT HAVE PROVED IT ALMOST *INDESTRUCTIBLE!*

"WITH CRANIUS'S TELEPATHIC POWERS *'HOMED IN'* ON YOUR MIND, WE SET OFF IN *PURSUIT* OF YOU--

"--AND SINCE THESE SYNTHETIC FORMS REQUIRE NO *FOOD* OR REST, IT DID NOT TAKE US TERRIBLY LONG TO *SWIM* THE ATLANTIC OCEAN!"

TRACKING YOU BACK *HERE* TO YOUR SWAMPY HOME TOOK ONLY A FEW DAYS LONGER--AND NOW THE *PRIZE* I SO FAITHFULLY SOUGHT IS WITHIN MY *GRASP!*

WE WILL TAKE YOU *BACK* WITH US TO MY HIDDEN *LABORATORY*--AND THEN--

--AND THEN... YOU'LL STEAL MY *BODY...*?

YOU MAY *THINK* YOU CAN, MADMAN...

...BUT YOU HAVEN'T GOT... A FLAMING CHANCE IN *HELL*....!

WATCH HIM, YOU FOOLS--HE'S BREAKING *FREE!*

I'VE *BROKEN* FREE, ARCANE... AND NOW...

SO, MY FRIEND--YOU SEEK TO MAKE ME *EARN* YOUR BODY?

VERY *WELL*, THEN --IF YOU *INSIST*--

--IT WILL ONLY MAKE MY EVENTUAL *VICTORY* THAT MUCH *SWEETER!*

WHOMP

STAY BACK, MY PETS-- *STAY BACK!*

IF I CANNOT DEFEAT HOLLAND *ALONE*--I DO NOT *DESERVE* TO OWN HIS BODY!

AN *IMPRESSIVE* *SPEECH*, ARCANE...

...A SHAME YOUR *WORDS* ARE AS HOLLOW ...AS YOUR *HEAD*...!

BROK!

WELL *STRUCK*, DOCTOR! YOU'RE A MOST *WORTHY* ADVERSARY!

IT WOULD SEEM I AM IN FOR THE *BATTLE* OF MY LIFE!

A PITY, THEN, THAT THE BATTLE WILL BE SUCH A *SHORT* ONE!

YOU *FORGET,* DOCTOR HOLLAND --I'VE *STUDIED* YOUR BODY--

--I KNOW ALL ITS *WEAK* AND *STRONG* POINTS--

--SO IT WILL NOT BE *TOO* DIFFICULT FOR ME TO *CONQUER* YOU WITHOUT HARMING YOUR MOSSY FORM!

AFTER ALL, I'LL NEED A BODY THAT'S IN *PERFECT* CONDITION IF I'M GOING TO *ENSLAVE* THE...

--UNNFF!

A SUDDEN GUST OF *WIND* WELLS UP AT THE MENTION OF --THE *WORD*--

--A COLD WIND WHOSE WHISPER SEEMS THE *MOAN* OF TORMENTED SOULS--

--BUT THOSE WHO BATTLE IN THIS GRISLY ARENA CHOOSE TO *IGNORE* THE WIND--

--FOR THE *ELEMENTS* ARE AS NOTHING BEFORE THEIR OWN PRIMORDIAL *HATE*...

FALL, HOLLAND! WHY DON'T YOU *FALL*?

--RATHER THAN LIVE ON AS A *SLAVE*!

I'D THINK A MAN SUCH AS *YOU* WOULD PREFER TO PERISH *NOW*--

AGAIN THE *WORD* IS SPOKEN--AND THE *WIND* GROWS HARSHER STILL--

--ITS WHISPERED MOAN BECOMING MORE LIKE A *MURMUR*--

STOP *STRUGGLING*, DOCTOR--AND *DIE*!

IT'S REALLY FOR THE BEST, YOU KNOW!

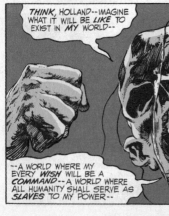

THINK, HOLLAND--IMAGINE WHAT IT WILL BE *LIKE* TO EXIST IN *MY* WORLD--

--A WORLD WHERE MY EVERY *WISH* WILL BE A *COMMAND*--A WORLD WHERE ALL HUMANITY SHALL SERVE AS *SLAVES* TO MY *POWER*--

AND THE MURMURING GROWS *DEEPER*-- COMING IN FRUSTRATED *HOWLS*--

YOU SHOULD CONSIDER YOURSELF *FORTUNATE,* DOCTOR--

--THAT YOU WILL *NOT* BE AROUND TO *SEE* SUCH A WORLD!

AND AS THE BARELY-CONSCIOUS *SWAMP THING* TOPPLES INTO THE DIRT...

IT IS *FINISHED,* MY PETS!

THE BODY I HAVE SO LONG *COVETED* WILL SOON BE *MINE!*

WE NEED ONLY *RETURN* WITH IT TO MY HIDDEN LABORATORY --*TRANSPLANT* MY BRAIN INTO ITS MOSSY CONFINES--

--THEN BEGIN A WELL-CALCULATED WAVE OF *TERROR* THAT WILL EVENTUALLY *SWEEP* MANKIND'S UNDESERVED FREEDOM FROM THE FACE OF THE EARTH--

--AND LEAVE *ARCANE* THE UNDISPUTED *MASTER OF THE WORLD!*

AND WITH THAT, THE WINDSWEPT *MOANS* -- THE GUSTY *MURMURINGS* -- BECOME A MUFFLED *CRY* OF OUTRAGE AND DESPAIR--

--A SOUND EVEN THE MEGALO-MANIACAL *ARCANE* AND HIS SYNTHETIC SERVANTS CANNOT LONG *IGNORE*...

THUS THEY STAND TRANSFIXED AS THE MOURNFUL CRY *CONGEALS* --INTO THE ANGUISHED HYSTERICAL *VOICES* OF CREATURES NO LONGER TRULY OF *THIS* WORLD--

--VOICES THAT SCREAM OUT FOR THE RIGHTEOUS *REVENGE* SO MANY YEARS *DENIED* THEM--

--AND THE SCREAMING GROWS *LOUDER, MORE DESPERATE*-- TILL THE ANCIENT WOODEN HEADSTONES SEEM TO *SHUDDER* AT THE SOUND--

--TREMBLING IN MOCK *FEAR* OF WHAT THEY KNOW MUST SHORTLY COME...

THEN, A TOMBSTONE *FALLS*--

--AND *ANOTHER* QUICKLY FOLLOWS--

--AND, AT LAST, THE MUSTY CEMETERY GROUND *ERUPTS* IN UNNATURAL FURY--

--HURLING THE REMAINING HEADSTONES *SKYWARD*--SHRIVELING THE YELLOWED GRASS--SPEWING UP GREAT CHUNKS OF DECAYING *DIRT*--

--*FREEING* THOSE WHO HAVE SLEPT A MOST *FITFUL* SLEEP BENEATH THIS UNHALLOWED SOIL FOR A COUNTLESS SCORE OF YEARS...

WH-WHO *ARE* YOU ALL? WHAT BUSINESS HAVE YOU *HERE*?

WE HAS COME TO REPAY A *DEBT!*

THE BIG BLACK MAN GROWS *SILENT* THEN--AS HE AND HIS SOMBER COMPANIONS MOVE SLOWLY, HESITANTLY, FORWARD, THEIR DARK EYES ALMOST *GLOWING* IN ANTICIPATION--

--AND ARCANE, IN TURN, WONDERS IF PERHAPS HIS *OWN* SYNTHETIC EYES HAVE SUDDENLY GONE *FAULTY*--FOR HE WOULD SWEAR HE CAN SEE CLEAR *THROUGH* THE GRIM-VISAGED THRONG APPROACHING HIM--

--AND THE *SWAMP THING?* HIS MOSS-HOODED EYES GO WIDE IN SURPRISE--AS HE REMEMBERS THE *TALE* HE'D HEARD SCANT MINUTES BEFORE--OF A GREAT BLACK *GIANT* WHO'D DIED AT THE STAKE--

--A GIANT WITH ONLY *ONE ARM!*

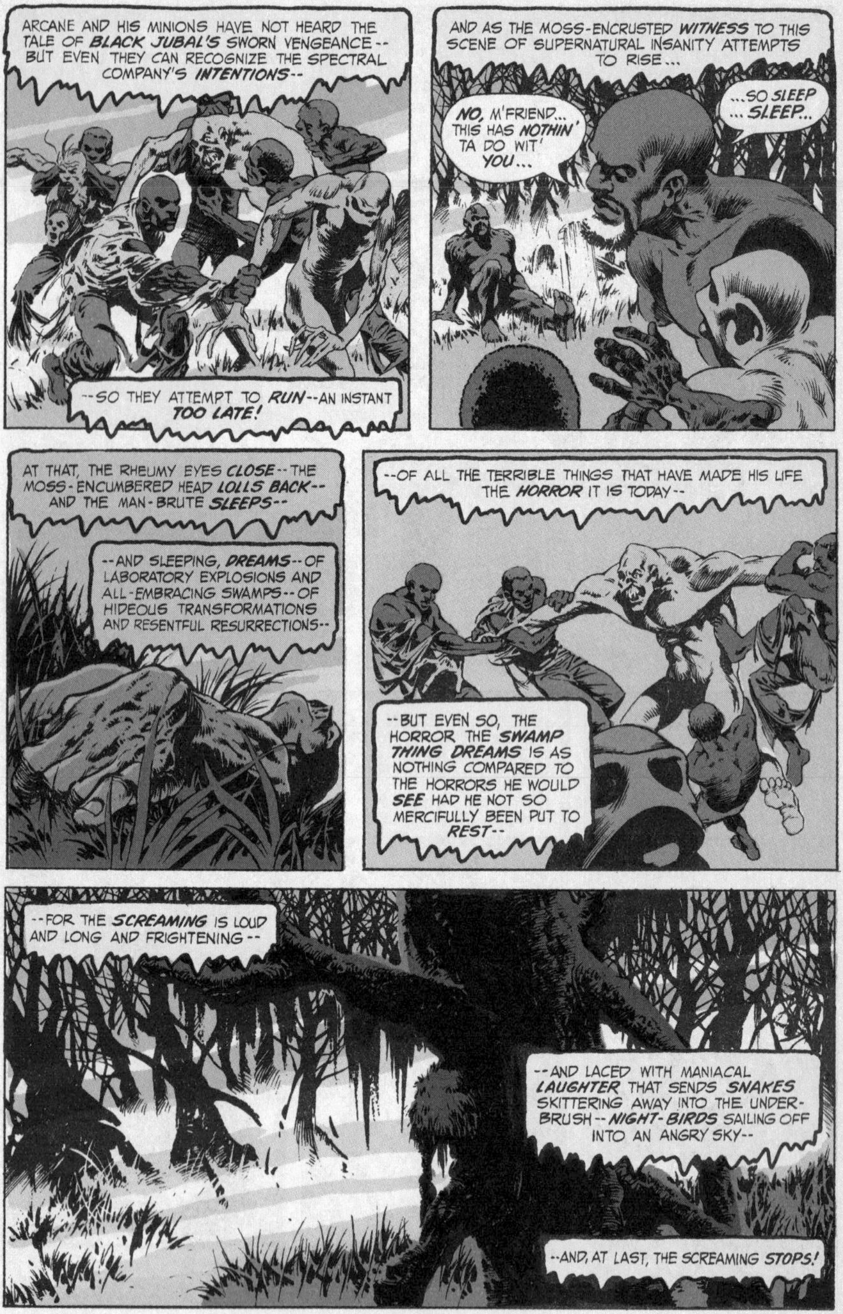
ARCANE AND HIS MINIONS HAVE NOT HEARD THE TALE OF BLACK JUBAL'S SWORN VENGEANCE -- BUT EVEN THEY CAN RECOGNIZE THE SPECTRAL COMPANY'S INTENTIONS--
--SO THEY ATTEMPT TO RUN--AN INSTANT TOO LATE!
AND AS THE MOSS-ENCRUSTED WITNESS TO THIS SCENE OF SUPERNATURAL INSANITY ATTEMPTS TO RISE...
NO, M'FRIEND... THIS HAS NOTHIN' TA DO WIT' YOU...
...SO SLEEP ...SLEEP...
AT THAT, THE RHEUMY EYES CLOSE--THE MOSS-ENCUMBERED HEAD LOLLS BACK--AND THE MAN-BRUTE SLEEPS--
--AND SLEEPING, DREAMS--OF LABORATORY EXPLOSIONS AND ALL-EMBRACING SWAMPS--OF HIDEOUS TRANSFORMATIONS AND RESENTFUL RESURRECTIONS--
--OF ALL THE TERRIBLE THINGS THAT HAVE MADE HIS LIFE THE HORROR IT IS TODAY--
--BUT EVEN SO, THE HORROR THE SWAMP THING DREAMS IS AS NOTHING COMPARED TO THE HORRORS HE WOULD SEE HAD HE NOT SO MERCIFULLY BEEN PUT TO REST--
--FOR THE SCREAMING IS LOUD AND LONG AND FRIGHTENING--
--AND LACED WITH MANIACAL LAUGHTER THAT SENDS SNAKES SKITTERING AWAY INTO THE UNDER-BRUSH--NIGHT-BIRDS SAILING OFF INTO AN ANGRY SKY--
--AND, AT LAST, THE SCREAMING STOPS!

IT IS ALMOST *DAWN* WHEN THE SWAMP THING *AWAKENS*, RUBBING THE FILTH OF SLEEP FROM HIS EYES--

--TO FIND HE IS--*ALONE!*

ARCANE--BLACK JUBAL--THE OTHERS-- ARE *GONE,* AND THE CENTURIES-OLD CEMETERY IS JUST AS IT WAS BEFORE--

--OR IS IT?

FOR NOW THERE ARE SEVEN *NEW* HEADSTONES RISING AGAINST THE MIST-- SIX SMALL AND ONE LARGE--

--AND THE SWAMP THING WONDERS IF PERHAPS HE SHOULD WAIT FOR THE RISING *SUN* TO EXAMINE THIS NEW MYSTERY MORE CLOSELY.

HE WONDERS THIS FOR ONLY AN INSTANT, THEN *SANITY* PREVAILS--

--AND HE TURNS AWAY, SHAMBLING OFF INTO THE MISTY HALFLIGHT OF *MORNING...*

FOR THERE REALLY IS NO *NEED* FOR HIM TO STAY...

ARCANE

IN HIS HEART, THE SWAMP THING *KNOWS* WHAT HE WILL FIND!

EPILOGUE: DAWN IS IN FULL BLOOM WHEN THE SHAMBLING SWAMP BRUTE AT LAST FINDS HIS WAY BACK TO THE CLEARING WHERE A CERTAIN ANCIENT WOMAN HAD SAT THE NIGHT BEFORE...

ONLY TO FIND SHE IS--

...*GONE*... THE SHACK... THE CAULDRON... AUNTIE BELLUM... ALL OF THEM...

...*GONE*...

...THIS *IS* THE RIGHT CLEARING... I RECOGNIZE THE FOLIAGE... BUT...

...IN GOD'S NAME ...WHAT HAPPENED TO THE *HOUSE* THAT WAS HERE... LAST NIGHT...?

HAVE I GONE *MAD*...? DID I IMAGINE IT ALL HAPPENED...?

SUNLIGHT... GLINTING OFF SOMETHING IN THE BUSHES... COULD IT BE HER CAULDRON OR...?

EAGERLY, THE SWAMP THING TEARS THE FOLIAGE ASIDE TO REVEAL...

...A GRAVESTONE... AND THAT INSCRIPTION ..."ELSBETH BELLUM"...

ELSBETH BELLUM

BLACK JUBAL'S ELSBETH, I'M CERTAIN...! SO *THAT'S* WHY SHE HAD NOWHERE ELSE TO GO.

THEN ...SHE WASN'T HERE LAST NIGHT...IT *WAS* ALL A DREAM...

I HAVE TO KEEP TELLING MYSELF THAT... IT WAS ONLY A *DREAM*...

...AND MAYBE SOME DAY...I'LL MAKE MYSELF *BELIEVE* IT!

THE END

232